IMAGES
of America

PARIS

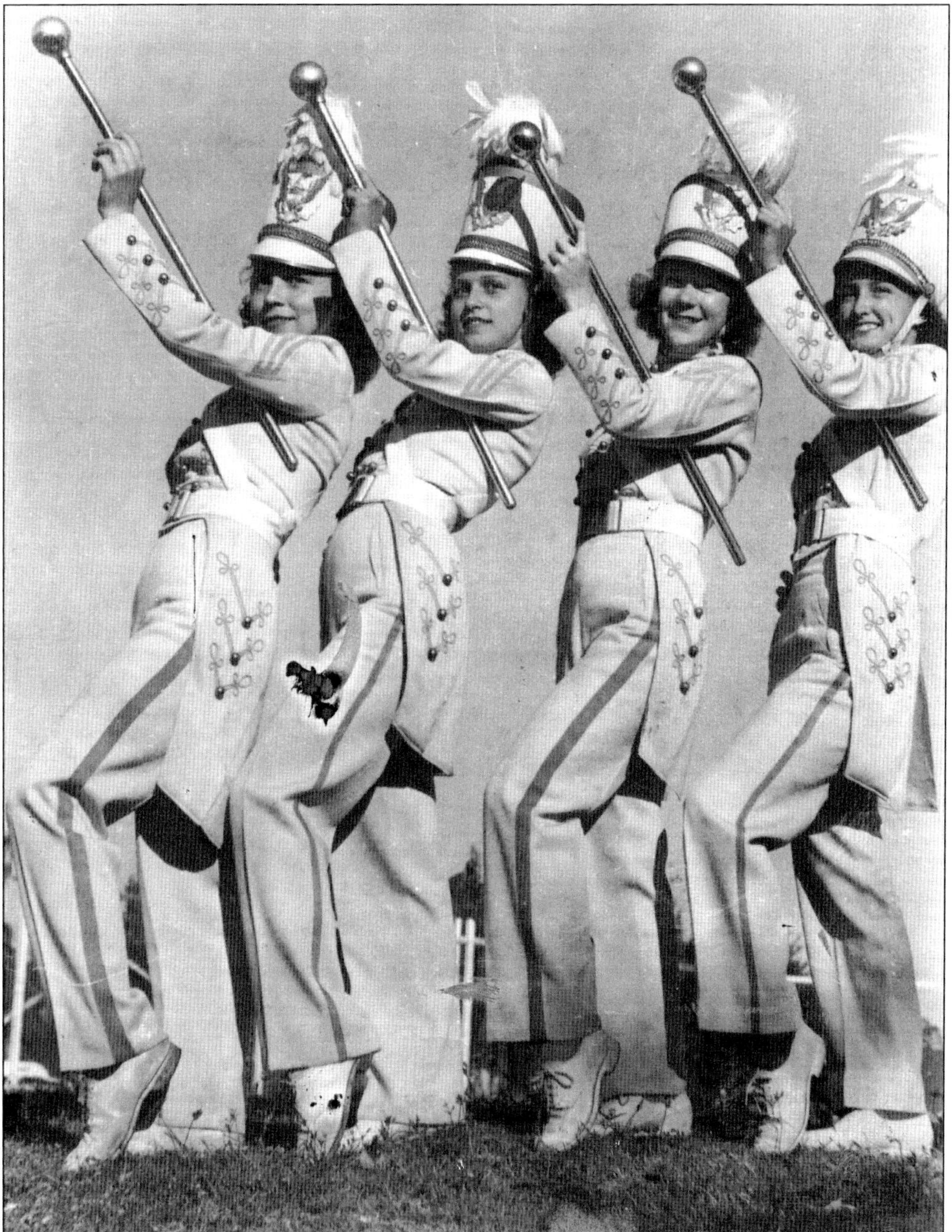

PARIS MAJORETTES IN THE 1950S. Nothing says "Texas" like drum majorettes. These proud majorettes exude the pride and confidence that is so typical of the citizens of Paris, Texas. (Courtesy of the A.M. & Welma Aikin Jr. Regional Archives.)

ON THE COVER: ADVERTISING, 1950S. This inventive Lamar Creamery advertising display probably dates from the 1950s. The robot's name is "Roby the Robot." This name is probably a play on "Robby the Robot," a character most notably associated with the 1956 production of the classic science fiction film *Forbidden Planet*. (Courtesy of the A.M. & Welma Aikin Jr. Regional Archives.)

IMAGES
of America

PARIS

Timothy G. Grammer with Jim Bell

ARCADIA
PUBLISHING

ISBN 978-0-7385-8526-0

Published by Arcadia Publishing
Charleston, South Carolina

Printed in the United States of America

Library of Congress Control Number: 2011936431

For all general information, please contact Arcadia Publishing:
Telephone 843-853-2070
Fax 843-853-0044
E-mail sales@arcadiapublishing.com
For customer service and orders:
Toll-Free 1-888-313-2665

Visit us on the Internet at www.arcadiapublishing.com

To my grandchildren Edan Cole and Eliza Marie

Contents

ACKNOWLEDGMENTS

I have been quite gratified during the production of this book with the helpful, courteous, and enthusiastic support I received from the people of Paris. There are, however, several things that this book is not. It makes no claim to be a history of Paris—there are several fine historians in Paris who are much more skilled with the town's history than I. Rather, this book attempts to examine what might be called "Images of Paris." I hope I have succeeded. All errors of omission and commission are entirely my own.

I wish to thank first and foremost Daisy Harvil, archivist of A.M. & Welma Aikin Jr. Regional Archives on the Paris Junior College campus. This book would not have been possible without her support. Citizens of Lamar County should be proud that they possess such a fine archive. I also wish to thank my coauthor, Jim Bell, of Paris, Texas, for the many hours of work he put into this book.

I also wish to recognize Chief Ronnie Grooms of the Paris Fire Department and Chief Robert Hundley of the Paris Police Department for their help; both of these dedicated civil servants are keenly proud of their organizations and their city. The staff of the Lamar County Historical Society Museum was an invaluable resource as well. I must thank Patrick Graham, publisher of the *Paris News*, for his gracious assistance. Others, too, helped in small ways, like Kristi Wolfe of the Coca-Cola Company and the staff of Paris City Library, which was, with one exception, gracious and helpful. In addition, the staff of the Texas State Library & Archives Commission: Prints & Photographs Collection in Austin as well as Texas Department of Transportation (TxDOT) made valuable contributions to this book.

As those who know me know, I am what might be called "technology challenged." This book was only made possible, technically speaking, through the help of many people. In particular, I received great assistance from Quinten Bell of Paris and Meghan Foster of Title III at Texas Wesleyan University. Quinten taught me the esoteric art of scanning photographs, and Meghan gave me a primer on the manipulation of digital images. In the same vein, I wish to thank all my colleagues at Texas Wesleyan University in Fort Worth; without them, this book would not have been possible. This book was inspired by my wife, Janet, as well as my mother-in-law, Margie Bell of Paris.

Unless otherwise noted, all photographs are courtesy of the A.M. & Welma Aikin Jr. Regional Archives at Paris Junior College.

INTRODUCTION

The area that is now Lamar County was inhabited by human beings many centuries before Europeans arrived. Various archaeological sites in the area testify to sophisticated Indian societies living here even before the coming of the Caddo Indians around 500 AD. French explorers were probably the first Europeans to visit what would become Lamar County. They established a post on the Red River north of Paris in the second decade of the 18th century. Neither the French, nor later the Spanish, would make serious efforts at colonizing East Texas, however. After 1816, small groups of Americans began to move into the Red River Valley. By 1839, George Wright had built a home in what is now Paris. By 1844, the village of Paris (whose original name was Pinhook) was firmly established and designated as county seat of the newly created Lamar County. The origin of the name "Paris" is shrouded in mystery, but by 1841, that name had replaced Pinhook. There are various conflicting stories as to how this name became attached to the town.

The people of Paris did not remain isolated on the frontier for long. The Civil War had a dramatic and lasting impact on Paris. Interestingly, Lamar County delegates at the secession convention voted against breaking away from the United States. Still, once Texas seceded from the Union, the sons of Paris and Lamar County served the Confederacy bravely. The 9th Texas Infantry Regiment (originally called "the Lamar Rifles") was formed from citizens of Lamar and surrounding counties and was under the command of Sam Bell Maxey. After a period of initial training, the 9th Texas had its baptism of fire at Shiloh in April 1862. After Shiloh, the 9th continued to serve. During that service, the 9th endured a number of bloody battles, including Chickamauga in 1863. The 9th Texas Infantry surrendered when the Confederacy collapsed in 1865 near Mobile, Alabama.

After the Civil War, Paris enjoyed an economic boom. This boom was fueled, to a large degree, by cotton. The world's appetite for cotton seemed boundless, and Paris greatly benefitted from this demand. The demand for cotton brought affluence to Paris, and Paris entered what was arguably its most prosperous period. This prosperity brought a strong "can-do spirit" to Paris, and this spirit is reflected in how the city sprang back from the devastating fire of 1877. That fire ravaged the central business district. But despite the damage, Paris quickly rebounded.

After the Civil War, Texas and the American South underwent a period of cultural, economic, political, and social change in the wake of the abolition of slavery and America's rapid industrialization. Like other parts of the South, and indeed the nation at large, the road to racial equality was not always smooth in Lamar County. Still, even in the 19th century, freed slaves could, and did, rise to prominence in Paris. A notable example of this is US Marshal Bass Reeves. Reeves was born a slave in 1838. Reeves clearly possessed a fine intelligence and became fluent in a number of Indian languages as a young man. His language skills served him in good stead later in life. In 1875, Reeves was hired as a US Marshal and worked for the federal court, under the famous "Hanging Judge" Isaac Parker. In 1883, Reeves was transferred and worked for the East Texas Federal Court in Paris. He was transferred again in 1895 to the federal court in

Muskogee, Indian Territory. Reeves died in Arkansas in 1910 and will always be remembered as one of the first, if not the first, African American federal marshals west of the Mississippi. Today, there is a statue honoring his service in the Paris Courthouse.

The greatest disaster to befall Paris was the great fire of 1916. The 1916 fire destroyed much of the center of Paris and caused millions of dollars in damage. The 1916 fire changed the face of Paris forever. In the wake of the fire, the architecture of Paris was dramatically altered. Gone were numerous dilapidated wooden structures. Many of the older Victorian structures in Paris were destroyed, and in their place, a new downtown plaza and many new homes and business establishments were built, which still grace the city today. In the wake of the fire, local businessman J.J. Culbertson donated a fountain to the city to honor both the disaster and, more importantly, the rebuilding of Paris. There were some notable buildings that survived the fire, however. These include the Gibraltar Hotel and the Sam Bell Maxey House.

Like other parts of the United States, the Great Depression hit Paris hard. Once the nation mobilized for war in the wake of the Japanese attack on Pearl Harbor, Paris entered into another boom period. This economic boom was fueled, to a large degree, by the establishment of Camp Maxey just a few miles north of Paris. Two infantry divisions, the 102nd and 99th, went through training at Camp Maxey. Paris's economy was not only fueled by soldiers spending their paychecks at local business establishments but also by contracts for food, general supplies, and building material.

After the war ended, Paris, like other towns in the United States, underwent a baby boom. This baby boom necessitated investment in the local infrastructure to include secondary schools, hospitals, and Paris Junior College. Unfortunately, Paris was hit by yet another disaster in 1982 when a tornado struck the town. This tornado left many dead and injured and millions of dollars in property destroyed and damaged. Paris suffered during the great recession that swept the nation and the world beginning about 2007. Still, Paris was not hit as hard as many towns and cities. Although some employers either shut down or cut back operations during the recession, major employers, such as Kimberly-Clark, Campbell's Soup, local hospitals, and Paris Junior College, served as anchors to the area's economy and ameliorated, to a certain degree, the effects of the economic downturn on Paris.

Although Paris has a long and sometimes tragic history, the people of Paris still possess, even during the recent recession, the can-do spirit that characterized their frontier ancestors.

One

To the Fire of 1916

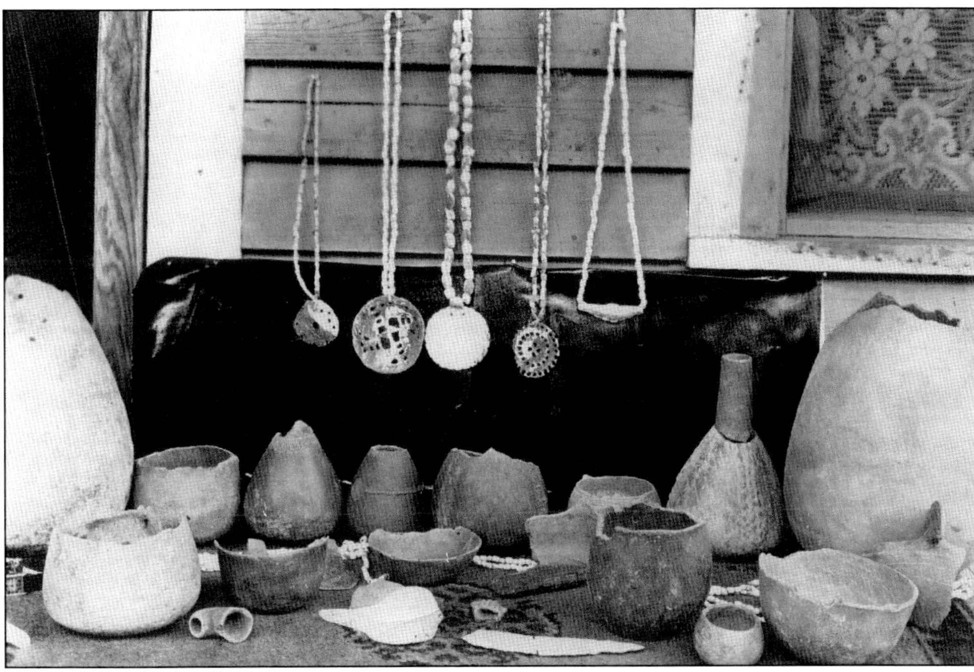

Archaeological Artifacts in Lamar County. Artifacts of daily life, like those pictured here, tell much about the lives of ancient peoples. The quality of this pottery suggests the high level of development possessed by ancient Lamar County Native Americans. Although Native Americans had inhabited the region for over 1,000 years, the group best identified with the area is the Caddo Indians. The Caddo Indians were primarily agriculturists and arrived in the area around 500 AD.

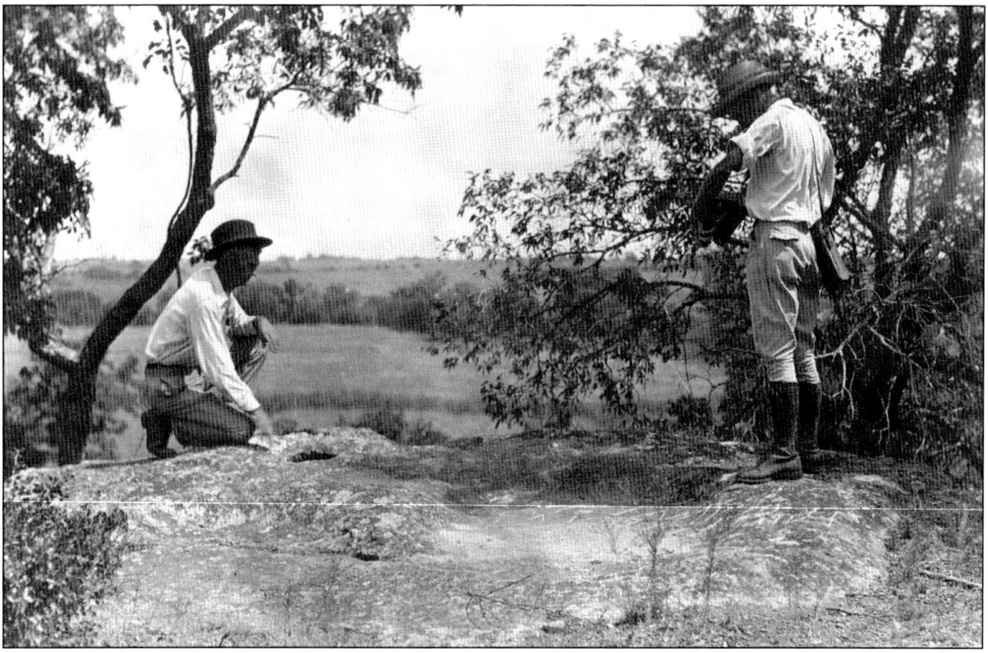

An Archaeological Dig Near Paris in the 1930s. During the Great Depression of the 1930s, the federal government provided funds for a number of works projects. One of these projects was the financing of archaeological digs. The archeological dig near Paris, pictured here, was perhaps funded by a works project.

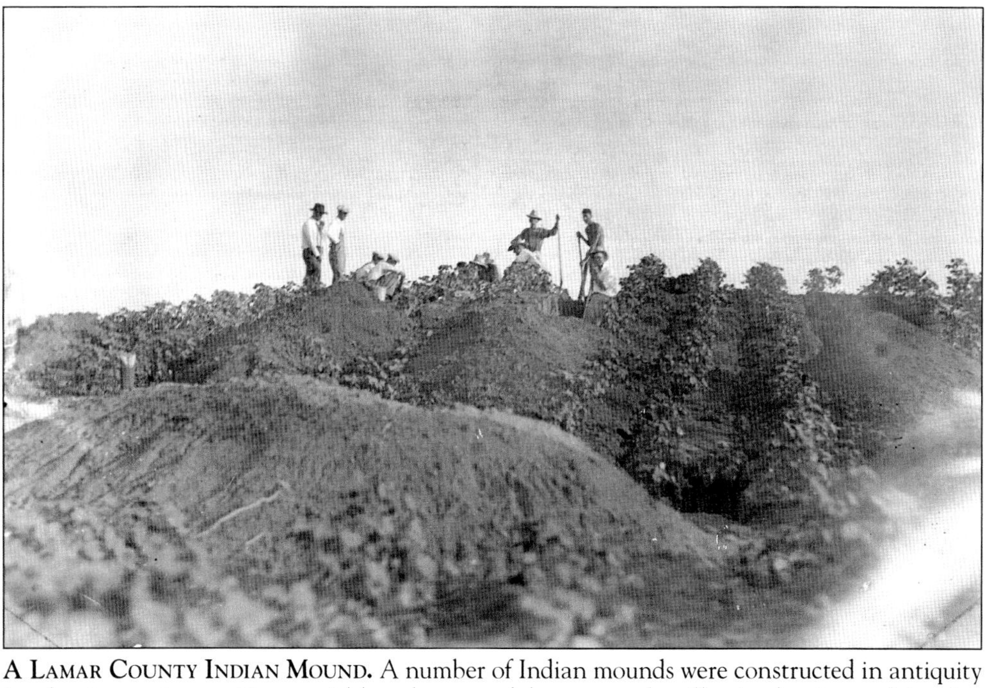

A Lamar County Indian Mound. A number of Indian mounds were constructed in antiquity in what is now Lamar County. Although some of these mounds still exist, looting and farming activities have destroyed many over the years. This mound near Paris, however, survived long enough to be investigated by archeologists.

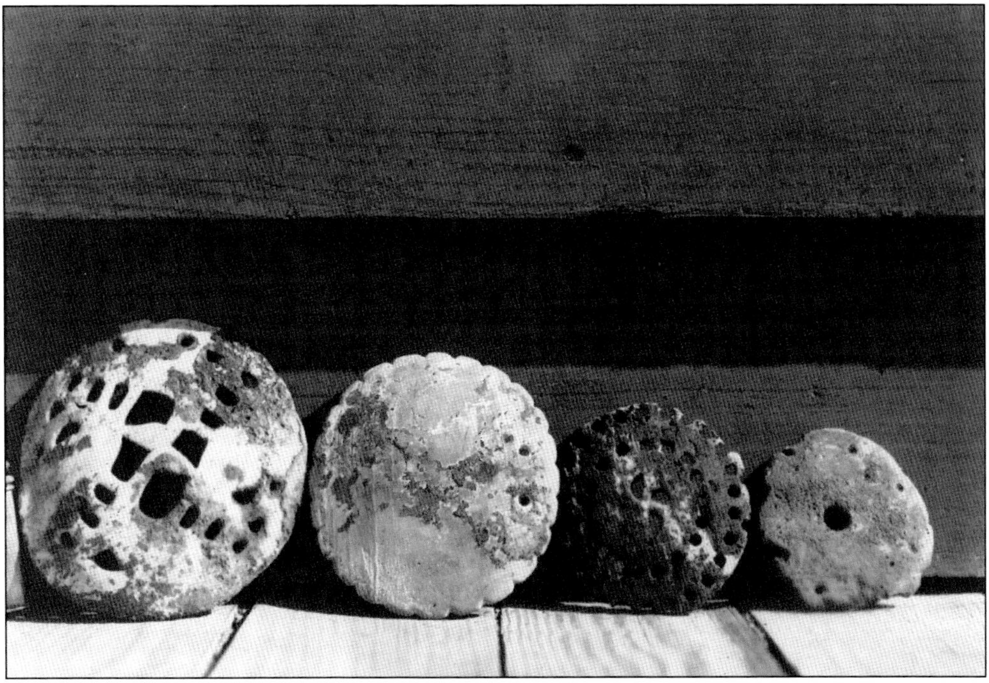

Indian Artifacts. The artifacts pictured here suggest that settled, agrarian societies inhabited Lamar Country long before the arrival of the Europeans. Native Americans established villages in the Lamar County area during the Formative Caddoan Period (900–1000 AD).

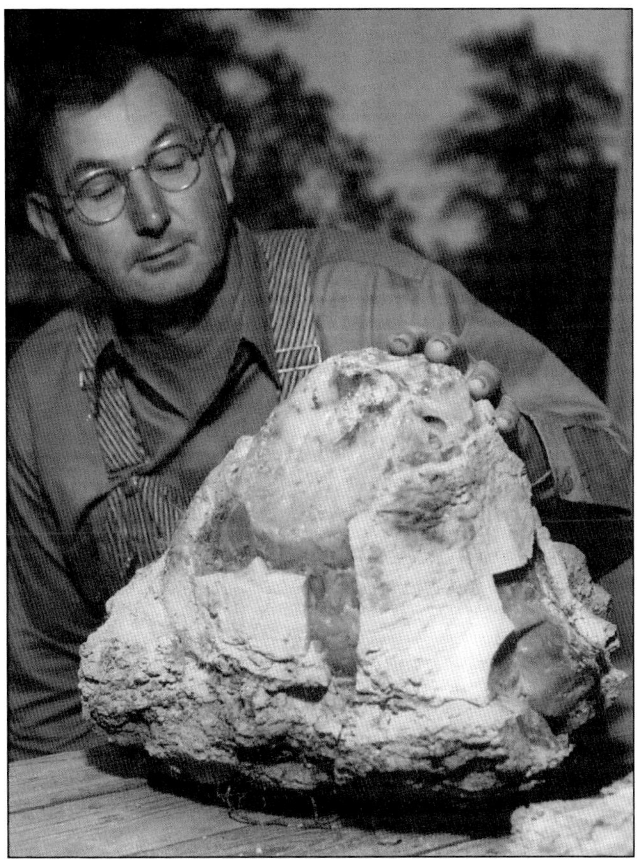

A Farmer Inspecting an Archeological Artifact Unearthed on His Land. There are numerous archaeological sites in Lamar County. Local Indian mounds were constructed during the Middle Caddoan Period (1100–1300 AD).

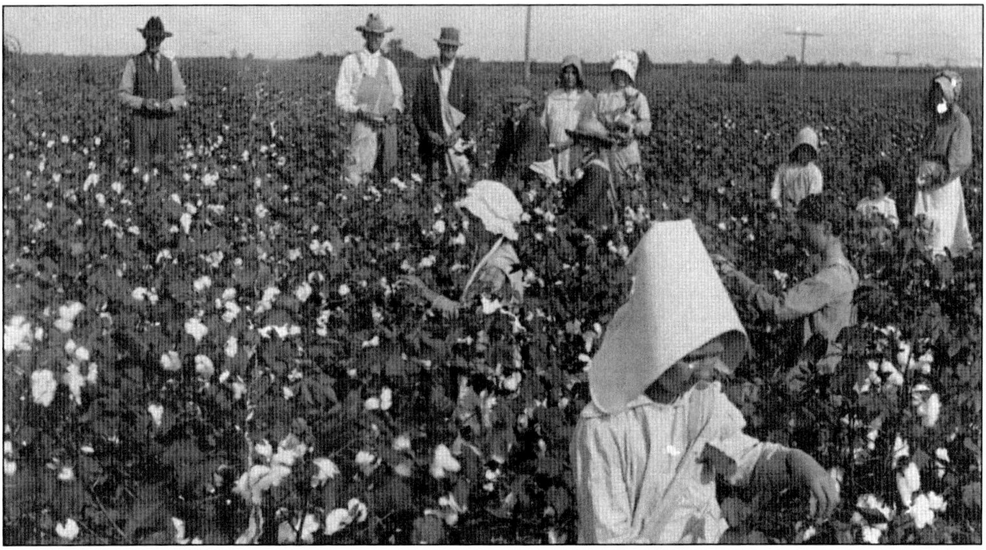

COTTON BOLLS BEING PICKED. "King Cotton" was the backbone of the Southern economy. This truism is certainly true when one considers Paris, Texas. Arguably, the most affluent period of Paris's history was fueled by cotton. Cotton production was often a family affair. In many ways, cotton made Paris and Lamar County. Red River steamboats, and later railroads, gave Lamar County cotton producers access to national and international markets. Cotton production, and the international demand for cotton, exploded during the 1850s. Paris, like much of the South, benefitted from the Industrial Revolution in Britain, particularly the rapid growth of textile plants, and the demand for machine-made clothing.

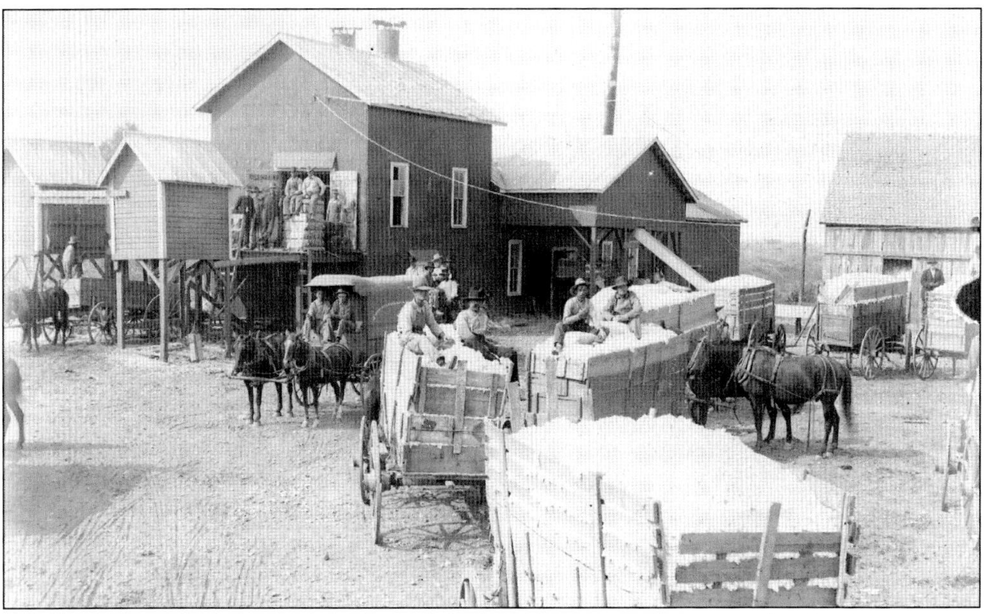

A LAMAR COUNTY COTTON GIN. Once picked, the cotton was transported to local cotton gins to have the seeds removed. It was the cotton gin that made large-scale commercial production a profitable business in the South. Cotton production reached a commercial level in Lamar County in the 1850s. More than 20 cotton gins operated in Lamar County at the height of the cotton boom. This cheap cotton spurred the development of industrialization in the United States.

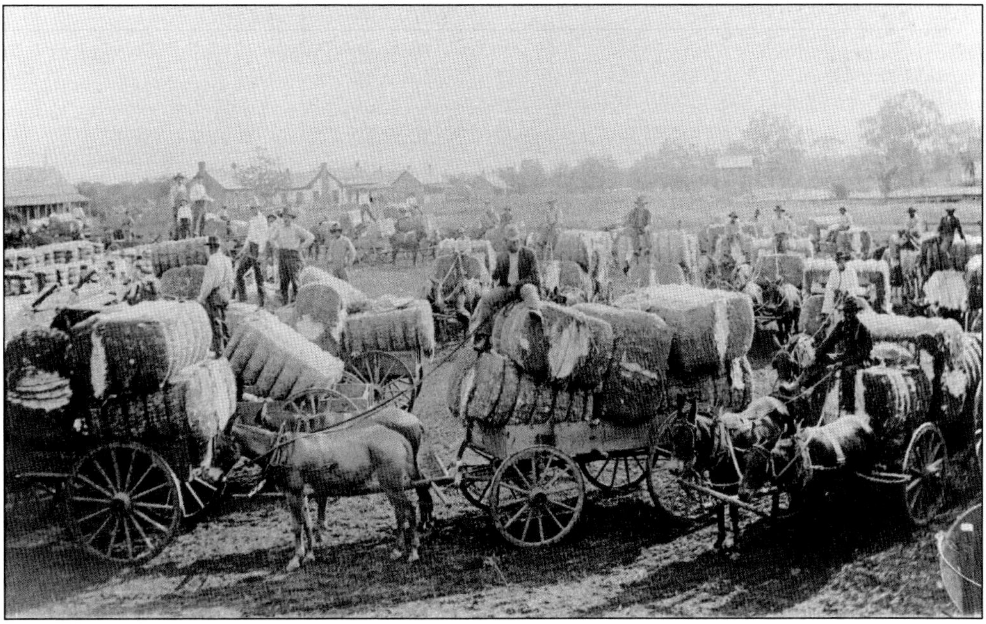

COTTON BAILS READY FOR MARKET. This image gives an impression of the vast cotton harvests that were reaped from the fertile land around Paris. At its height, over 100,000 acres of land in Lamar County were devoted to the raising of King Cotton. But, Paris has had, and still has, a diversified economy. Because of this, Paris was able to weather economic storms that brought ruin to other East Texas towns.

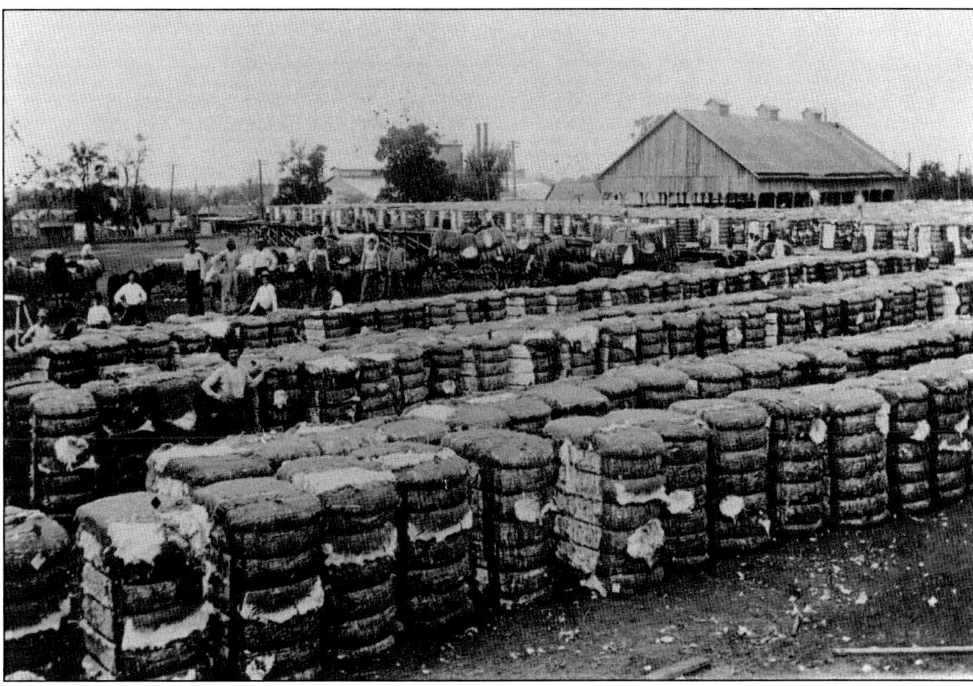

COTTON BAILS AWAITING TRANSPORT. Once processed at the gin, the cotton was baled and stored until transported to the local market. Cotton, the Red River trade, and the fact that the earliest settlers were merchants, all helped create a diversified economic structure in the area.

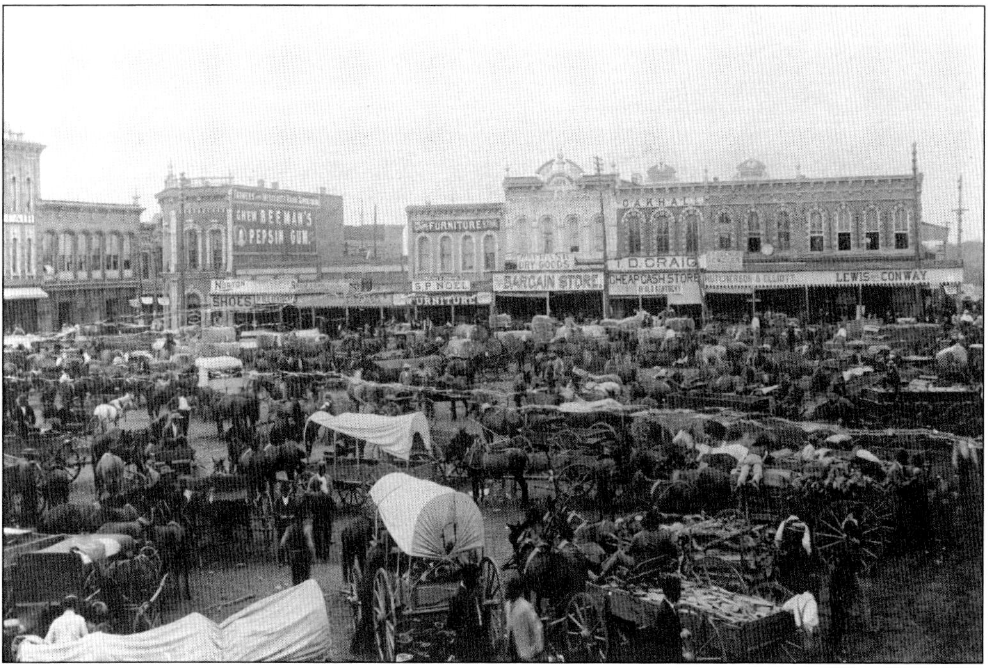

Market Day in the Square. Downtown Paris was the center for the buying and selling of cotton. Cotton production grew dramatically between 1880 and 1920. Exactly 24,623 bales were produced in 1880. In 1920, the peak year for cotton production, 69,264 bales were produced in Lamar County. After 1920, however, cotton production declined, with less than 2,000 bales produced in 1982.

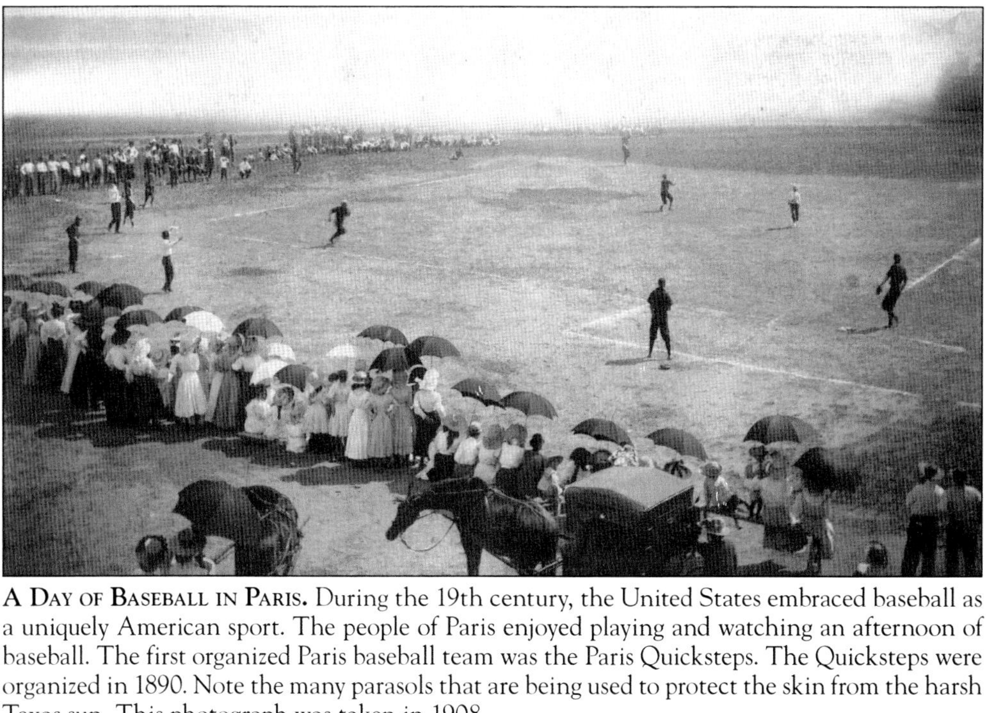

A Day of Baseball in Paris. During the 19th century, the United States embraced baseball as a uniquely American sport. The people of Paris enjoyed playing and watching an afternoon of baseball. The first organized Paris baseball team was the Paris Quicksteps. The Quicksteps were organized in 1890. Note the many parasols that are being used to protect the skin from the harsh Texas sun. This photograph was taken in 1908.

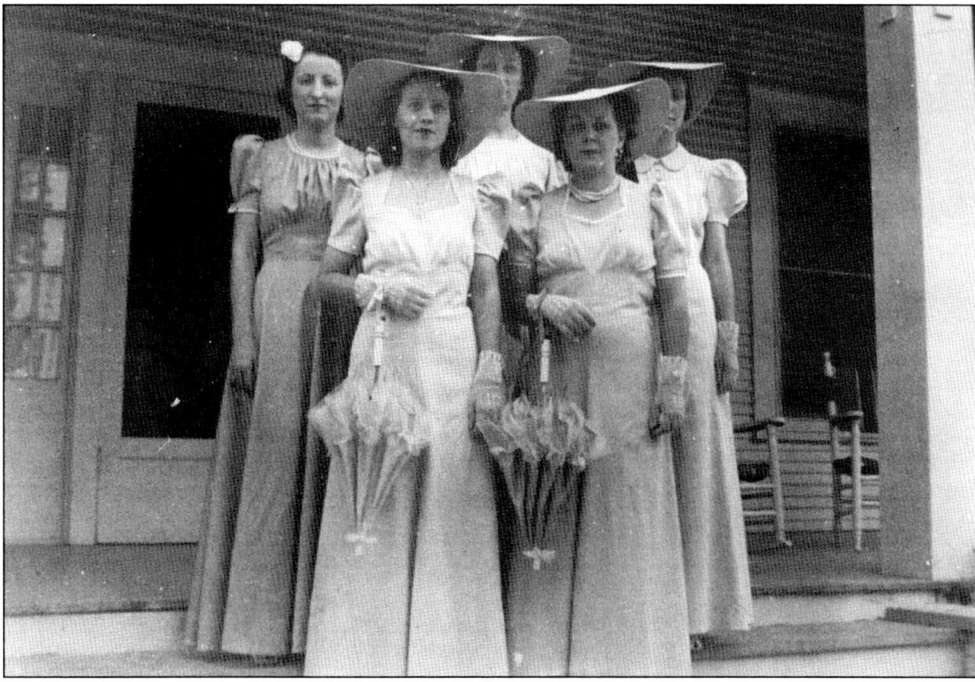

Elegant Paris Ladies. These well-dressed Paris ladies are perhaps preparing for a wedding ceremony. The quality of these dresses indicates the level of affluence in Paris at the time. This particular photograph is undated. It could have been taken anytime from about 1900 to the Great Depression of the 1930s.

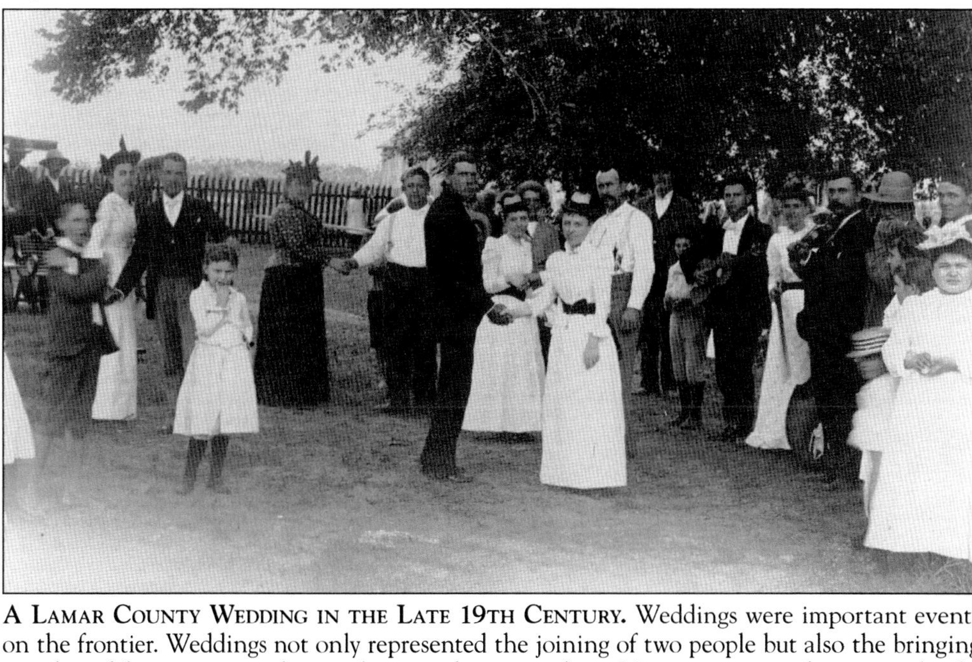

A Lamar County Wedding in the Late 19th Century. Weddings were important events on the frontier. Weddings not only represented the joining of two people but also the bringing together of the community for socializing and merry-making. Upon examining this image closely, two musicians are visible on the right-hand side of the photograph; one man is playing a guitar, while the other is playing a fiddle.

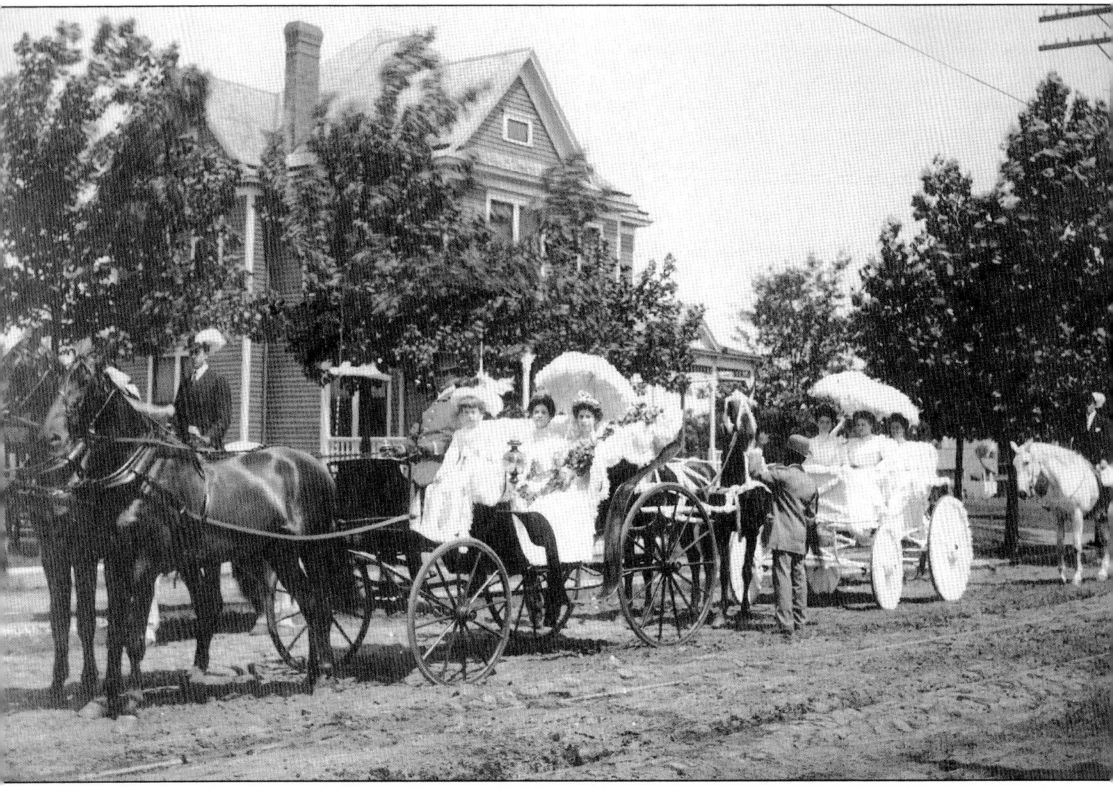

AN EARLY PARADE IN PARIS. The people of Paris have always enjoyed parades. Here, six members of the King's Daughters organization prepare to participate in a parade. The King's Daughters were organized in Paris in 1887 and involved themselves heavily in charitable work. Rails used by the Paris trolley system are visible in the unpaved street.

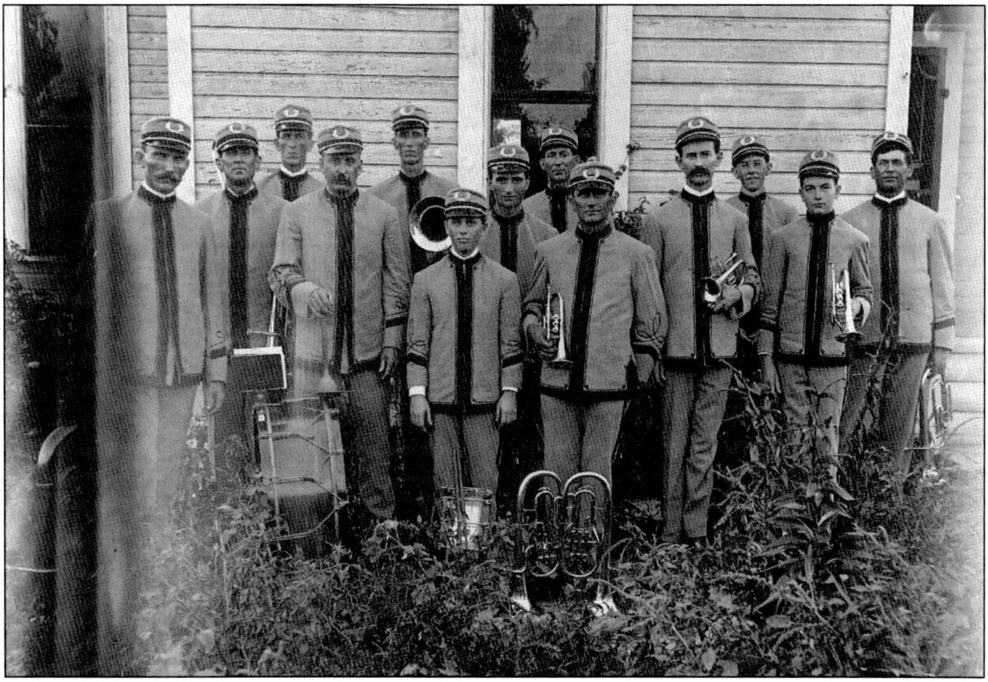

The Milton Band about 1907. Parades and marching bands go hand in hand. Interestingly, the band's uniforms have been modeled on West Point cadet uniforms, grey with black piping. The caps worn by members of the band are not, however, modeled on West Point uniforms. A close examination of the cap badges reveals that inside wreath are the letters "MCB." Perhaps this is short for "Milton Community Band."

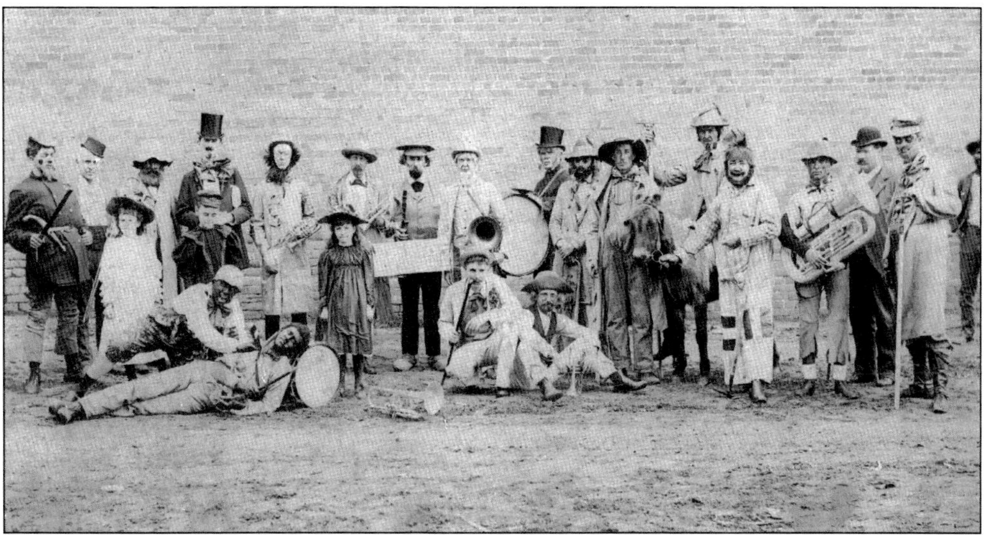

A Comically Attired Group of Parisians in the 19th Century. Not all parades were serious affairs. The group pictured here is comically attired. Several amusing stereotypes are represented in this group. On the left is a "police officer" (identified by the baton). To the right of the police officer are two white men in black face (a common comic motif in the late 19th century). Barely visible on the right is an African American man. Perhaps, this group was dressed for a Mardi Gras celebration.

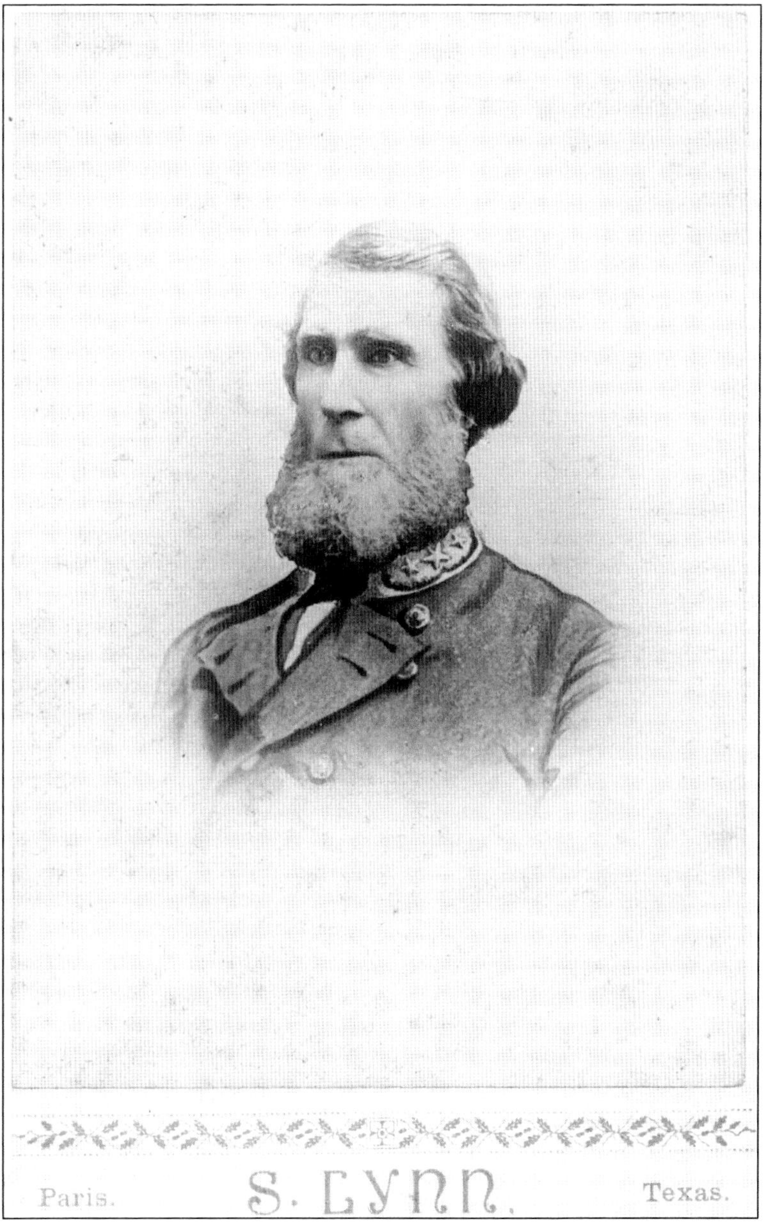

GEN. SAM BELL MAXEY. One of the best-known members of the Paris community was Sam Bell Maxey. Here, he is pictured in his Confederate general's uniform. Maxey was born in Kentucky and attended the United States Military Academy at West Point, where he was roommate for a time with Thomas "Stonewall" Jackson. He served with distinction in the Mexican-American War and resigned from the Army in 1849. After leaving the Army, Maxey went into law practice, moving to Paris in 1857. During the Civil War, he entered Confederate service and rose to the rank of major general. During that conflict, he served as commanding general of the Indian Territory between 1863 and the end of the war in 1865. At the end of Reconstruction, Maxey entered the US Senate and served two terms. After departing the Senate, Maxey returned to Paris and practiced law. His home on Church Street, built in 1867, survived the fire of 1916 and is a well-known historic site.

JOHN CHISUM. The famous cattle baron John Chisum was born in Tennessee in 1824. With his parents, 13-year-old John moved to what is now Lamar County in 1836. In 1852, Chisum became county clerk of Lamar County. He served in that capacity for only a short time, resigning to enter the cattle business. After leaving Paris, Chisum settled in New Mexico, where he was an important player in the infamous Lincoln County war and had dealings with Billy the Kid. Chisum is buried in Paris.

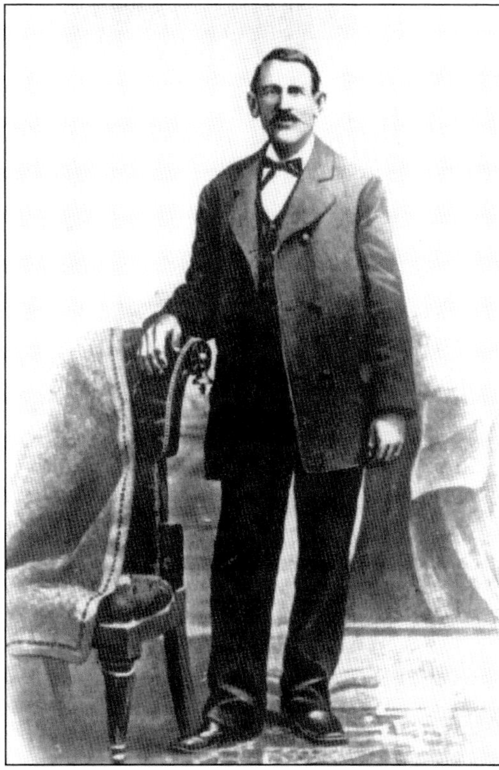

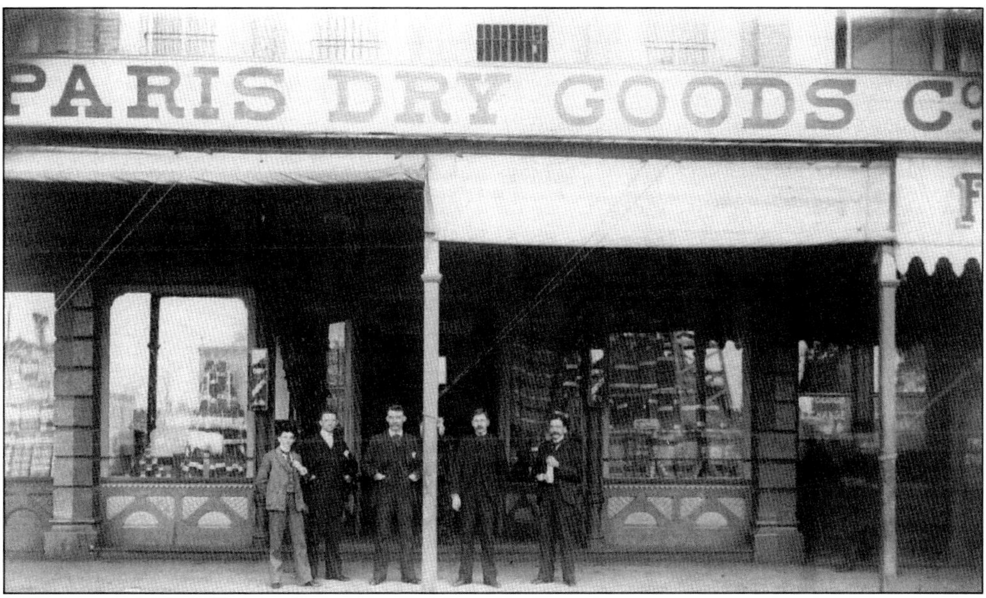

EMPLOYEES OF A PARIS DRY GOODS STORE. This photograph resides in the A.M. & Welma Aikin Jr. Regional Archives on the campus of Paris Junior College. It is claimed on the back of the photograph that one of the individuals in this picture is Frank James (1843–1915), brother of the notorious Jesse James. It is known that Frank James worked as a store clerk for a few months at A.G. Hubbard Dry Goods in Paris after "retiring" from his criminal career. As to whether this really is a photograph of Frank James . . . that may never be known.

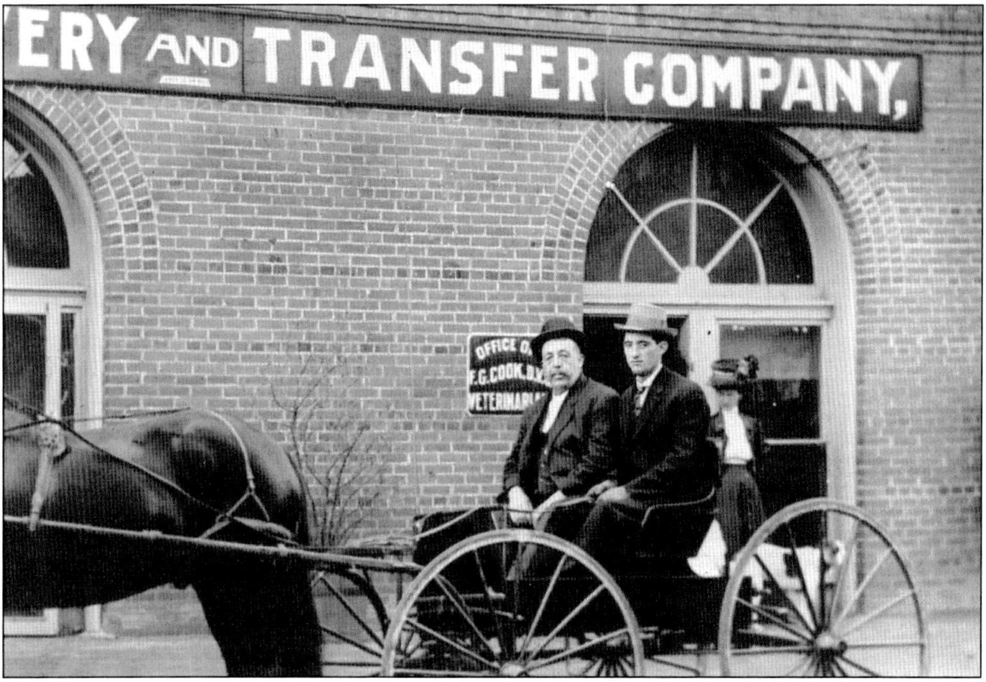

The Livery and Transfer Company of Paris. The iconic image of the livery stable is a staple of Western movies and American folklore. As befitted a town of Paris's importance during the 19th century, Paris had more than one livery stable. Livery stables provided a number of services and the expense varied depending on the services provided.

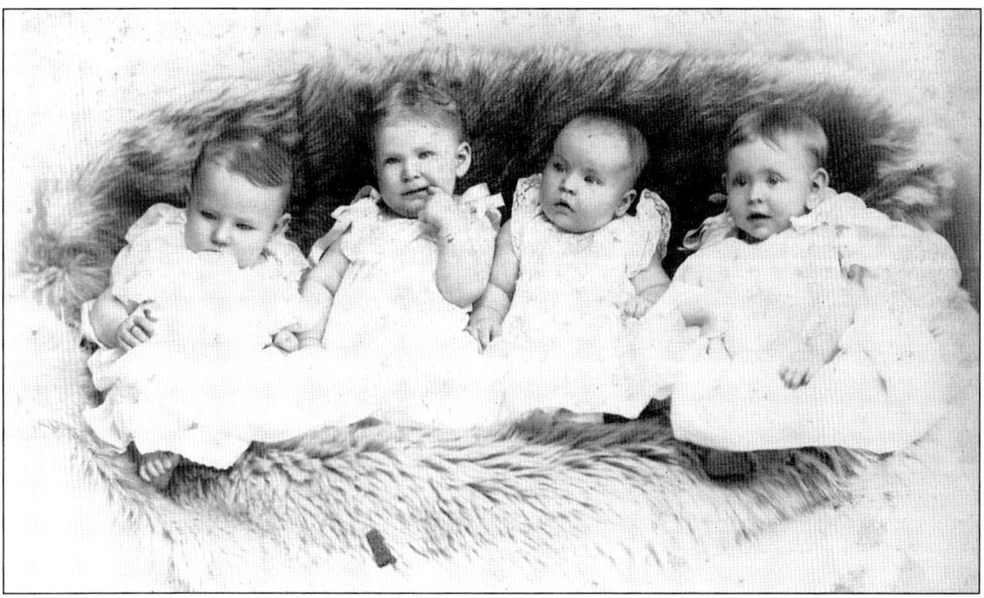

Paris Infants. As the science and art of photography improved during the late 19th century, people began turning the camera to things other than formal occasions and famous people. Parents were eager to use the new technology to preserve images of their children. Pictured here in 1896 or 1897 are four Paris infants. From left to right are Lavita Coleman, Verlinda Yates, Beth Coleman, and Jackie Jennings.

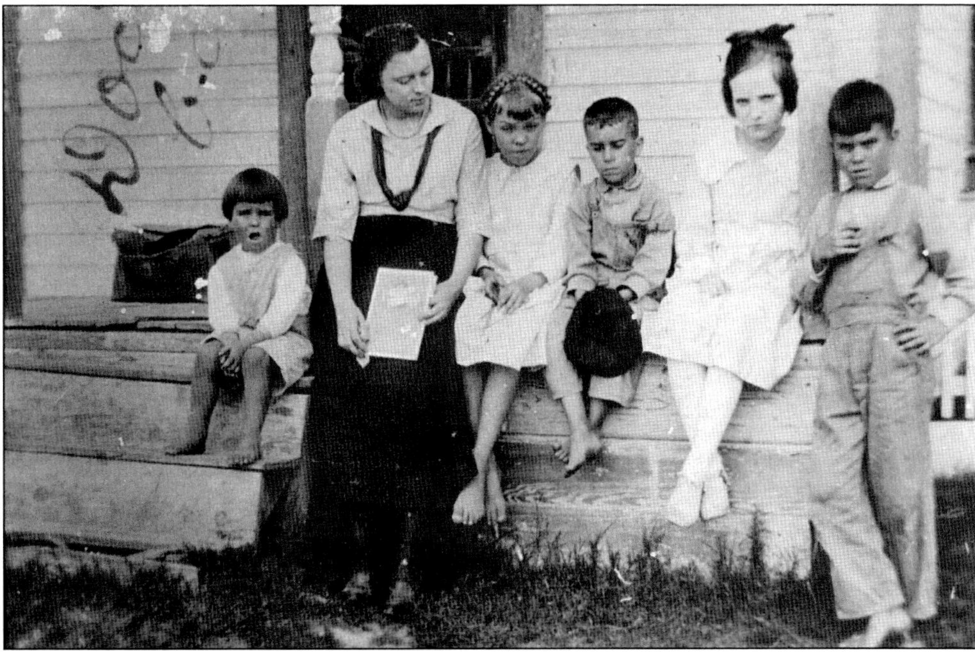

PARIS CHILDREN IN THE LATE 19TH CENTURY. These rather disgruntled children are either a family group or schoolchildren. The adult is holding what may be a textbook. As America expanded west, settlers outpaced the government and governmental institutions. Until local governments organized themselves, primary education was the responsibility of parents.

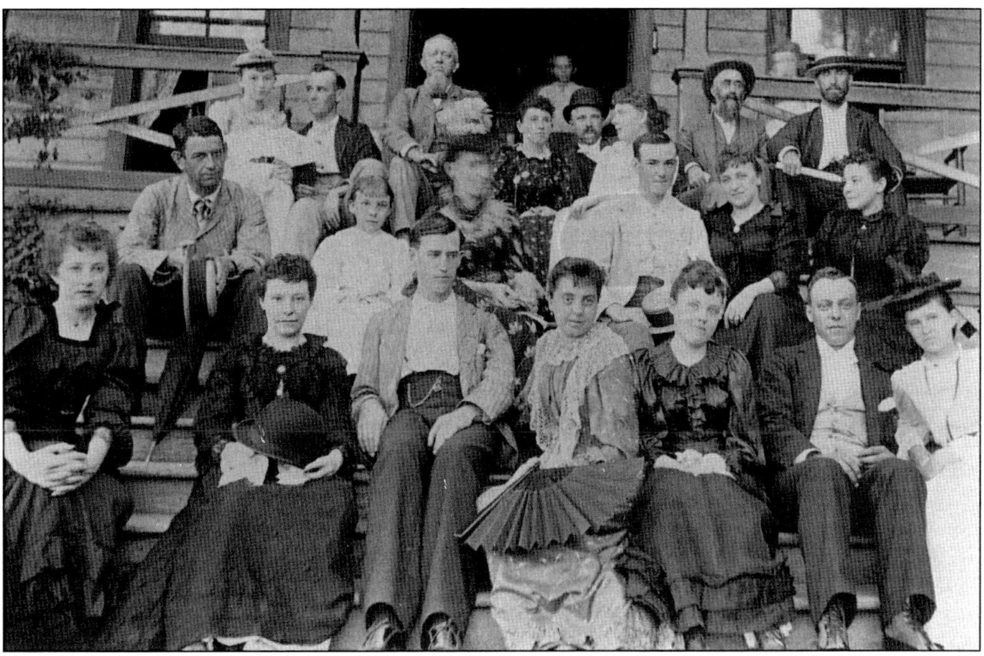

A FAMILY PORTRAIT. Families tended to live in close proximity to each other before the advent of the automobile. This Paris family is a good example of a late-19th-century extended family. The family patriarch is in the center of the top row. Once the automobile became widely available, families tended to shatter; the old paradigm of family members living in the same local fell apart.

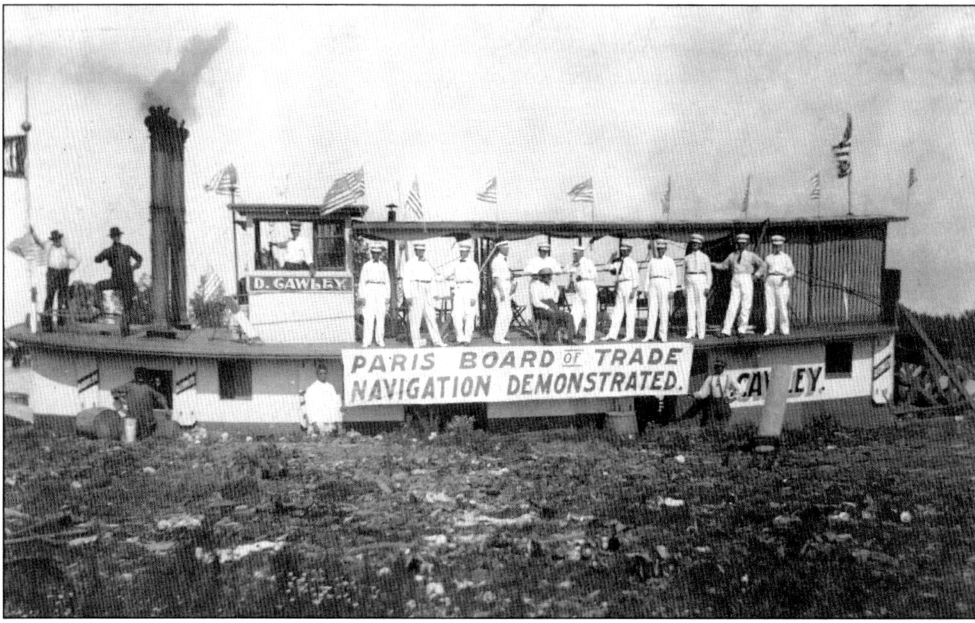

A Board of Trade Business Idea. Paris has always possessed a strong entrepreneurial spirit. With that said, not every business idea was successful. In 1908 (the date of this picture), the Paris Board of Trade attempted to demonstrate the feasibility of excursion trips along the Red River from Paris to Shreveport. Although his idea possessed great merit conceptually, this business scheme failed.

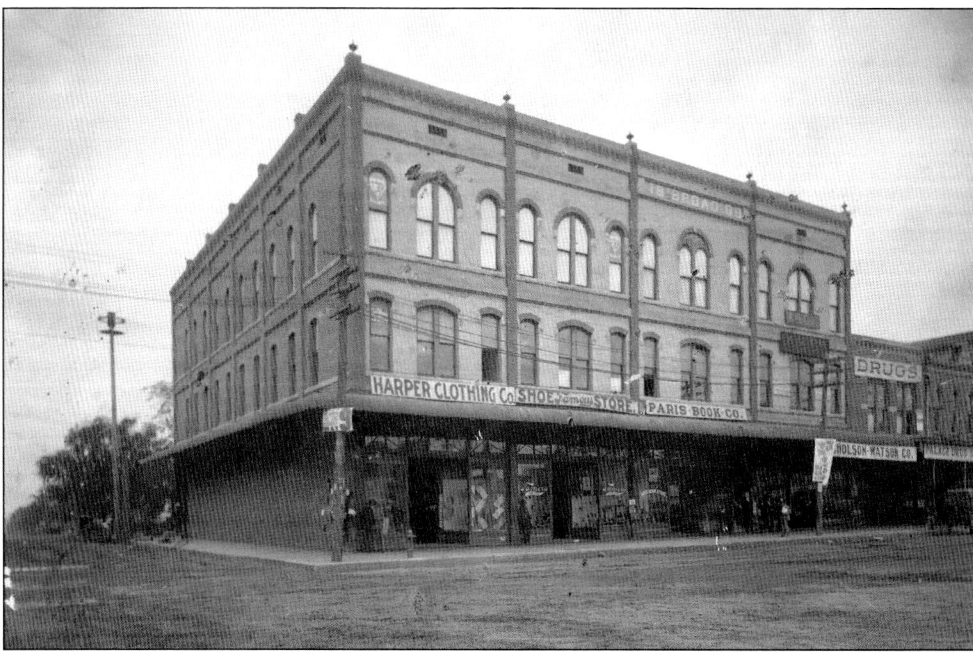

The Broad Brothers Building. The Broad Brothers Building pictured here was constructed in 1899. It replaced an earlier structure that had existed on the site since the 1870s. This building housed the Harper Clothing Company. Also visible is the Famous Shoe Store, Paris Book Company, and the Palace Drugstore. Like so many fine, old structures in Paris, it was destroyed in 1916.

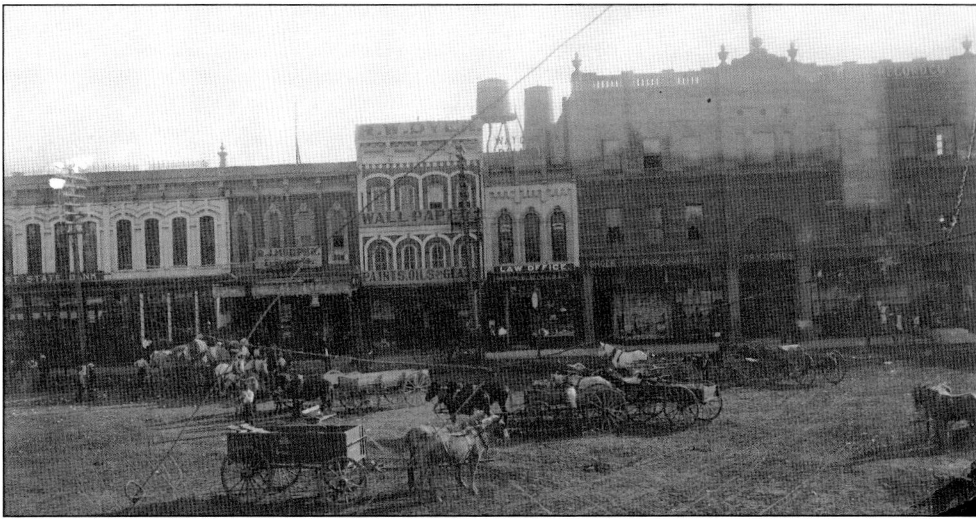

DOWNTOWN PARIS ABOUT 1900. Downtown Paris bustled with commerce at the turn of the century. The First State Bank is visible on the left, and Crook-Record Co. is on the right. The law offices of Noyes & Huber can also be identified in this photograph. The date of this photograph is uncertain.

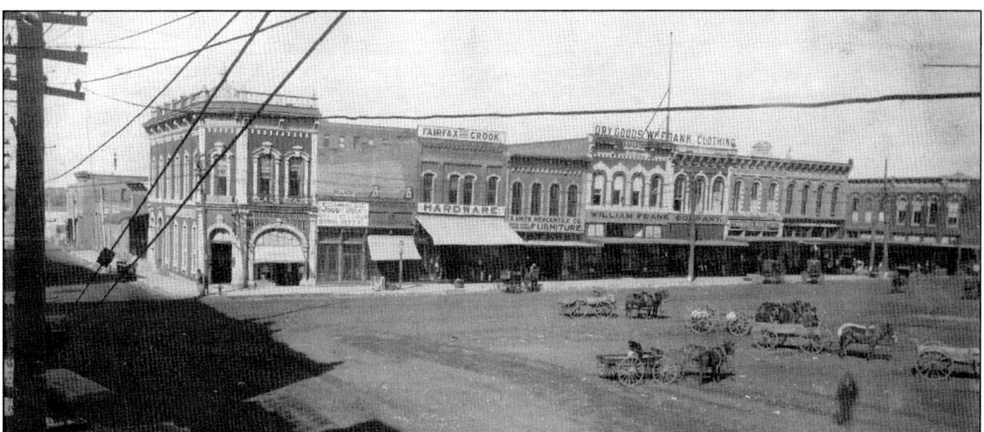

A PANORAMIC VIEW OF PART OF THE SQUARE. As is evident from this 1905 photograph, Paris had extensive telephone service at this time. Indeed, the Erie Telephone Company began operations in Paris in 1882. In addition, one can see that cement sidewalks have been installed. Fairfax and Crook Hardware is the most notable business that can be identified in this image.

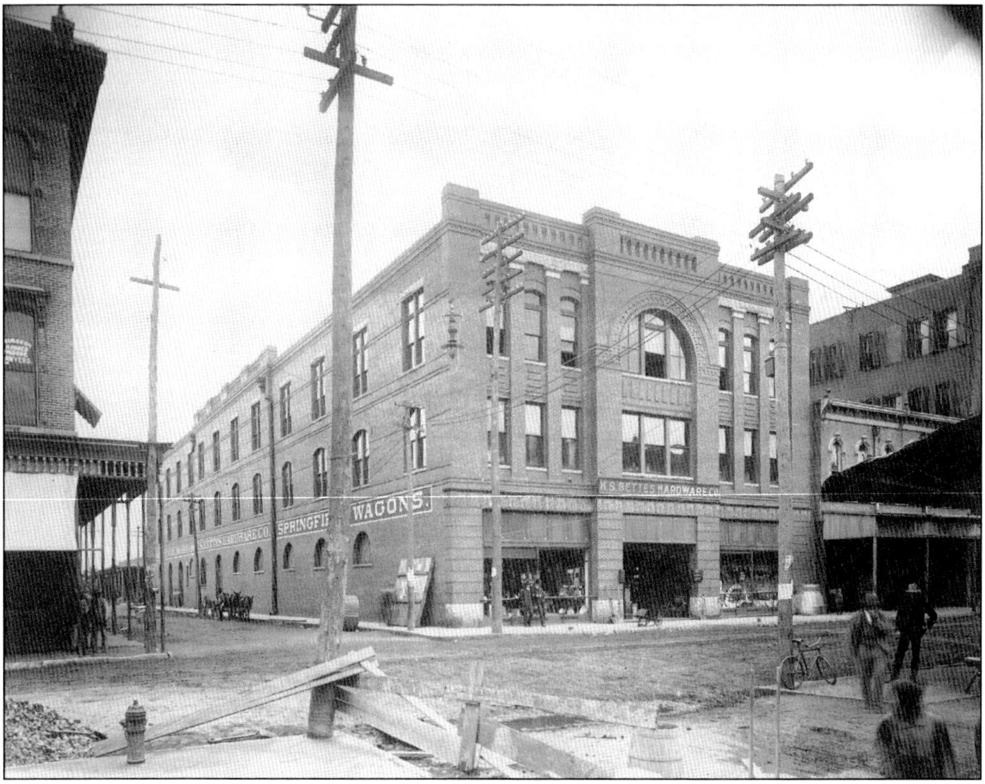

THE BETTES HARDWARE COMPANY. Bettes Hardware Company, pictured here, was a major supplier of hardware and building supplies to the Paris community. This photograph may have been taken about 1905. One can see cement sidewalks being constructed as well as a fire hydrant already in place. Paris acquired a public water system in 1877. In 1894, a city-operated sewer system was put into operation.

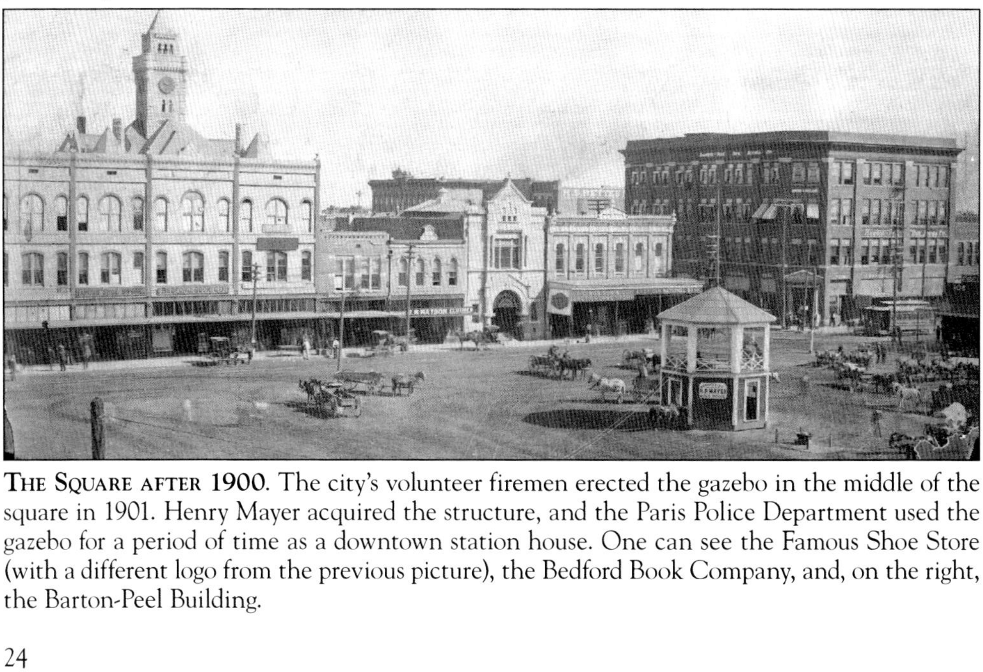

THE SQUARE AFTER 1900. The city's volunteer firemen erected the gazebo in the middle of the square in 1901. Henry Mayer acquired the structure, and the Paris Police Department used the gazebo for a period of time as a downtown station house. One can see the Famous Shoe Store (with a different logo from the previous picture), the Bedford Book Company, and, on the right, the Barton-Peel Building.

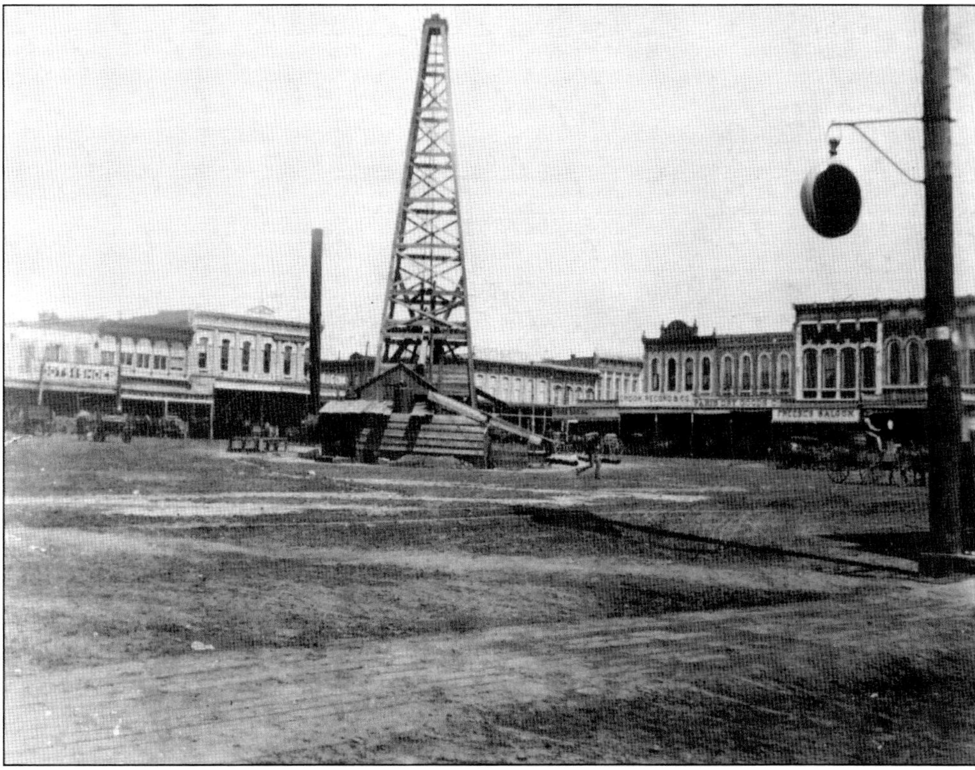

AN ARTESIAN WELL IN THE SQUARE. Between 1890 and 1893, an attempt was made to provide the city with a safe source of fresh water; the project failed. Visible in the background is Crook-Record Co. and Freeses Saloon. Although there is no evidence that Freeses Saloon ever had a shoot-out, there were a few quarrels in Paris. For example, Jim Reed, the first husband of Belle Starr, was killed by a deputy sheriff in Paris in 1874. Reed had been a member of the James-Younger outlaw gang at one time.

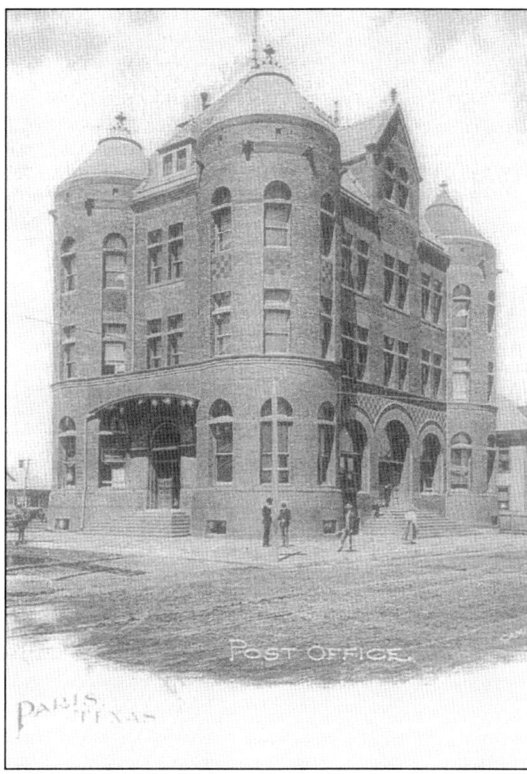

THE PARIS POST OFFICE. This old building was destroyed in the great fire of 1916. Free mail delivery came to Paris in 1889. A close inspection of this photograph reveals that it has recently rained, and rails for Paris's trolley car system in the unpaved street are also visible. (Courtesy of the Lamar County Historical Society Museum.)

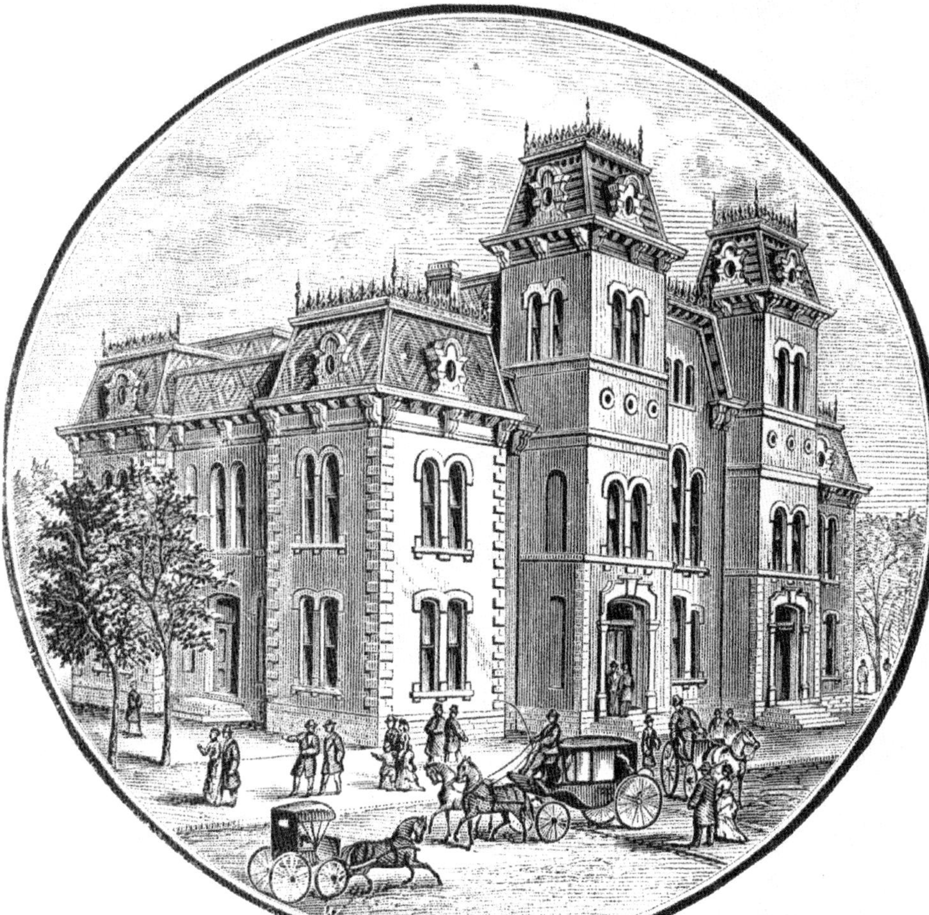

COURT HOUSE, PARIS.

A Period Artist's Rendering of the Second Courthouse in Paris. The structure pictured here was occupied in 1875 and replaced the earlier brick building that had been constructed in 1846. This second courthouse was designed by Charles Wheelock and built in the then-popular Second Empire style. The image itself was created by "W.T.&H. St. Louis."

THE OLD FEDERAL BUILDING IN PARIS. This structure was badly damaged in the fire of 1916. It was determined that the building could not be salvaged, and it was demolished. Considering that Paris had a federal building at all is a testament to the city's importance. Federal buildings were usually located in the seats of federal judicial districts.

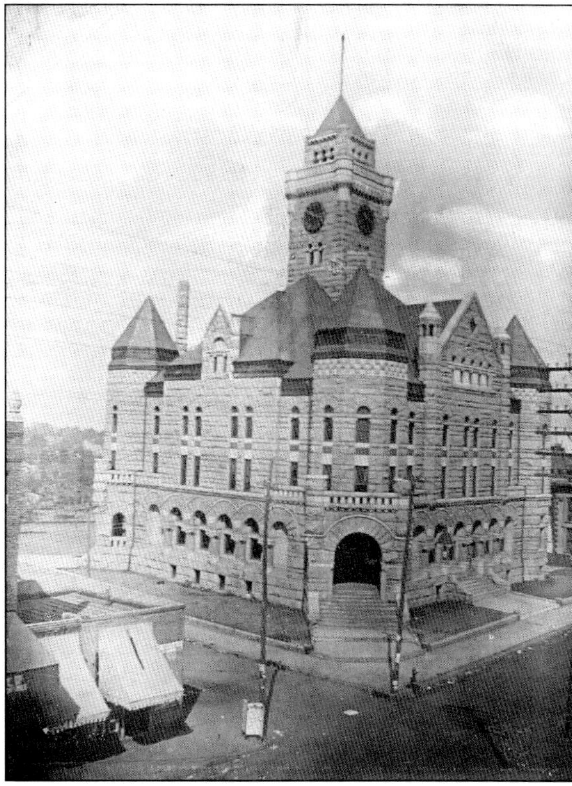

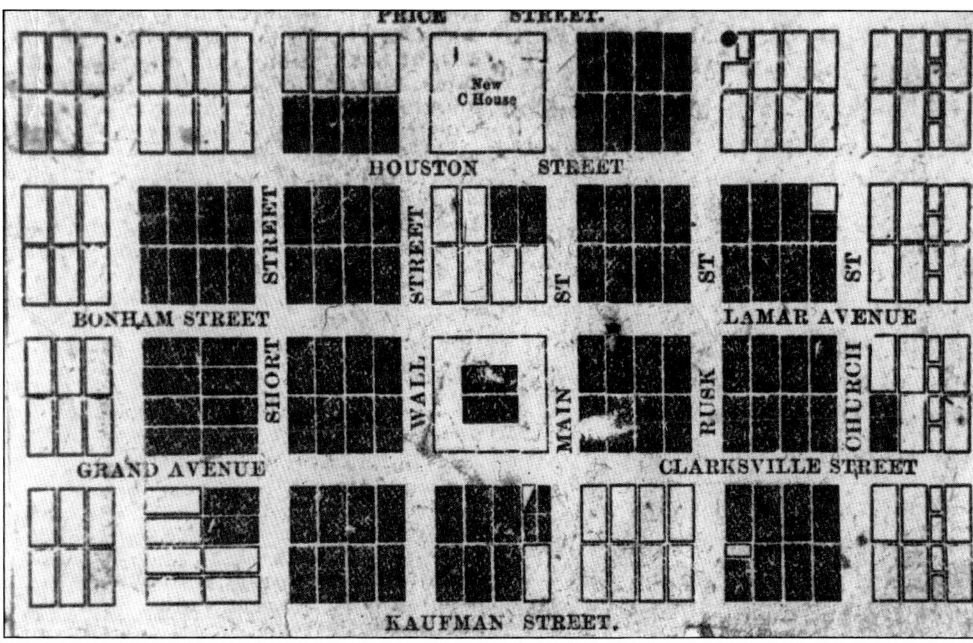

MAP OF THE 1877 FIRE. Paris was struck by the first of two great fires on August 31, 1877. The fire was as an act of arson by Taylor Pounds, who set the fire in a saloon on the south side of the square. A strong wind aided the fire's spread. About 10 acres of the central business district were destroyed. Pounds was convicted of the crime but soon escaped custody.

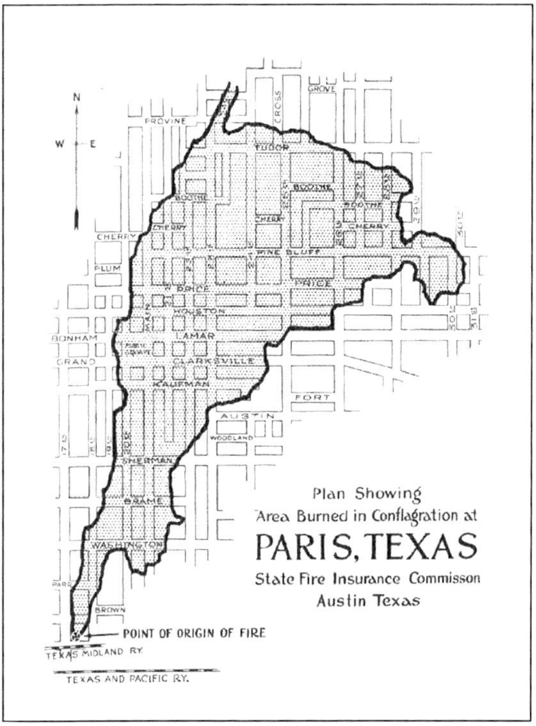

Map of the 1916 Fire. Perhaps the greatest challenge ever faced by Paris was the fire of 1916. The fire began during the late afternoon of March 21, 1916. The exact cause of the fire has never been definitively determined. It is speculated that either sparks from a passing train or children caused the fire. Wind gusts of up to 50 miles per hour, coupled with a drought, assisted in the spread of the fire.

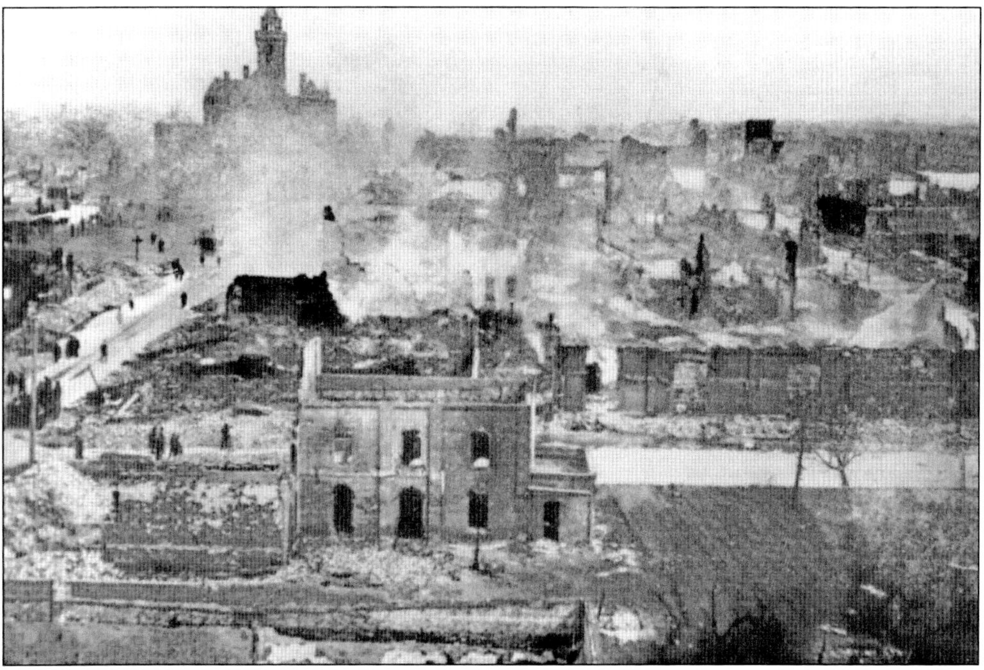

The Devastated Central Business District after the Fire. This photograph, looking north, was taken from the top of the damaged Gibraltar Hotel. About 1,440 buildings were destroyed. Sources disagree, but either three or four people died during the fire. The low number of deaths is credited to the fact that the fire began during daylight hours and to the bravery of the firefighters.

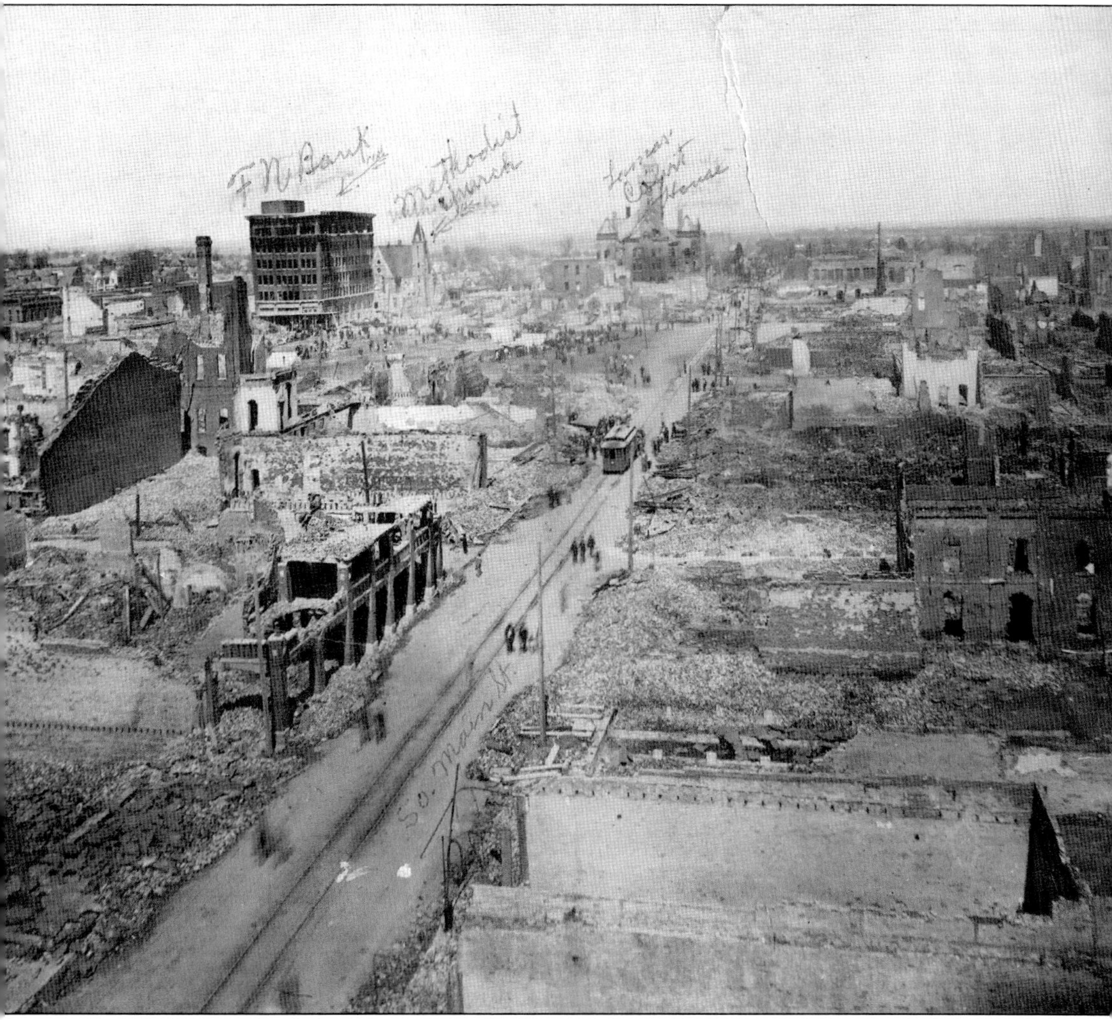

DEVASTATED PARIS. Governmental buildings were hit hard by the fire. The county courthouse, city jail, city hall, two fire stations, two schools, the post office, and federal courthouse were all destroyed. The destroyed or damaged First National Bank, Centenary Methodist Church, and Lamar Courthouse can be seen. The fire did not spare houses of worship. The Congregational, Central Presbyterian, First Baptist, Holy Cross Episcopal, Church of Christ, Methodist, and First Christian churches were all destroyed. Only three of the "white churches," as they were then called, survived the fire. Eight of nine African American houses of worship were also destroyed.

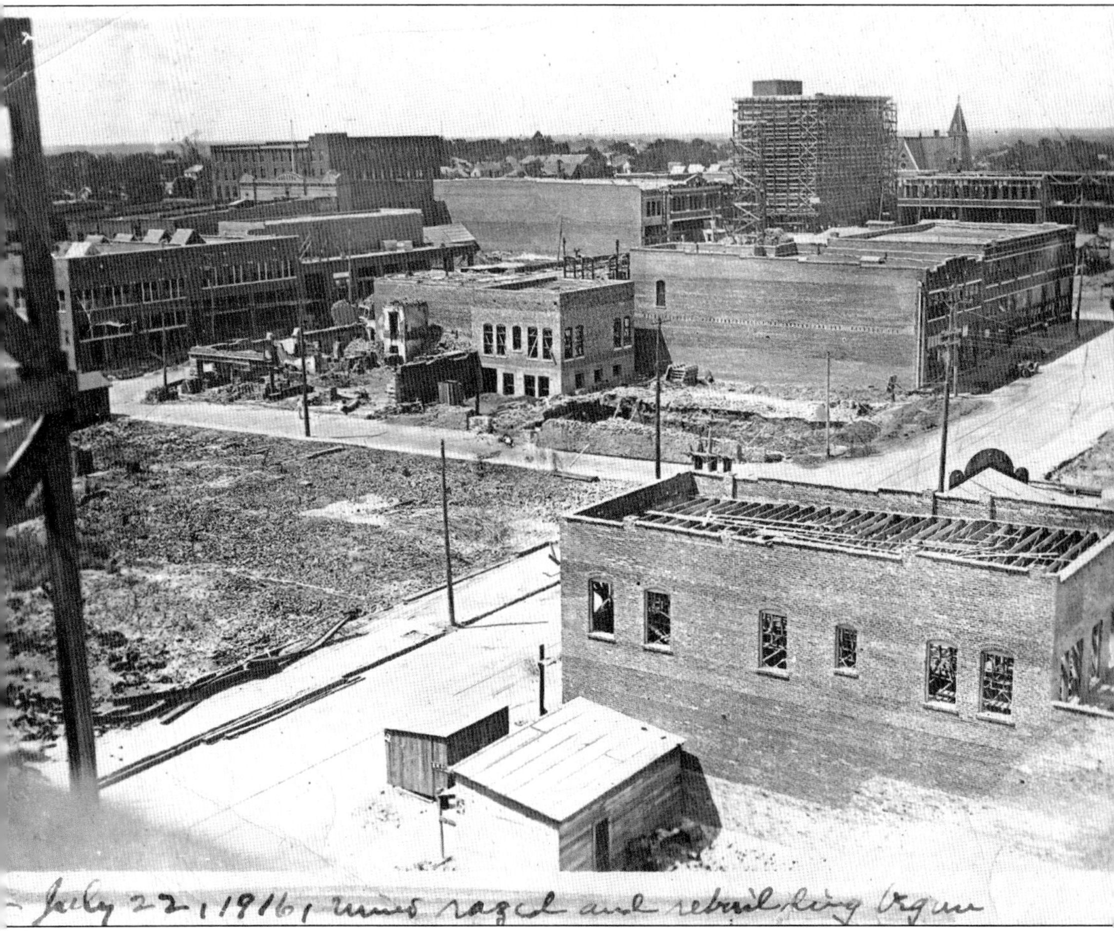

The Rebuilding of Paris. By July 22, 1916, just four months after the great fire, the rebuilding of Paris was well underway. This photograph was taken from the roof of the Gibraltar Hotel. The Gibraltar was built in 1912 and was damaged in the fire of 1916. The Gibraltar was a successful business for many years, serving rail passengers traveling between Dallas and St. Louis. The widespread availability of automobiles and the decline in rail passenger service spelled doom for the Gibraltar. As of 2011, attempts are being made to refurbish this once proud structure.

Two

Architecture and Landscape

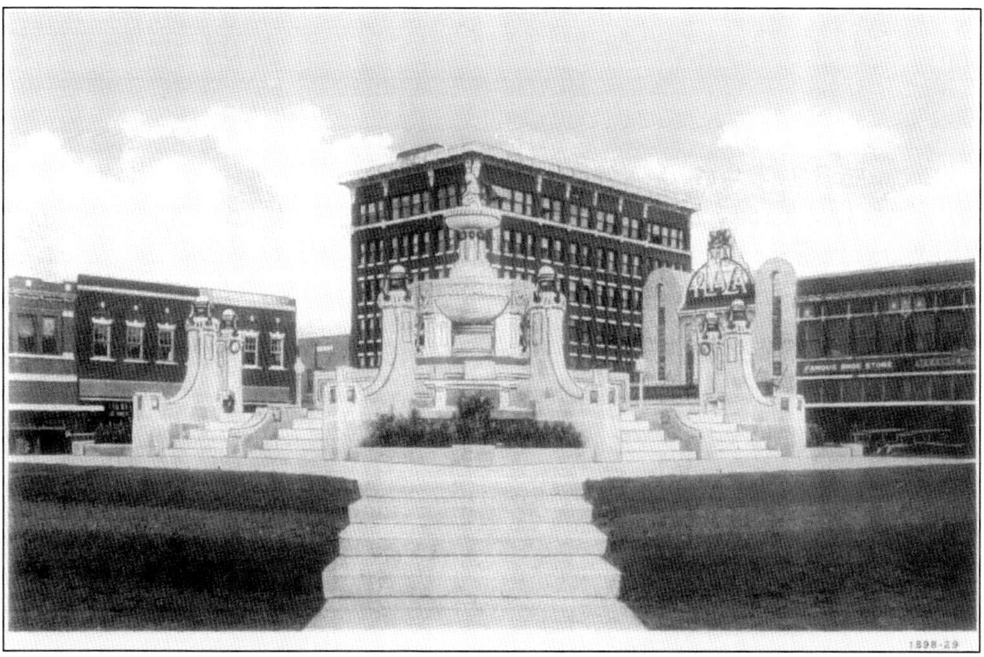

The Culbertson Fountain in the Downtown Plaza. The Culbertson Fountain was commissioned by John James Culbertson (1853–1932) and designed by German-born architect J.L. Wees. Culbertson was a great benefactor to the city. He presented the fountain to the people of Paris in 1927 as a memorial of the city's postfire renewal. It remains an enduring symbol of Paris and its history.

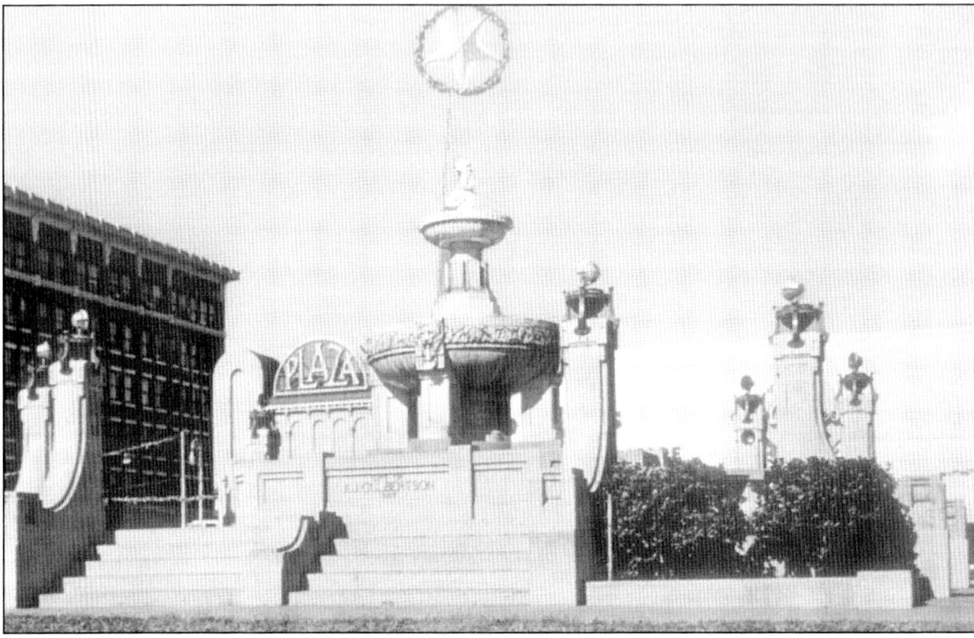

DECORATED CULBERTSON FOUNTAIN FOR CHRISTMAS. A mythological triton tops the fountain. The basin is formed of one piece of Carrara marble. If there is a "center" to Paris, it is the Culbertson Fountain. Even today, the fountain is decorated for local events. The fountain was restored as part of a bicentennial project.

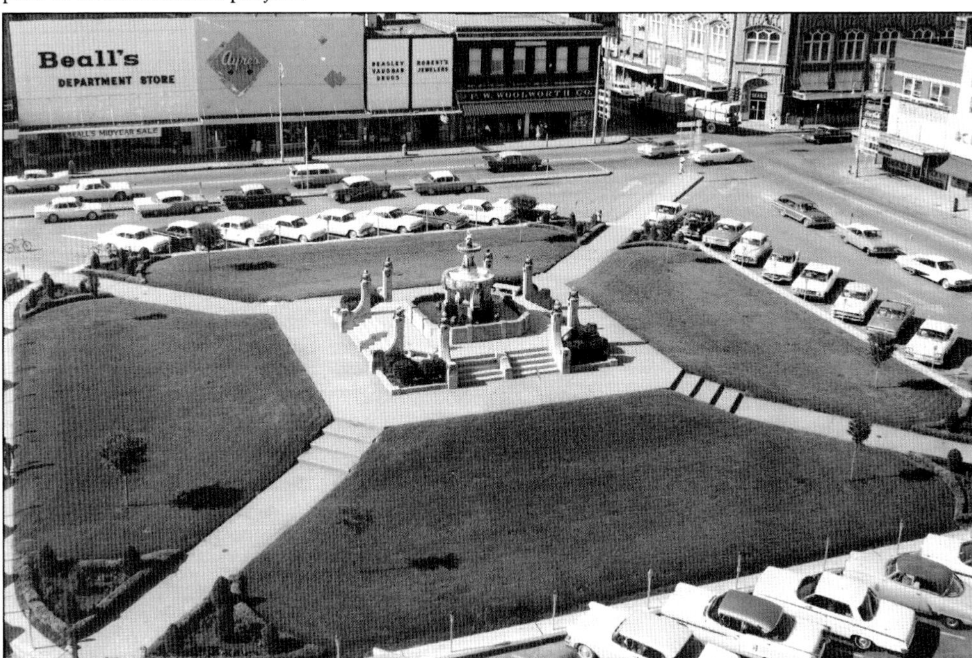

THE DOWNTOWN PLAZA IN THE LATE 1950S. The downtown plaza has always been a center of business and civic activity. One can identify F.W. Woolworth, the Palace Drugstore, and Sears as well as other stores, like Beall's Department Store. The downtown area was referred to as "the Square" until it was renamed "the Plaza" by the city council in July 1933.

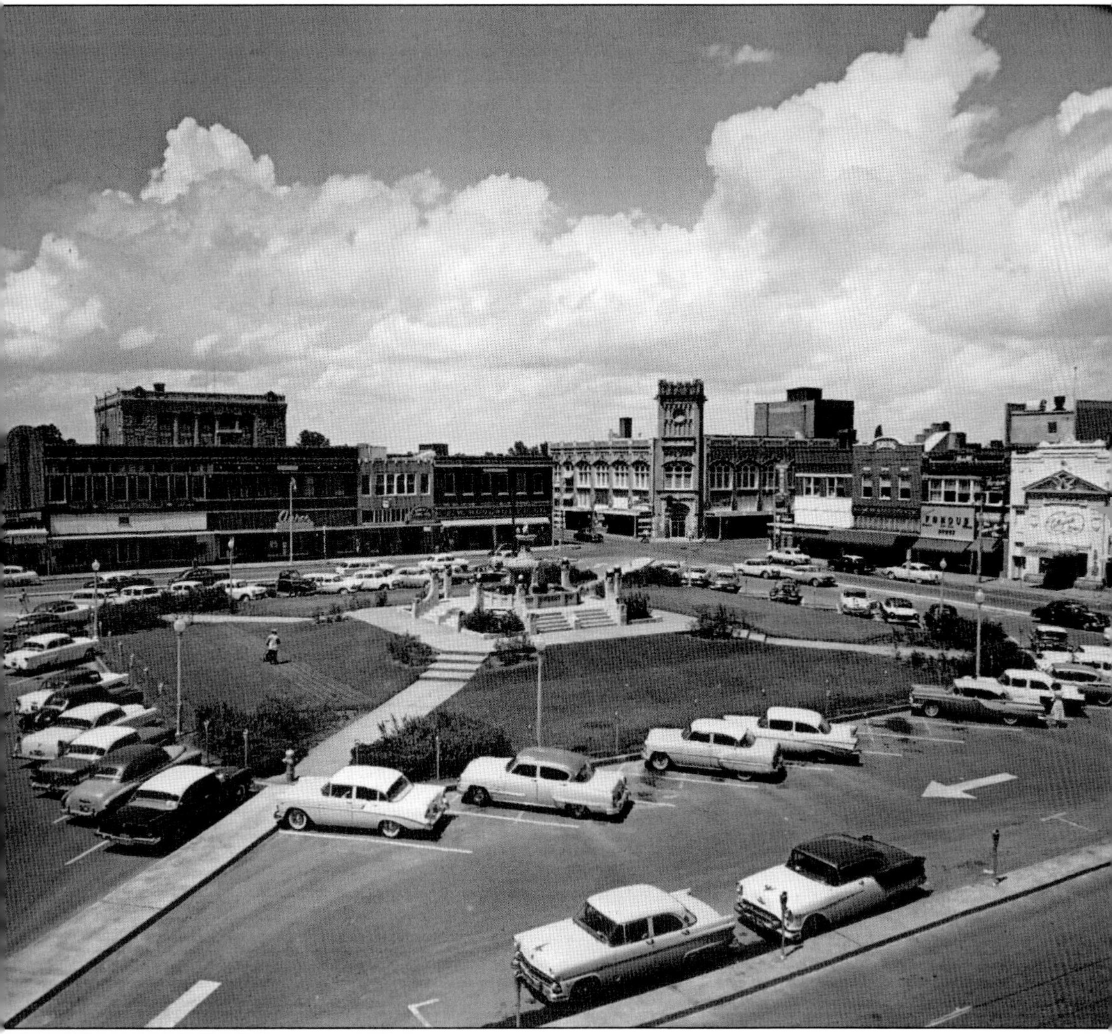

THE PARIS PLAZA IN THE 1950S. This photograph gives a good view of the downtown plaza. The courthouse can be seen on the skyline as well as the R.F. Scott Building with its distinctive tower. The R.F. Scott Building was designed by German-born architect J.L. Wees. Wees practiced architecture in St. Louis until he came to Paris to assist in the rebuilding in 1916. The R.F. Scott Building was completed quite quickly; it was ready for occupancy in 1917. It was built to house the Burton-Peel Dry Goods Store. In later years, the local Sears & Roebuck would call R.F. Scott home. Internal evidence within this photograph suggests that it was taken some years before the image on the preceding page.

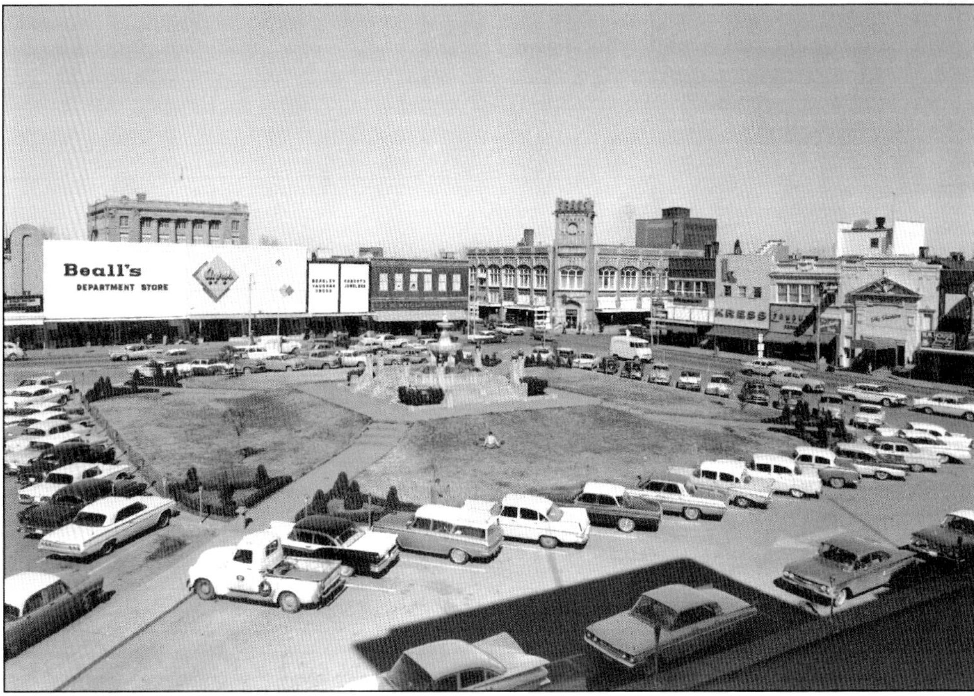

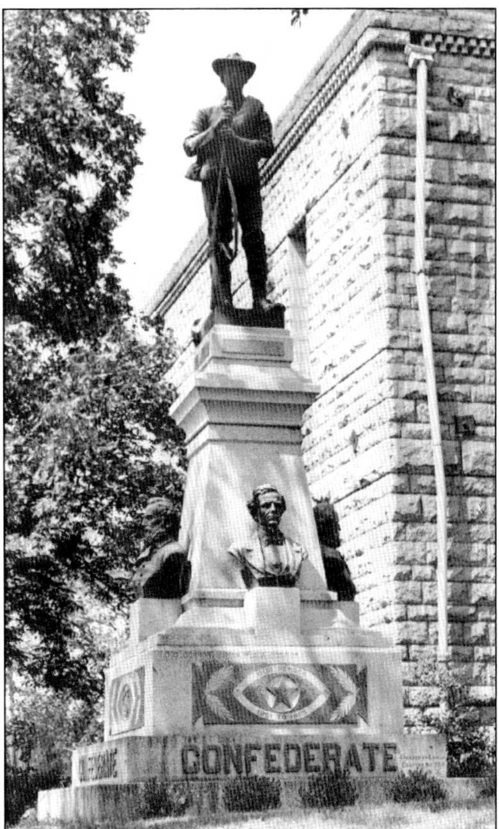

The Plaza. One can readily identify the Fashion Store and W.M. House Jewelry. Paris has always been a nationally known center of jewelry making and watch repair. Although this photograph and the one on page 32 are almost identical, they were taken at different times of the year. While the photograph on page 32 is probably a summer shot, this image was taken either in the late fall or early spring as evidenced by the foliage on the saplings around the fountain.

Monument to Confederate Soldiers. The Confederate memorial, located at the courthouse, was designed by architect Pompeo Copini and erected in 1903. It features an idealized Confederate soldier who is accompanied by four famous Confederate leaders, the president of the Confederacy, Jefferson Davis; Robert E. Lee; Thomas "Stonewall" Jackson; and Texan Albert Sydney Johnston. Both Jackson, killed in action in 1863, and Johnston, killed in action in 1862, were wartime Confederate heroes. Lee became the symbol of the Confederate war effort after his death in 1870.

The Chisum Monument in Paris. The photograph at right is an early-20th-century image of the Chisum monument in Paris. Cattleman John Chisum died in Arkansas at the age of 60 and is buried in Paris. In many ways, Chisum, cattlemen, and cowboys have been raised to mythic status by American film and television. Although Paris was never a major center of cattle raising, cattle were, and are, a component of the Lamar County landscape and economy. Cattle production peaked in Lamar County with 79,620 head in 1969. By 1982, the annual production of cattle was less than half of the 1969 total.

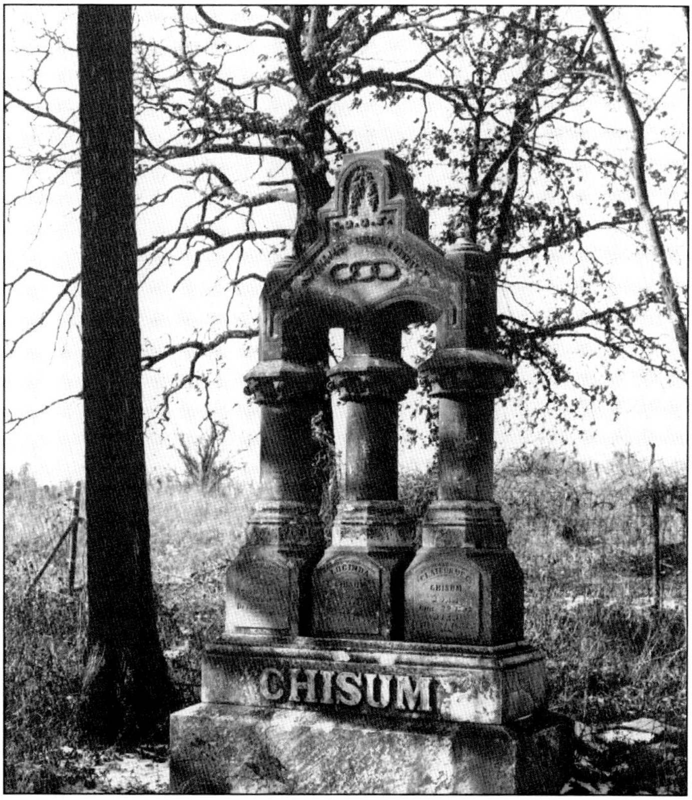

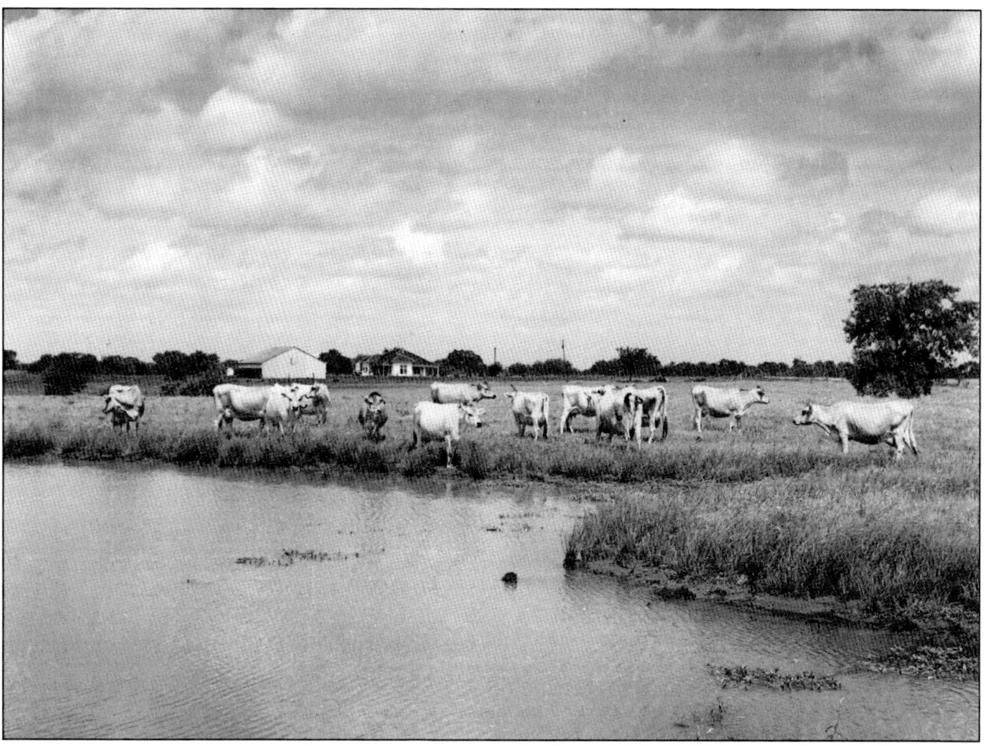

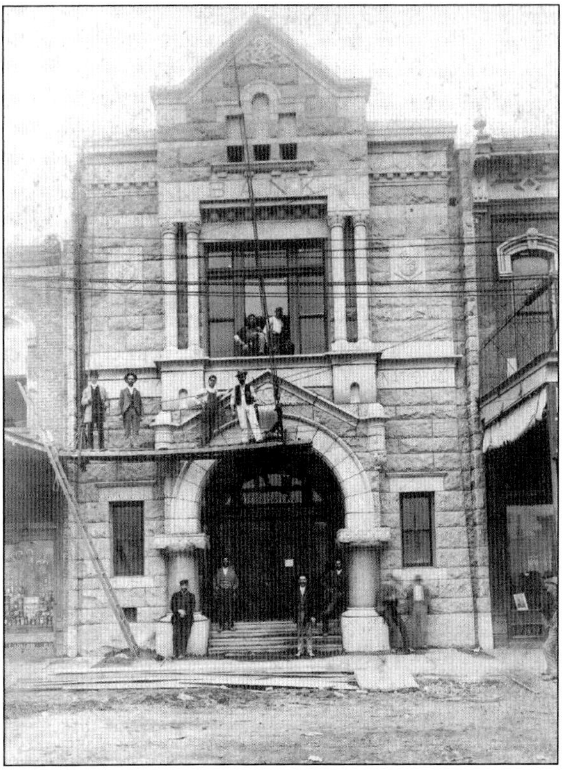

BANKS IN PARIS, TEXAS. When one thinks of the development of Paris, and indeed the United States, one does not often consider the critical role that banks played. Without banks, farmers, businessmen, and governments cannot take out loans to fund either business expansion or civic improvement. Because of this, banks played a critical, if unsung, role in the growth of Paris. The image at left is of City National Bank under construction, possibly in 1902. This building was destroyed only a few years later in 1916. The First National Bank was badly damaged in 1916. The structure was saved, however, and soon after the fire, First National was back in business, shown at right.

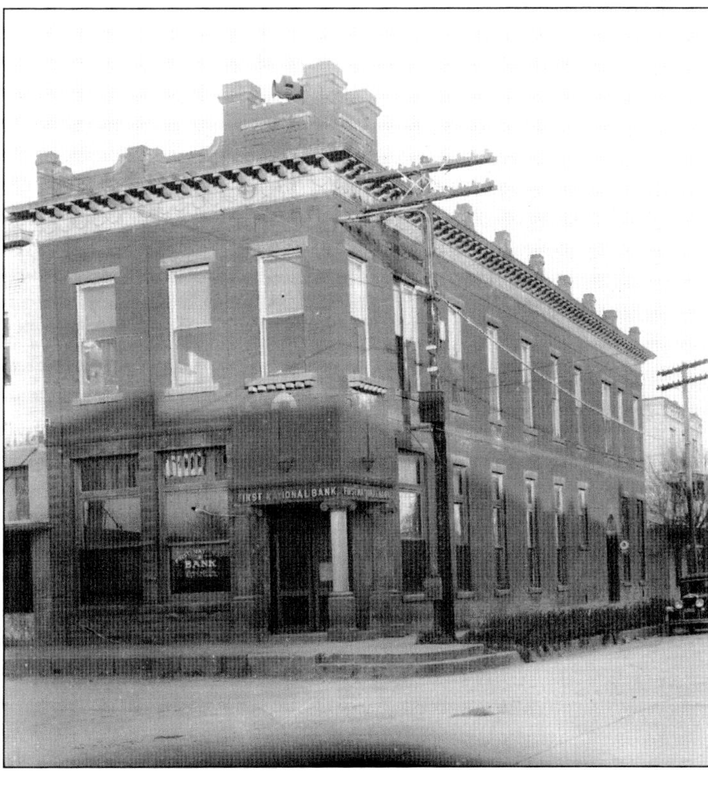

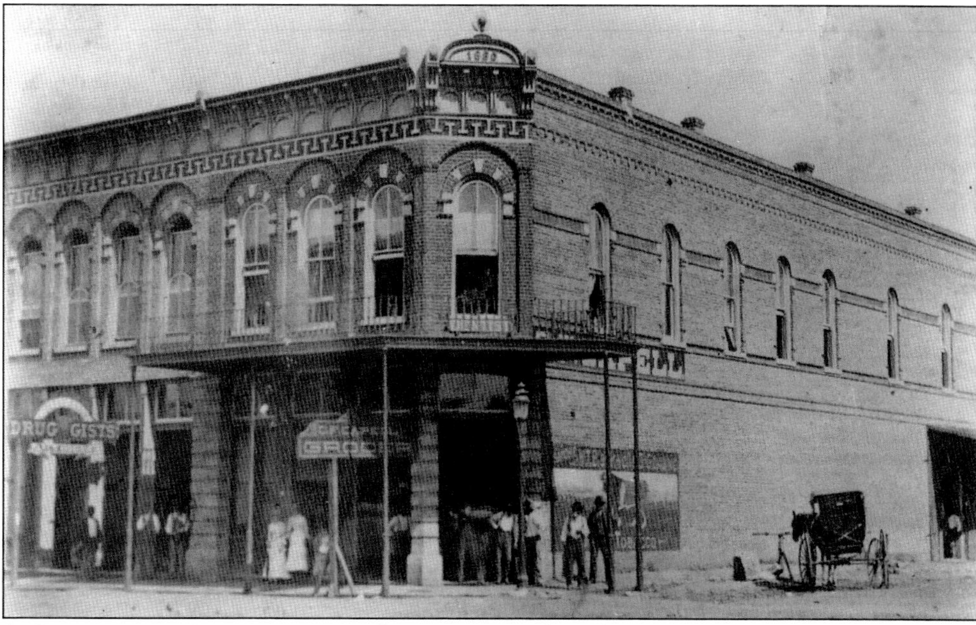

A Corner of the Square. C.F. Capell Grocers was a flourishing business during the 19th century. A close inspection of this photograph reveals that a dentist's office existed on the second floor of the building as well as a druggist shop (interestingly spelled "Drug Gists") to the left of the grocers. During the 19th century, drugstores sold all manner of patent medicines; most of which had no real curative effects.

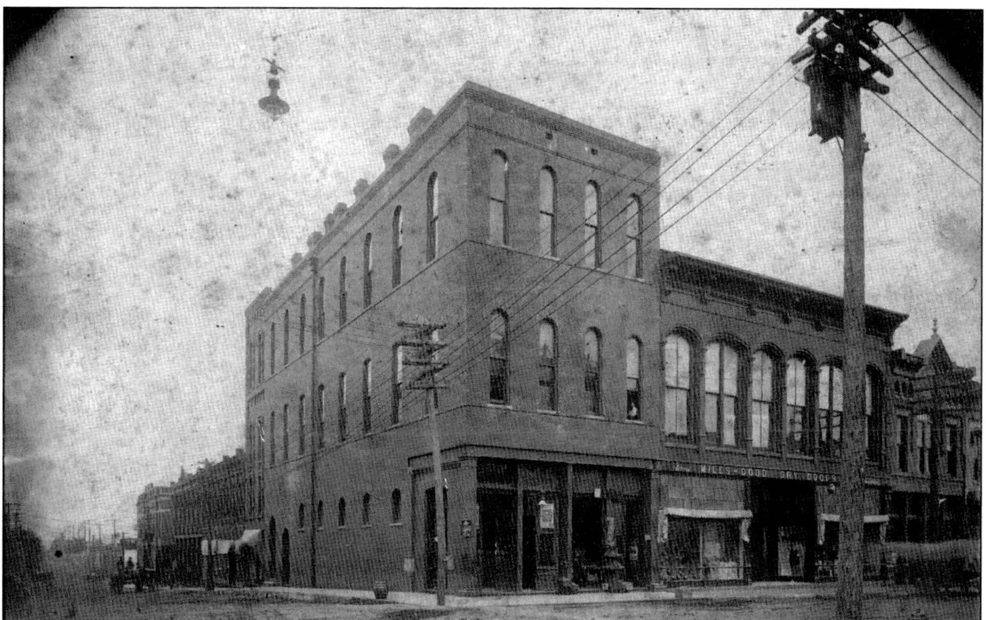

The Odd Fellows Building. The Odd Fellows Building was destroyed in 1916. A tavern was located on the first floor and sold Schlitz beer according to a sign in front of the establishment. Next to the tavern is Miles-Dodd Dry Goods. One can see a newly installed fire hydrant at the bottom right.

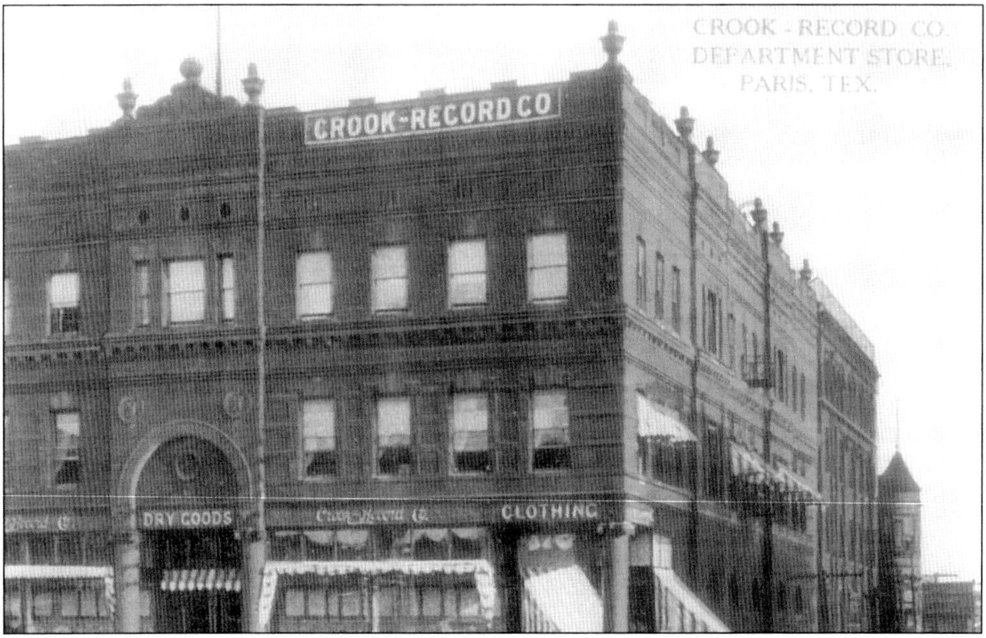

The Crook-Record Co. Department Store. The Crook-Record Co. and department store was a fixture in Paris downtown for many decades. W.P. Lane, who would go on to be comptroller of the State of Texas (1911–1914), worked at Crook-Record Co. in his early years. (Courtesy of the Lamar County Historical Society Museum.)

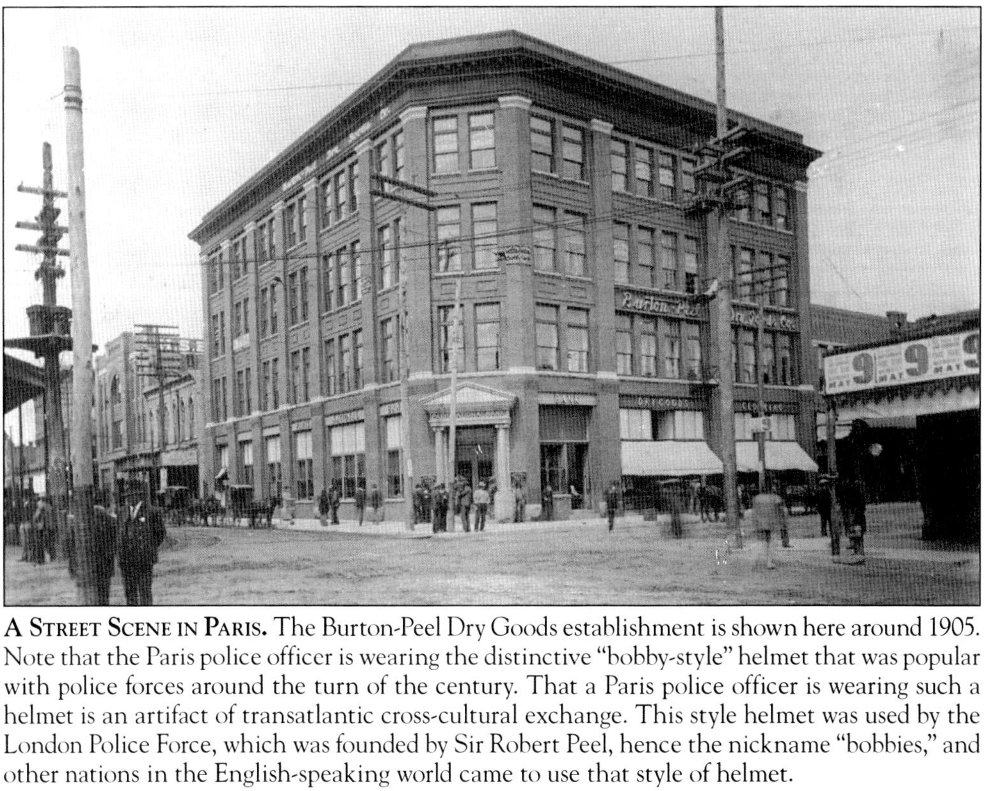

A Street Scene in Paris. The Burton-Peel Dry Goods establishment is shown here around 1905. Note that the Paris police officer is wearing the distinctive "bobby-style" helmet that was popular with police forces around the turn of the century. That a Paris police officer is wearing such a helmet is an artifact of transatlantic cross-cultural exchange. This style helmet was used by the London Police Force, which was founded by Sir Robert Peel, hence the nickname "bobbies," and other nations in the English-speaking world came to use that style of helmet.

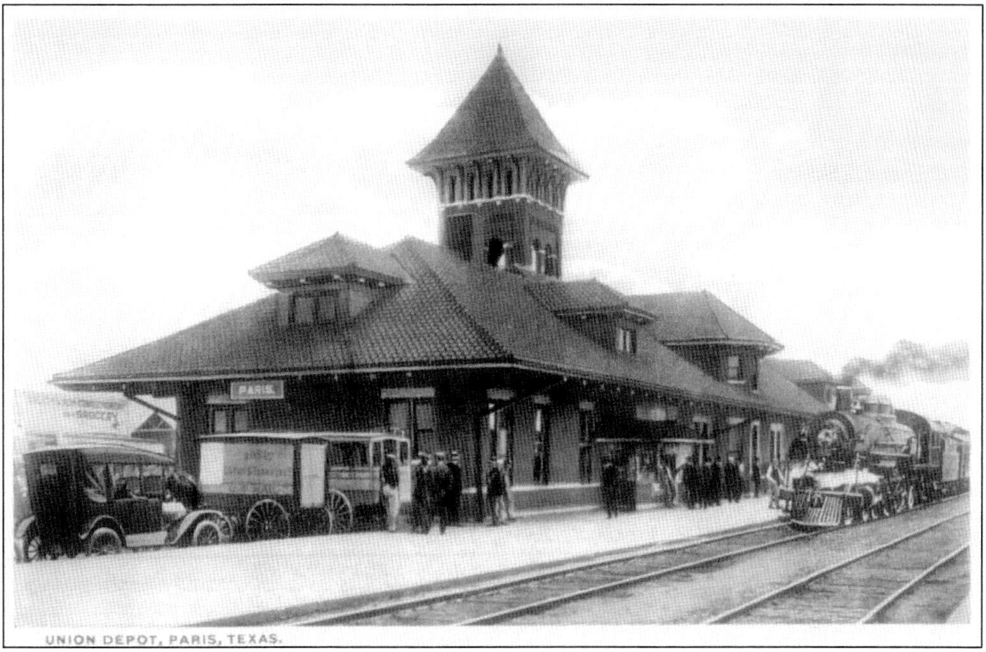

The Paris Train Station. The old Union Station depot is a distinctive landmark in Paris and houses the transportation museum. Next door to the station is the Lamar County Historical Society Museum. If one is interested in the history of Paris, the first place he or she should investigate is the Lamar County Historical Society Museum.

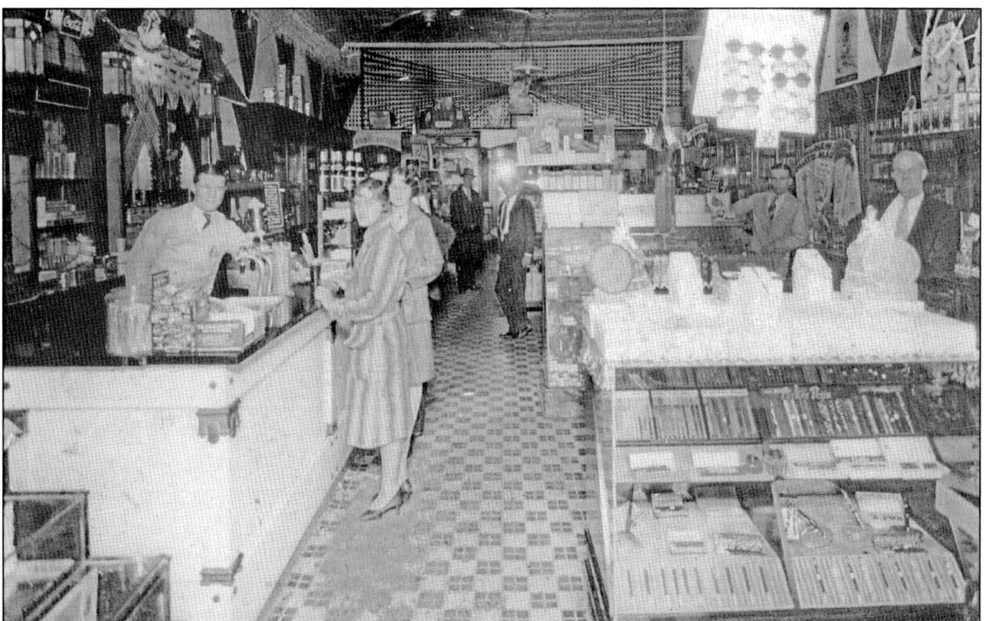

The Palace Drugstore. The Palace Drugstore was a fixture in downtown Paris from the 19th century through the mid–20th century. In this image from 1930, one can see the soda fountain that was so typical of drugstores prior to the development of nationwide, corporate drugstore chains. Parker pens are on display in the front case.

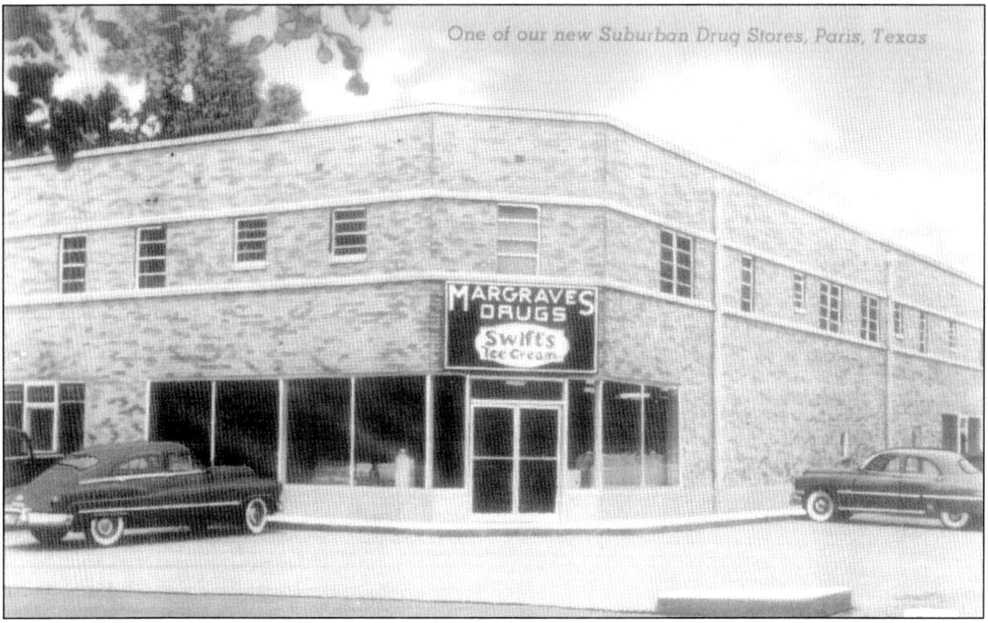

MARGRAVE DRUGSTORE. Margrave's was a favorite hangout for Paris teenagers in the 1950s and 1960s. Located across from the sanitarium, Margrave's had a soda fountain so typical of the period. During the "glory days" of community drugstores in the 1950s and 1960s, drugstores did more than sell prescription drugs. All manner of goods were sold at drugstores, and it almost always featured a soda fountain and often served hamburgers and other fast food items popular with teenagers at the time. (Courtesy of the Lamar County Historical Society Museum.)

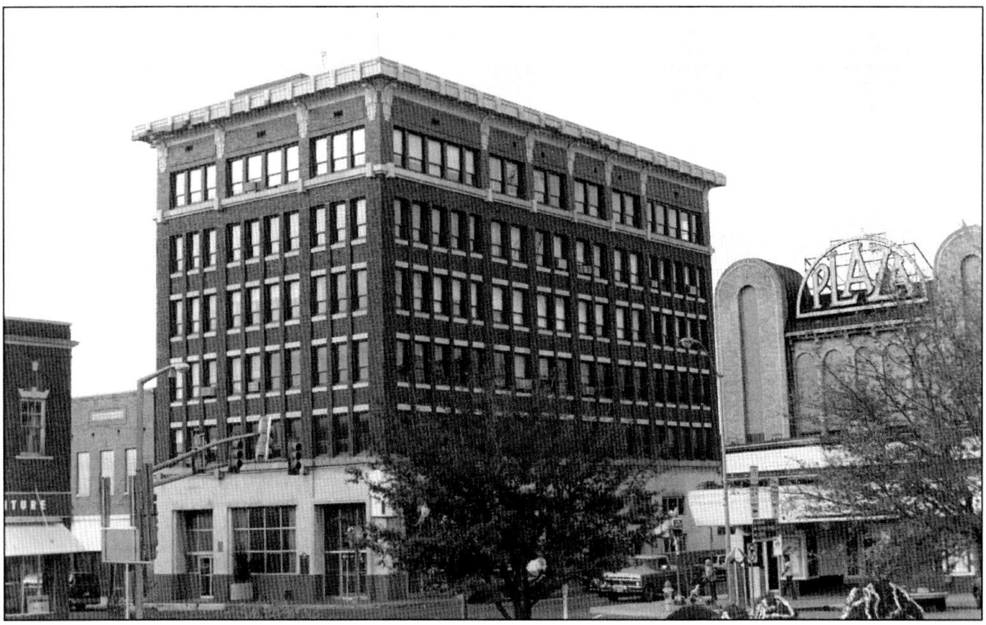

THE FIRST NATIONAL BANK AND THE PLAZA THEATER. In this photograph, the Plaza Theater can be identified. The Plaza Theater, with its distinctive sign, opened for business in July 1926. Although motion pictures are no longer shown at the Plaza, the theater is now the venue for Paris Community Theater stage productions.

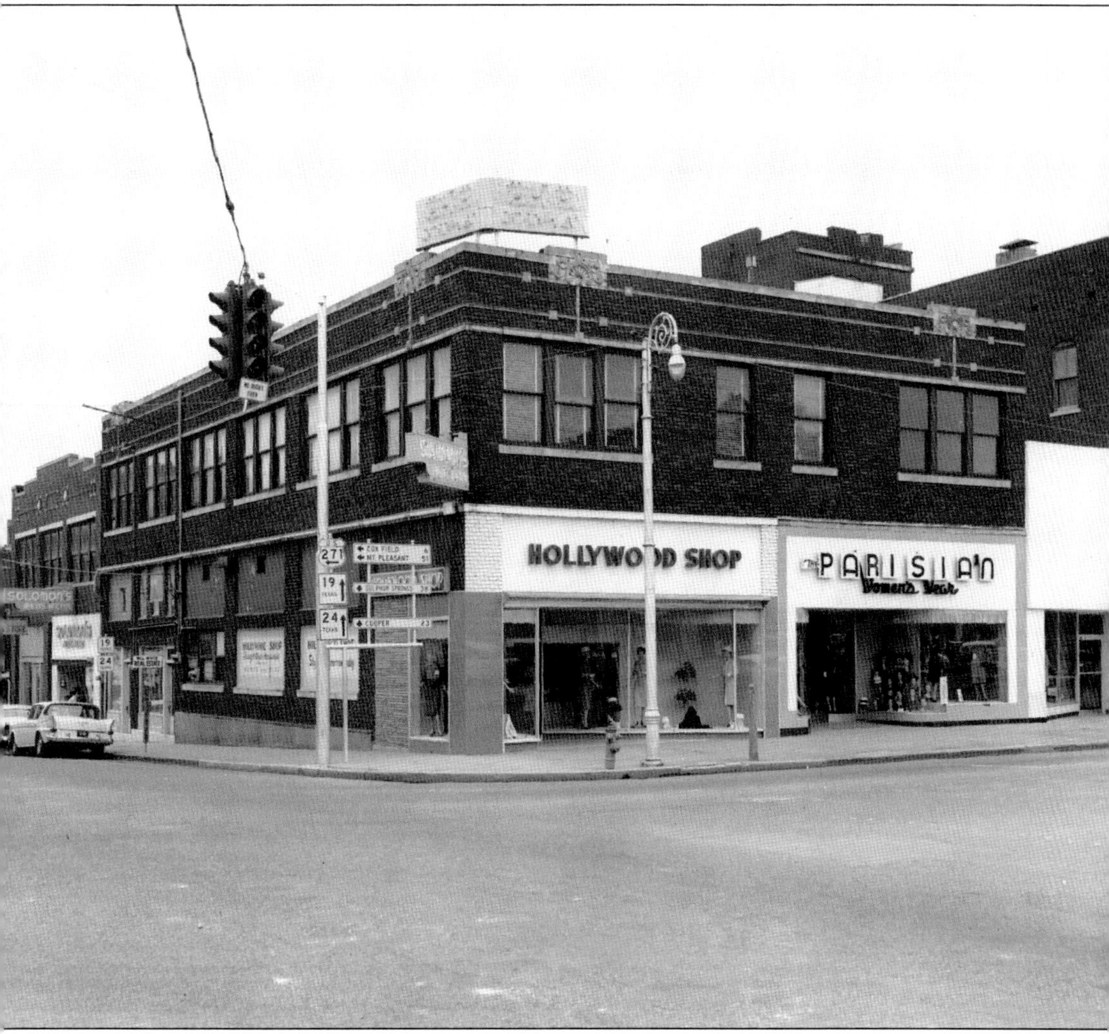

SHOPS ON THE PLAZA ABOUT 1963. The Hollywood Shop was a favorite shopping location; it was particularly well known for its women's hats. To the right of the Hollywood Shop is Parisian Women's Wear, a popular store for fashion-conscious Paris women. Solomon's Men's Wear and the office of Bill White Real Estate can also be identified in this photograph.

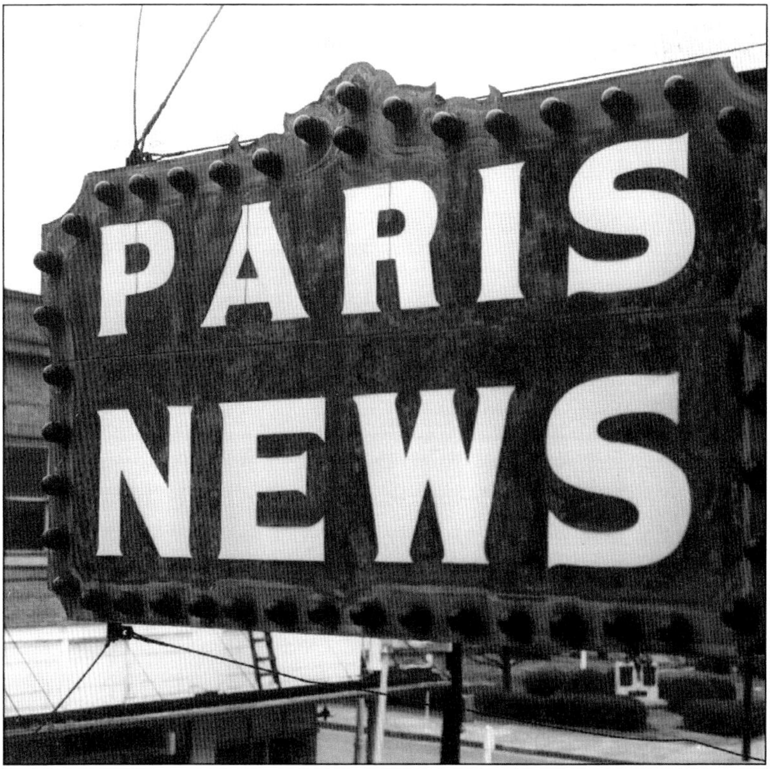

LOGO OF THE *PARIS NEWS*. The *Paris News* began operations as a weekly paper in 1869. Like many small towns across the United States in the 19th century, Paris had any number of daily and weekly papers. The *Paris News* was the one paper to stay in business. (Courtesy of the *Paris News*.)

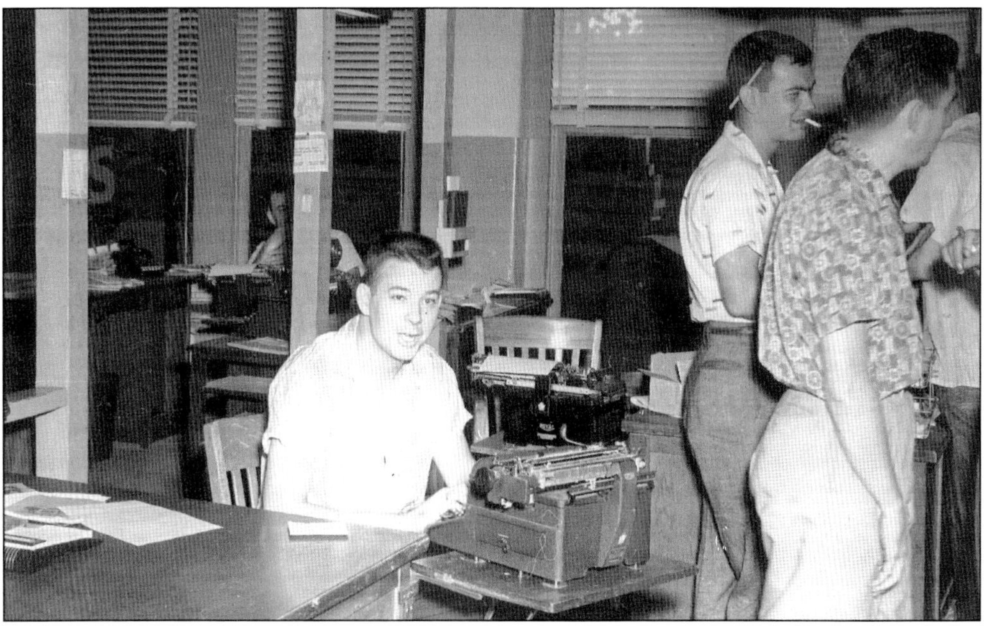

THE *PARIS NEWS* NEWSROOM. Here, reporters of the *Paris News* are discussing some current event around 1960. The *Paris News* has served Lamar County since the 19th century. Before the advent of the Internet and television news, people received local, national, and international news via the printed daily newspaper. With the advent of the Internet, local newspapers have struggled to survive. (Courtesy of the *Paris News*.)

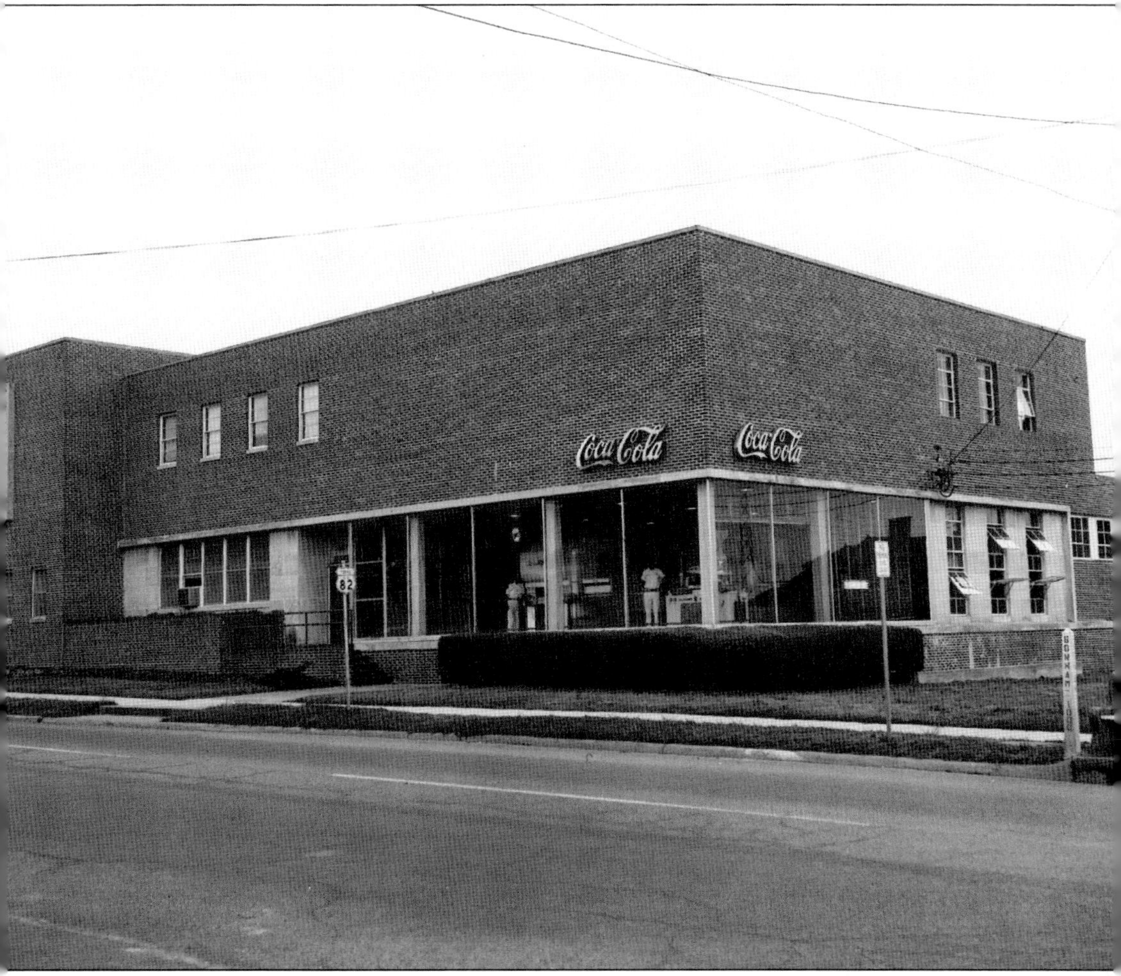

Paris Coke. The Coca-Cola bottling and distributing plant in Paris was founded by C.C. Smith in 1906. The business was sold in 1908 to George Griffith and Will Freeze. Griffith and Freeze subsequently sold out to the Rainwater organization in 1943. Coca-Cola Enterprises acquired the facility from the Rainwater family in 1986. The facility no longer bottled Coke products by the early 21st century; however, it still acts as a regional distribution center. Paris Coke employs 33 people and has a $1.3 million impact on the Paris economy. In addition, Paris Coke generously donates to the United Way and the Boys & Girls Clubs.

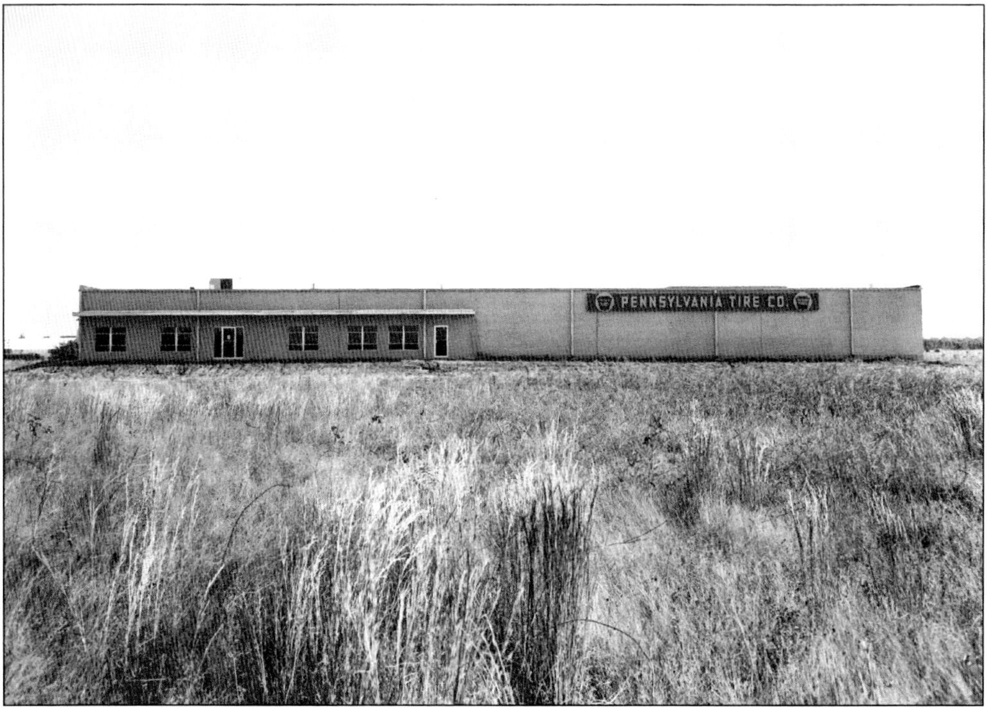

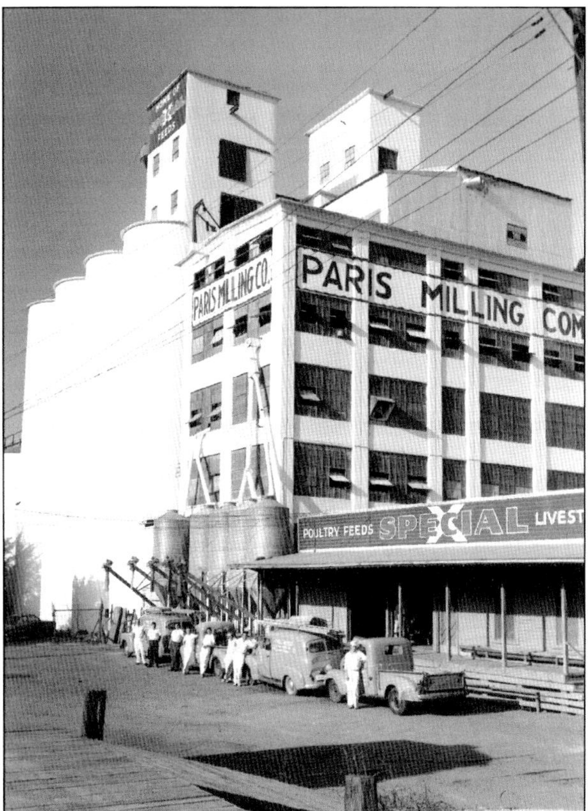

THE PENNSYLVANIA TIRE COMPANY. The Pennsylvania Tire Company was a major employer in Paris for many years. Prior to the late-20th-century business practice of outsourcing manufacturing overseas, small communities, such as Paris, benefitted greatly when corporations would locate facilities in their towns. Many small communities have been virtually destroyed when local corporations outsourced production overseas.

THE PARIS MILLING COMPANY. Employees of the Paris Milling Company pose for the photographer. This company's origins can be traced back to 1850 when Francis Bassano established a gristmill in Paris. Old-fashioned gristmills were simply places where grain was ground to flour. In other words, gristmills were required for any town that wished to advance beyond sustenance agriculture. The Paris Milling Company is no longer in operation.

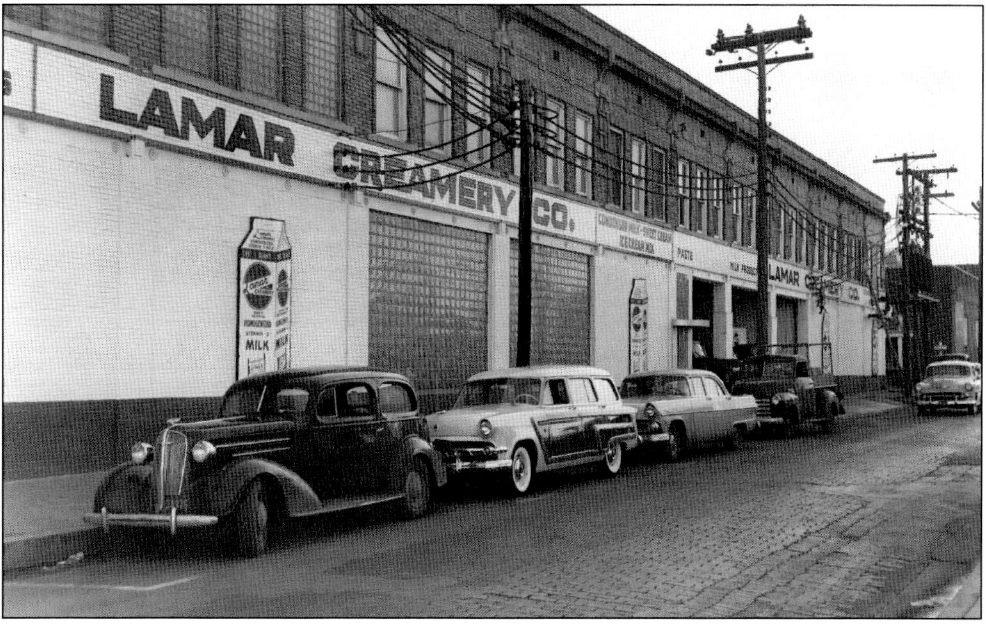

THE LAMAR CREAMERY. The Lamar Creamery was founded in 1928 and was a major employer in Paris for almost 40 years. Unfortunately, the facility suffered a devastating fire on May 18, 1964. With the facility destroyed, the management elected to relocate the plant to Sulphur Springs. Interestingly, the fire was so ferocious that local citizens were called in to help the firefighters battle the blaze.

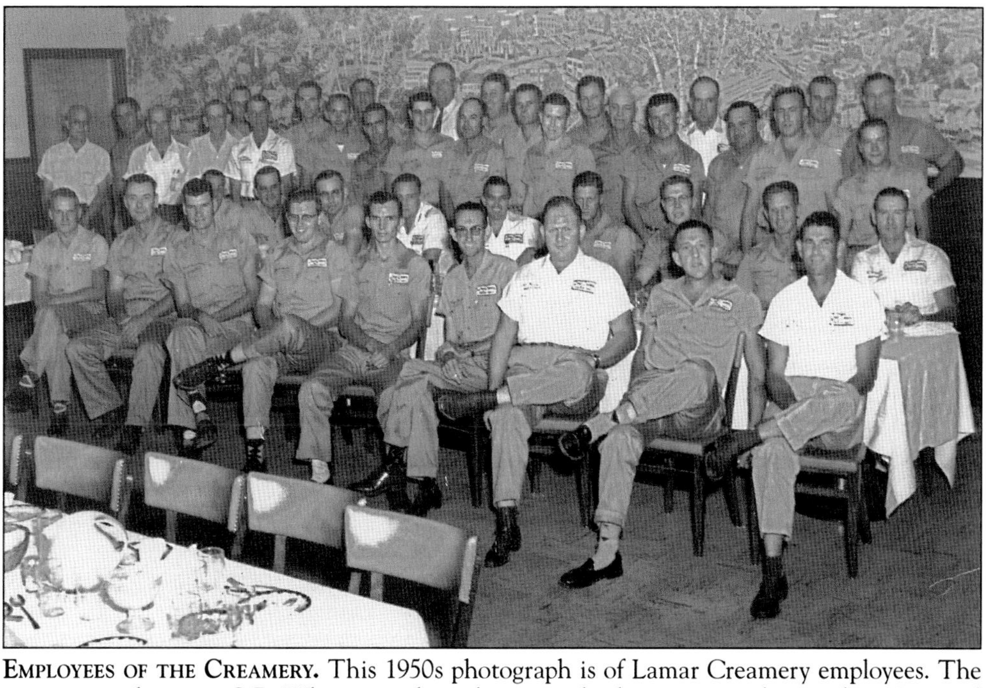

EMPLOYEES OF THE CREAMERY. This 1950s photograph is of Lamar Creamery employees. The manager at the time, O.B. White, stands at the center back, wearing a shirt and tie. Internal evidence in the picture seems to indicate that this photograph was taken during a holiday dinner given by the company for the employees.

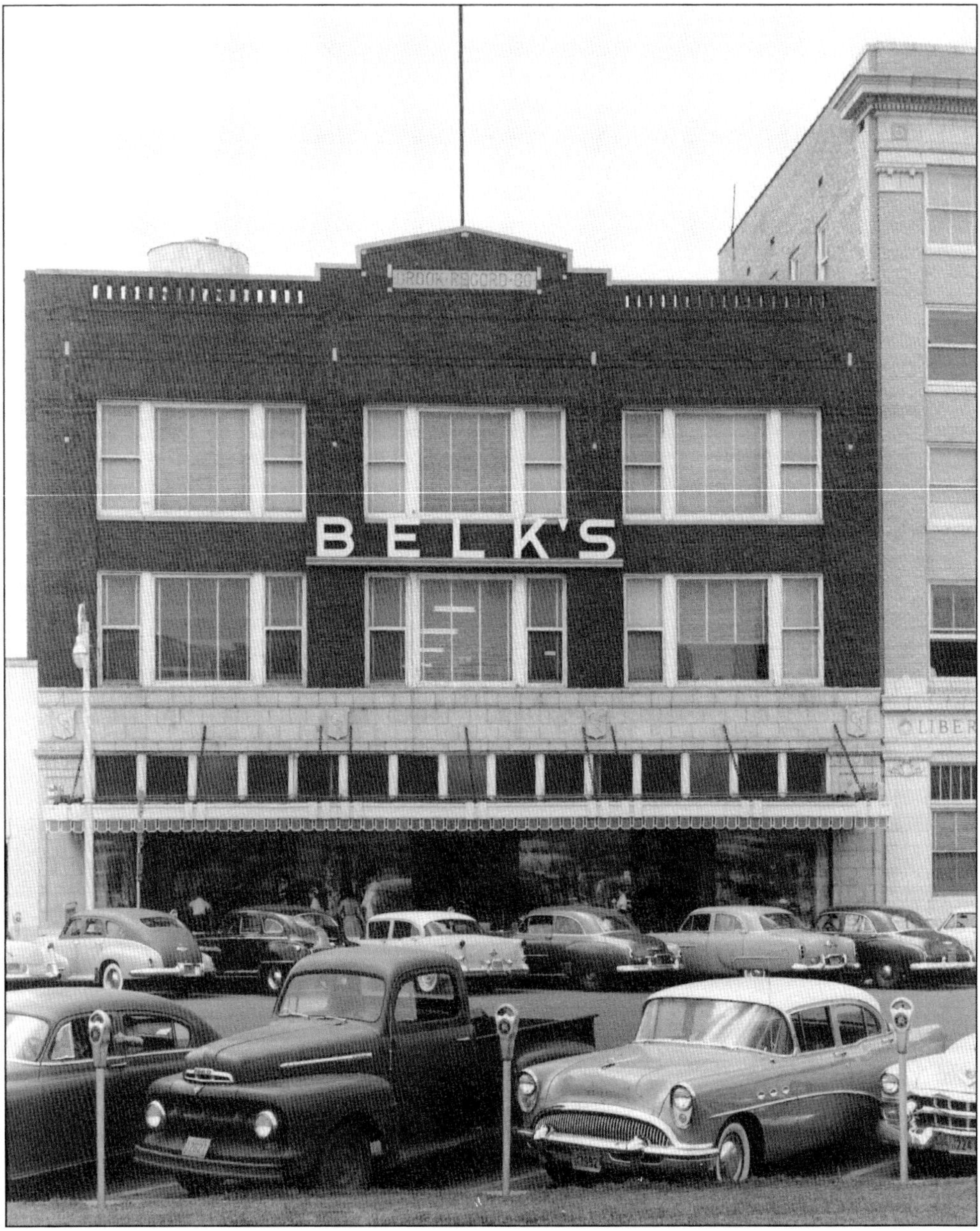

Belk's Department Store Downtown. Belk's Department Store was a longtime fixture of the downtown plaza. Here, Belk's occupies the old Crook-Record Co. Building. Belk's is a national chain of department stores located primarily in the South. The first Belk's was opened in Monroe, North Carolina, in 1888. Belk's is the largest privately owned department store chain in the United States. Today, the Belk's in Paris is known as Belk Paris Town Center and is located on Loop 286.

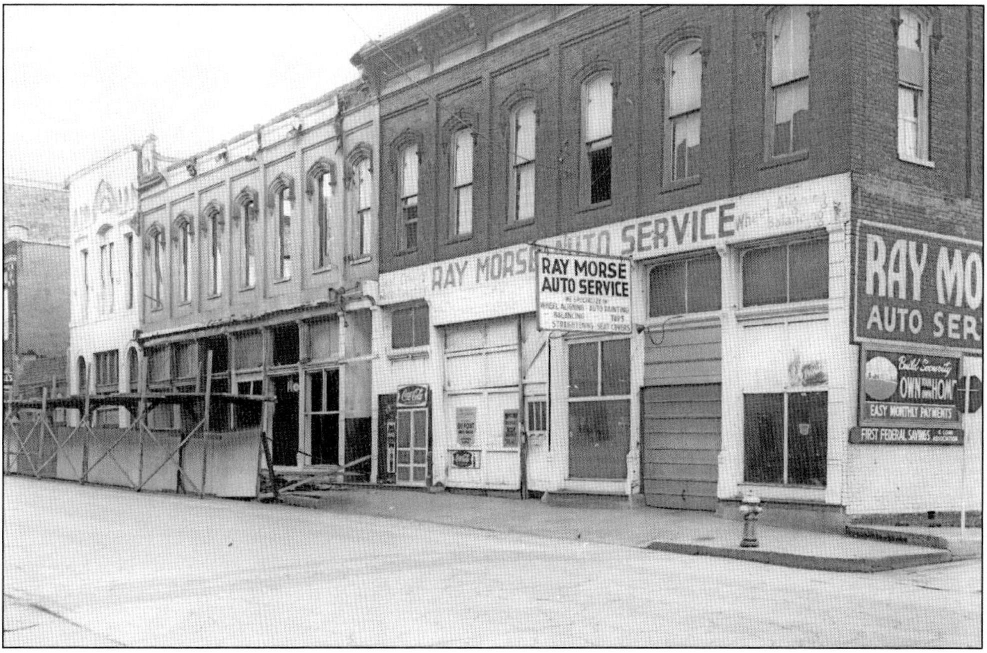

The Ray Morse Auto Service Company. The Ray Morse Auto Service Company stands next to a downtown building that has been gutted for renovation in 1960. The building being renovated may have housed a Bell Telephone office. The Bell system, "Ma Bell" as it was called, was broken up into separate companies in 1984 as a result of a lawsuit.

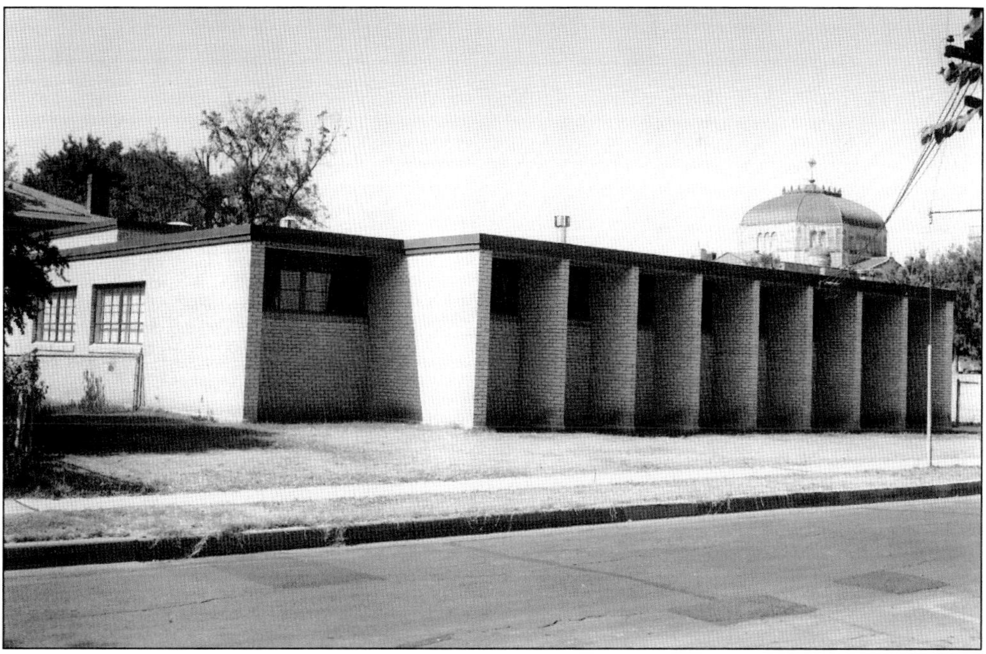

The Old Paris High School Music Annex about 1955. The music annex was used as a band hall by members of the Paris High School band. In 1975, the annex was converted into a day nursery operated by the King's Daughters. On the skyline is the distinctive cupola of the First Methodist Church.

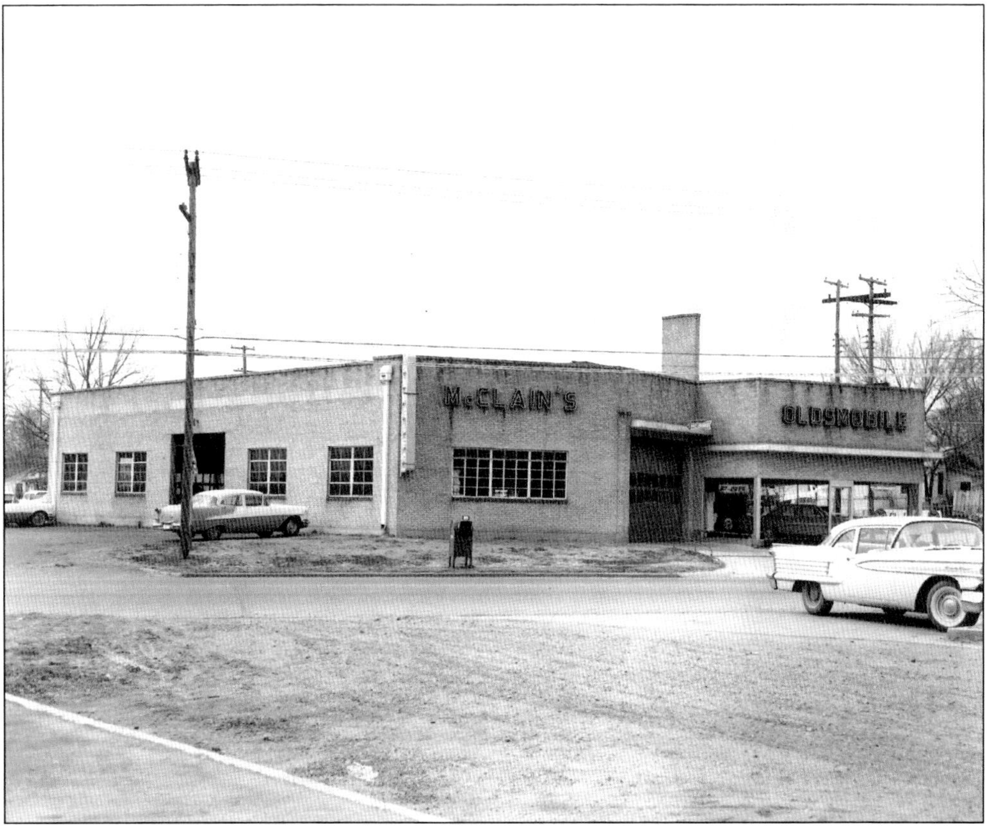

McCLAIN'S OLDSMOBILE DEALERSHIP IN THE 1950s. The first automobile in Paris seems to have been an Oldsmobile, owned by Col. R. Peterson, in 1898. The Oldsmobile line of automobiles first hit the road in 1897. In 2004, General Motors discontinued the Olds marquee and rolled the last Oldsmobile off the assembly line.

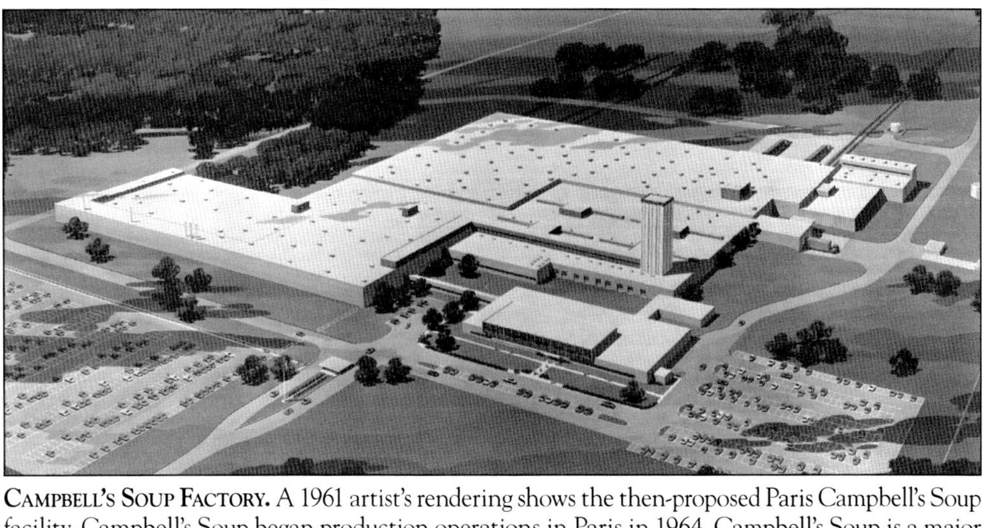

CAMPBELL'S SOUP FACTORY. A 1961 artist's rendering shows the then-proposed Paris Campbell's Soup facility. Campbell's Soup began production operations in Paris in 1964. Campbell's Soup is a major employer in Paris and contributes millions of dollars per year to the Paris economy. Campbell's Soup is a popular place to work as it provides good pay and benefits as well as job security.

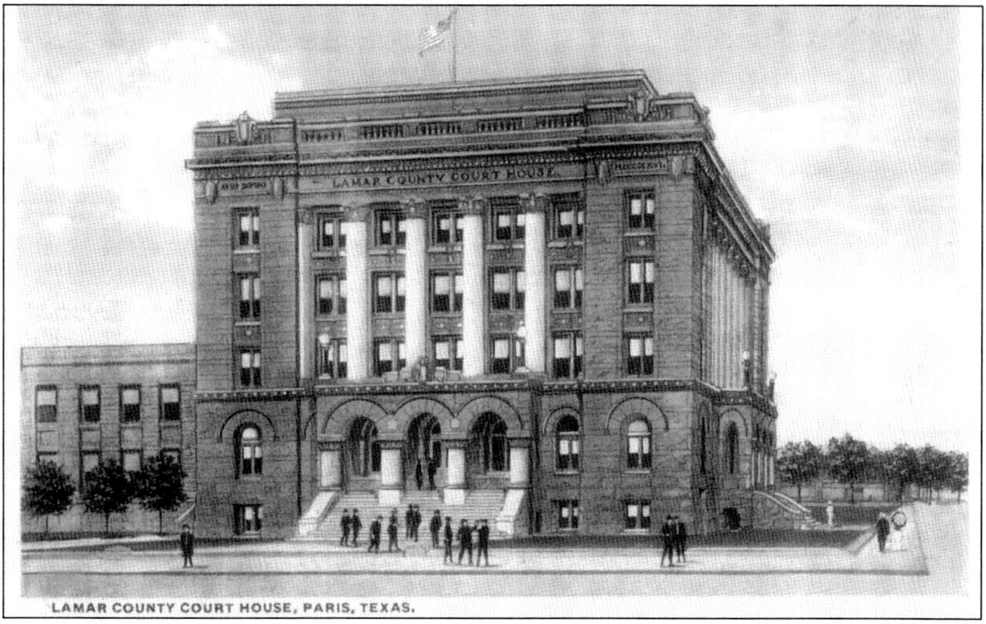

The Lamar County Courthouse in the 1930s. The old courthouse was destroyed in the fire of 1916. This structure was completed in 1917. The courthouse is the place where most people interact with the government, which is not always for criminal matters. (Courtesy of the Lamar County Historical Society Museum.)

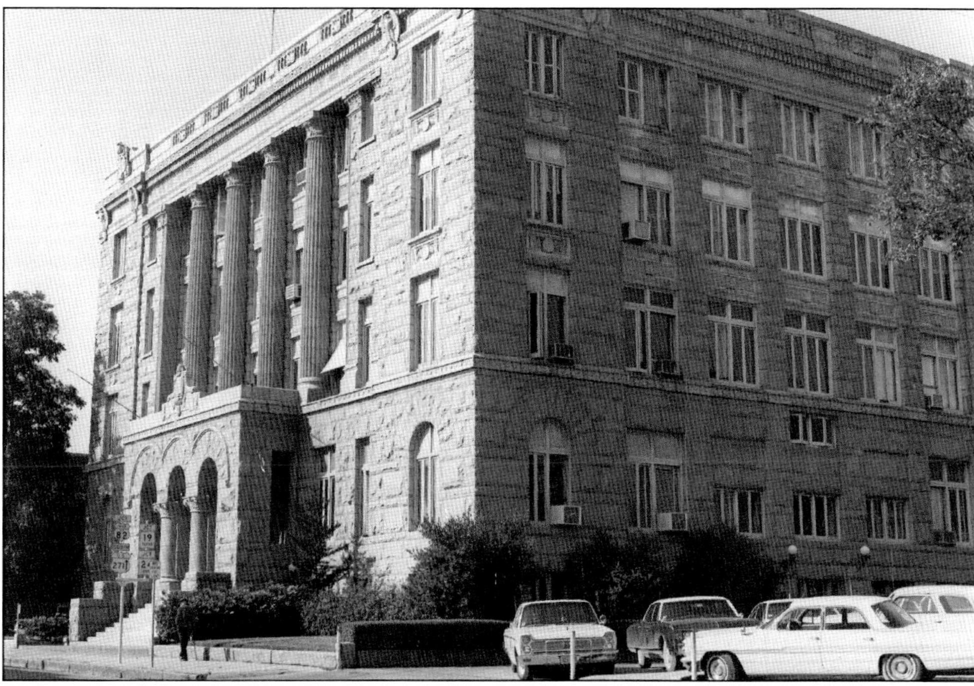

The Courthouse in the 1960s. The 1917 courthouse was restored in 2007 and is still in use. Courthouses provide all manner of services to communities. Marriage licenses are issued from courthouses. In addition, births and deaths are registered in those places. Deeds, business deals, and records are also kept at local courthouses.

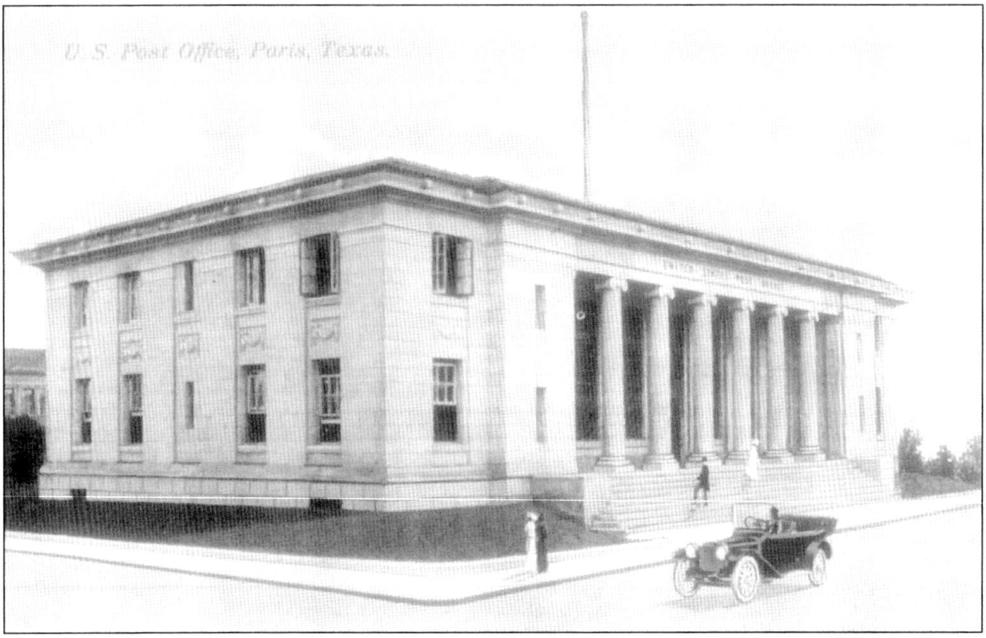

THE PARIS POST OFFICE ABOUT 1920. Previous post office facilities occupied a variety of different locations during the early years of Paris. The Paris Post Office Building in 1916 was seriously damaged by the fire. It is easy to forget that in the days before the Internet and cheap long-distance telephone service, it was the US Postal Service that, in many ways, bound the nation together. (Courtesy of the Lamar County Historical Society Museum.)

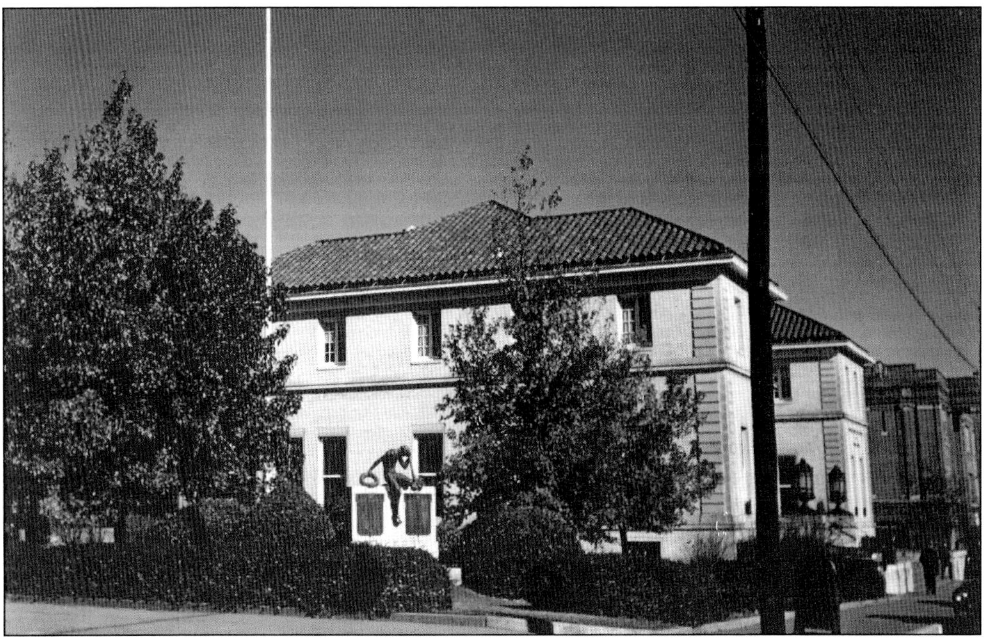

THE WORLD WAR I MEMORIAL IN PARIS. About 340 Lamar County residents served in the military during the World War I. Eleven were killed in action in France. Many of these men would have served in the 359th Infantry Texas Brigade, part of the 90th Division. The 359th saw severe fighting around St. Mihiel.

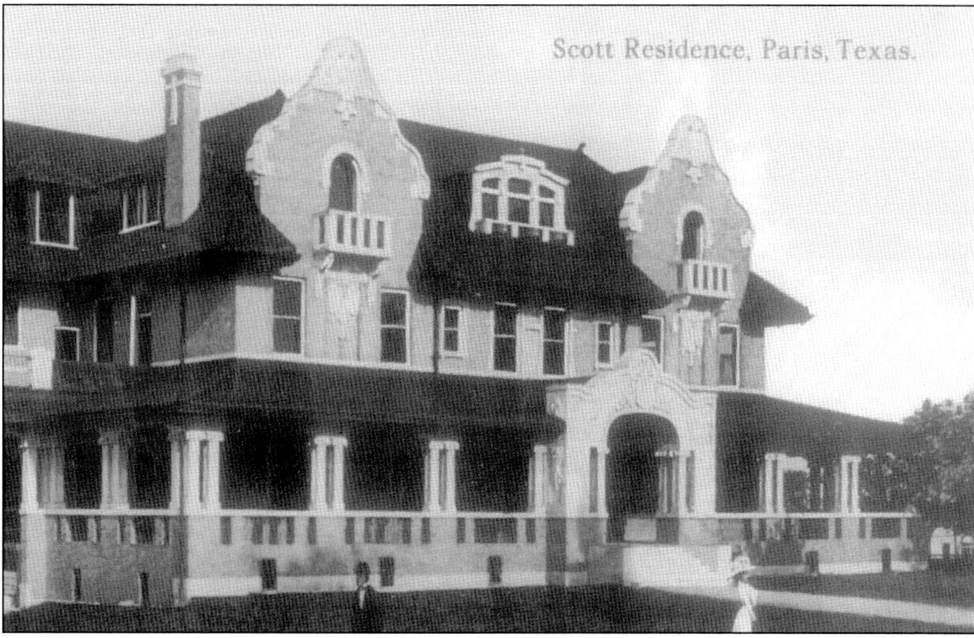

THE RUFUS F. SCOTT HOME IN THE EARLY 20TH CENTURY. This old house was completed in 1910 and was the home of R.F. Scott. The home was purchased by Gene Roden in 1938 and converted into a funeral home and operated by the Roden family for many years. The building is now the Starrett Funeral Home. (Courtesy of the Lamar County Historical Society Museum.)

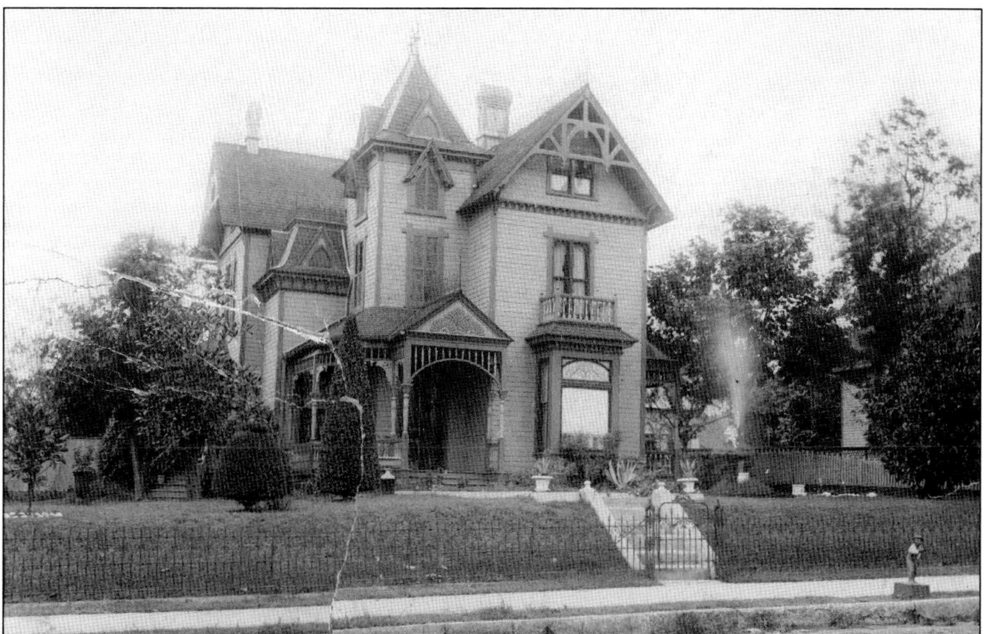

A WELL-KEPT VICTORIAN HOME. This is an excellent example of Victorian architecture. This home is also a visible demonstration of the prosperity of Paris before the great fire. At the time this photograph was taken, the street was not yet paved. In addition, a high-pressure water fountain is rather dramatically flowing. Also, potted aloe vera plants can be seen in the front yard.

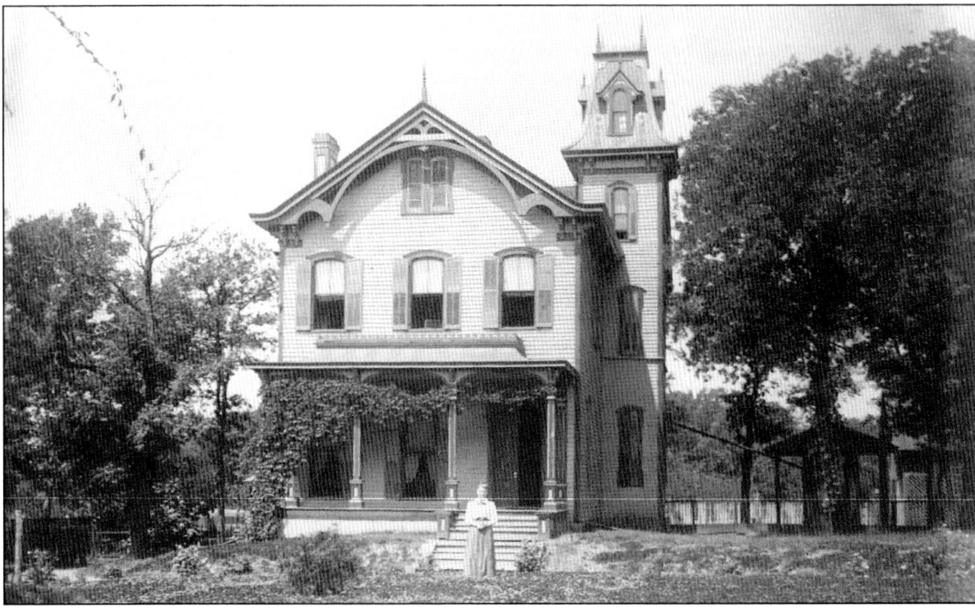

Kaufman Terrace about 1900. This home, located appropriately on Kaufman Street, is a wonderful example of the high level of skill and craftsmanship that went into home construction at the time. Kaufman Terrace was built for James Daniel, a Virginian, who came to Paris after the Civil War. Today, Kaufman Terrace has been restored to its previous glory.

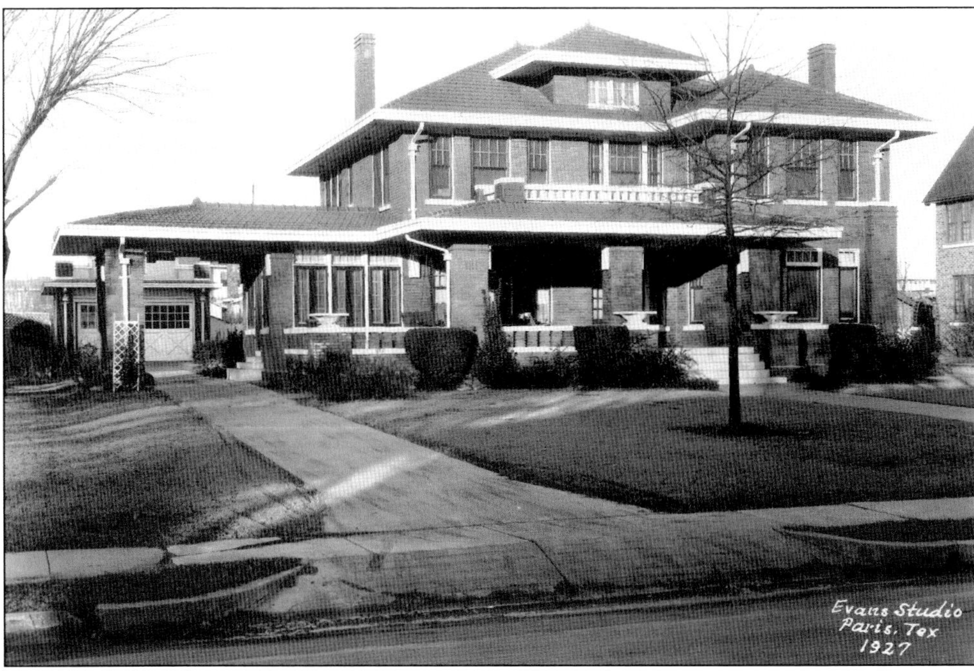

A Fine Old Home on Church Street. After the fire of 1916, Paris rebuilt itself, seemingly almost overnight. One might argue that, like a Phoenix, Paris rose reborn from the ashes. Fine houses, many still extant, came to grace the "new" Paris. This home on Church Street was built immediately after the 1916 fire. This photograph was taken in 1927. The young tree in front of this house was still standing in 2011.

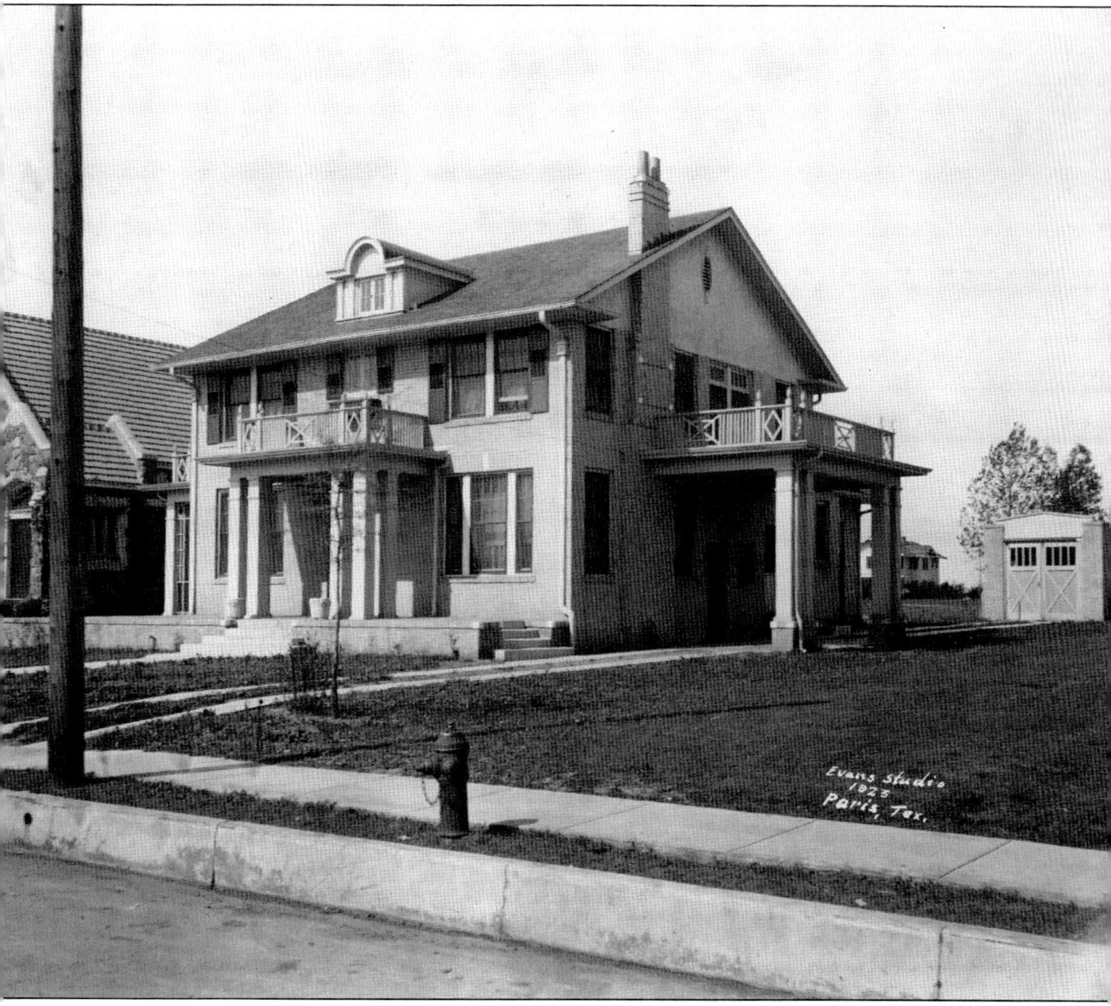

NEW CONSTRUCTION IN PARIS. This house next to Holy Cross Episcopal Church no longer exists. When this photograph was taken in 1923, it was still a private residence. Holy Cross Episcopal Church soon acquired the property. The building was converted into a school and used as an Episcopal elementary school for many years.

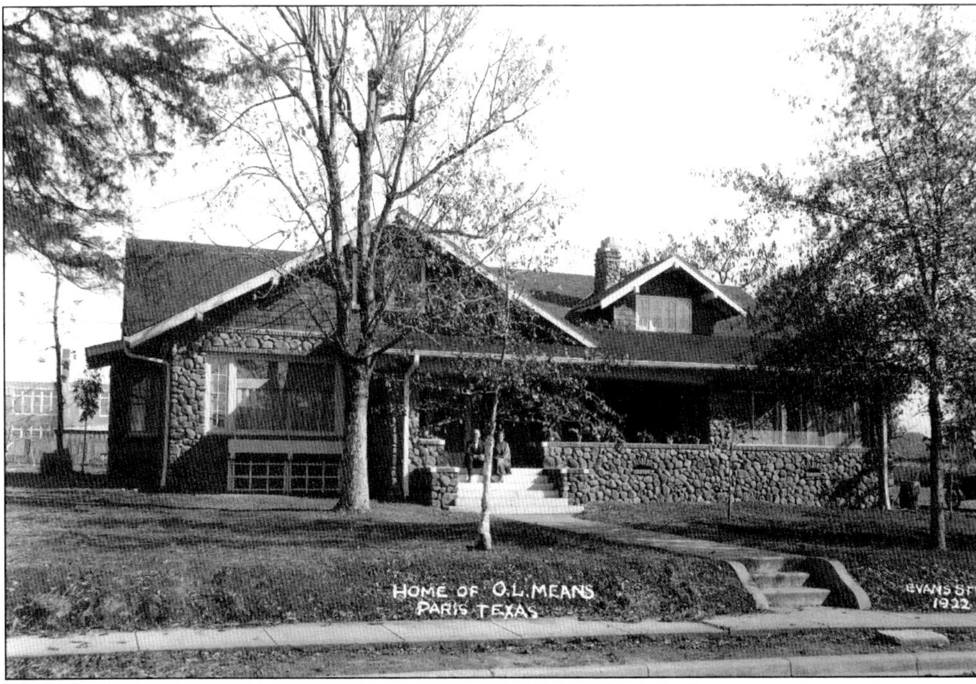

Two Homes Built after the Great Fire of 1916. After the fire, there was a burst of new home construction in Paris. The above image is of the Means home in 1922. This was the home of O.L. Means and his wife. The Means are posing on the front steps. In the background, a large brick building can be seen that may be a school. The image below is of the residence of L.L. Hardison in 1921. Hardison was elected to a county judgeship in Paris in 1906. This home is graced with many decorative flourishes.

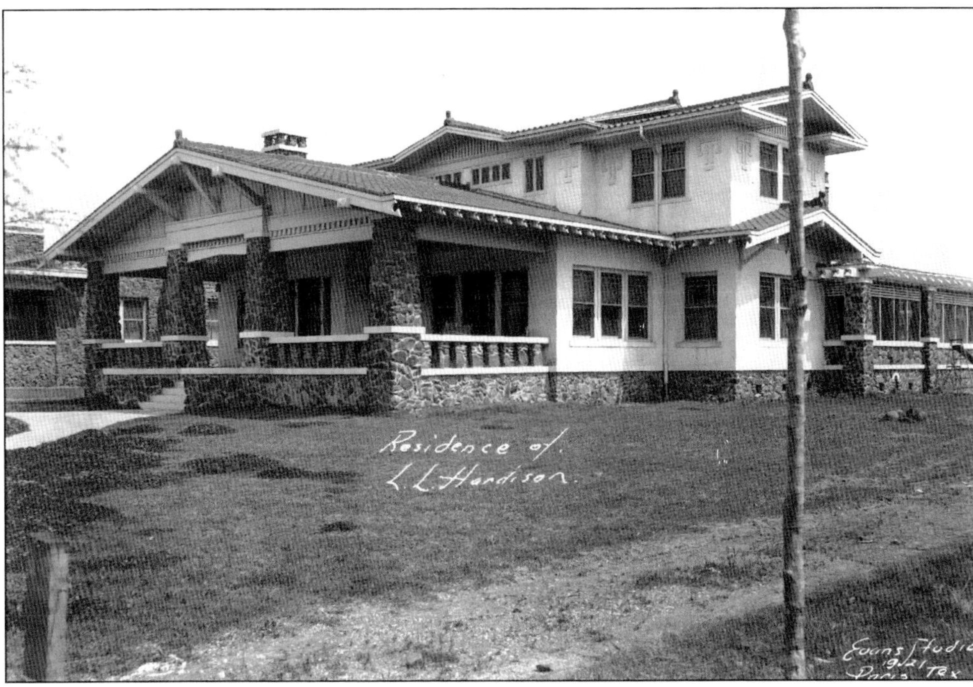

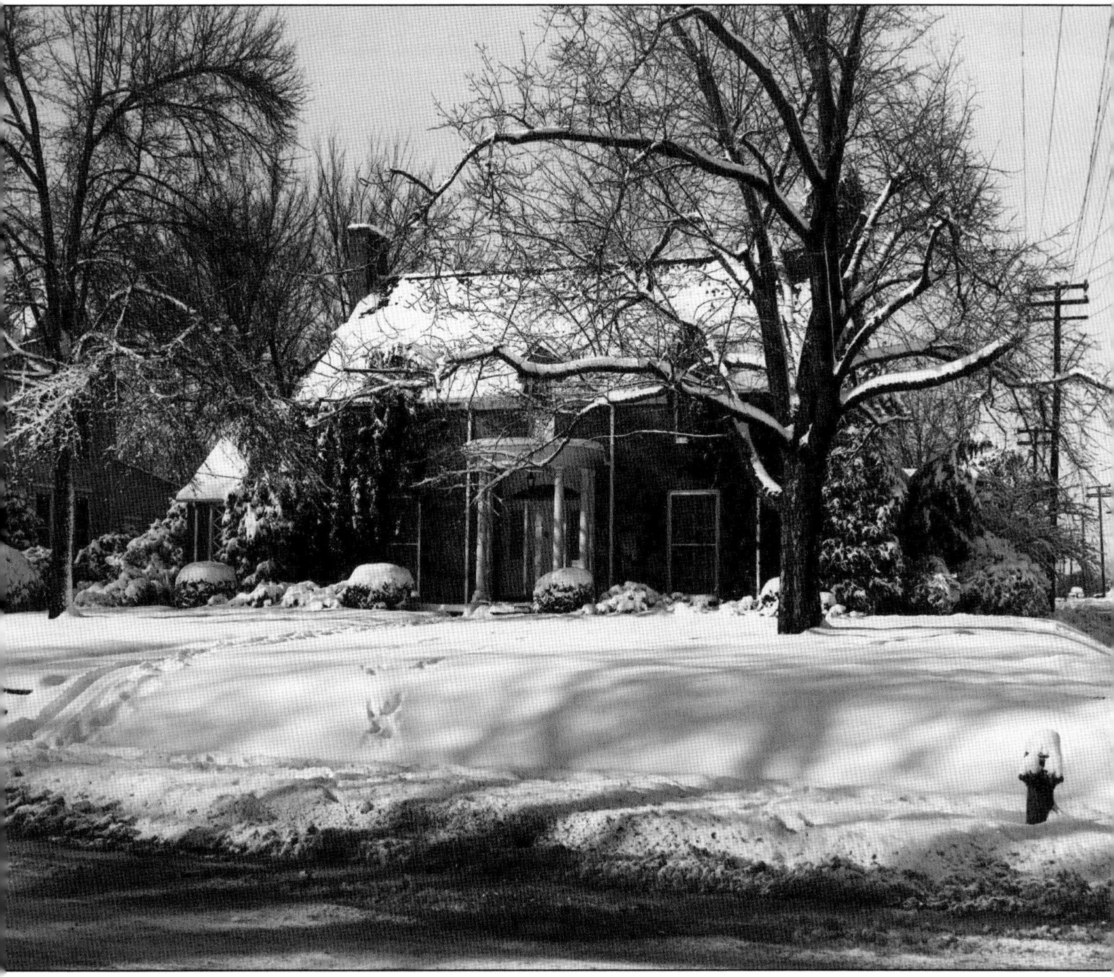

A SNOW-CLAD HOME IN 1951. There was a heavy snowfall in 1951, as can be seen in this image of a Church Street home. During that year, there was heavy snowfall in the United States, Europe, and even Australia. Heavy snowfall is rare but not unknown in Paris. It seems that when a heavy snow falls, people make sure to memorialize the event with photographs.

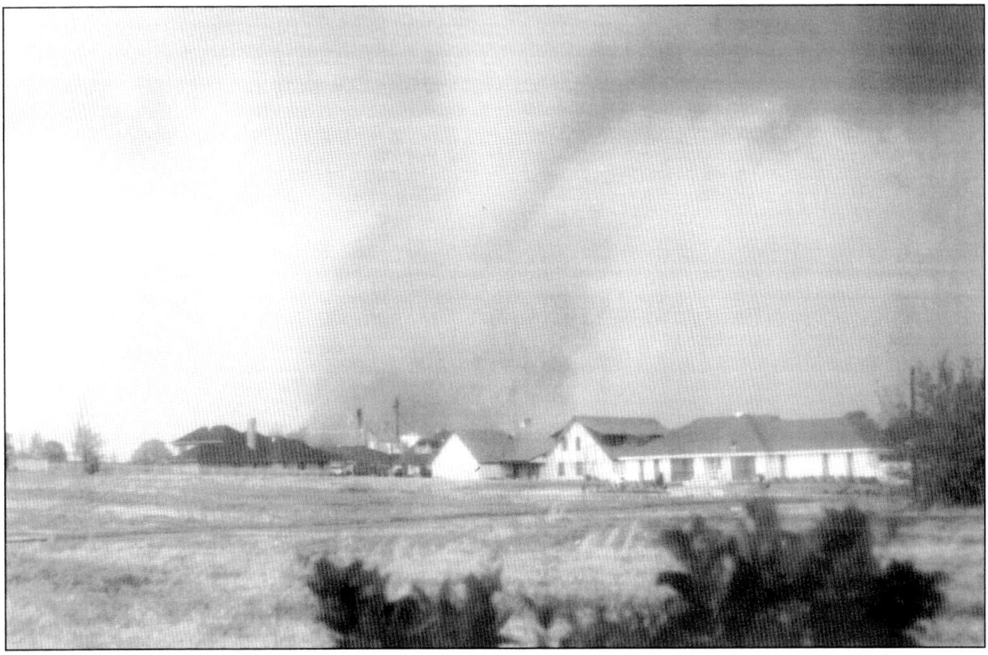

The Tornado That Struck Paris in 1982. On April 2, 1982, North Texas, including Paris, suffered a number of devastating tornado strikes. Although tornados are not an unusual event in Northeast Texas, the storm of 1982 was, in many ways, "A Perfect Storm," which devastated the region. (Courtesy of the *Paris News.*)

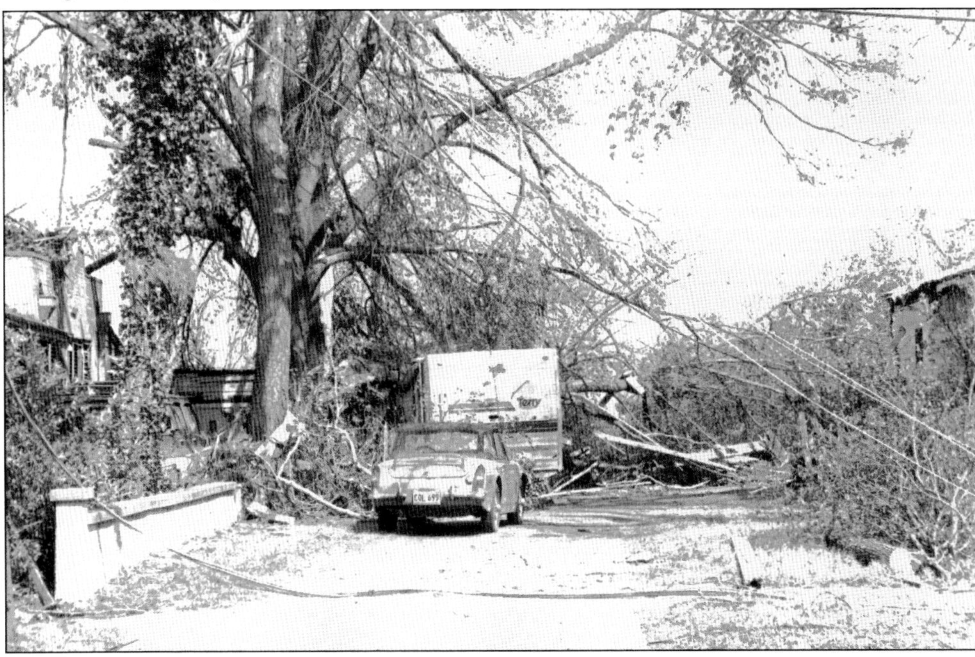

A Paris Street after the Tornado. The tornado of 1982 was the most significant disaster to befall Paris in the late 20th century. During the afternoon of April 2, a large super cell formed in North Texas and began moving east through Sherman in the direction of Bonham. By mid-afternoon, the storm arrived in the vicinity of Bonham. (Courtesy of the *Paris News.*)

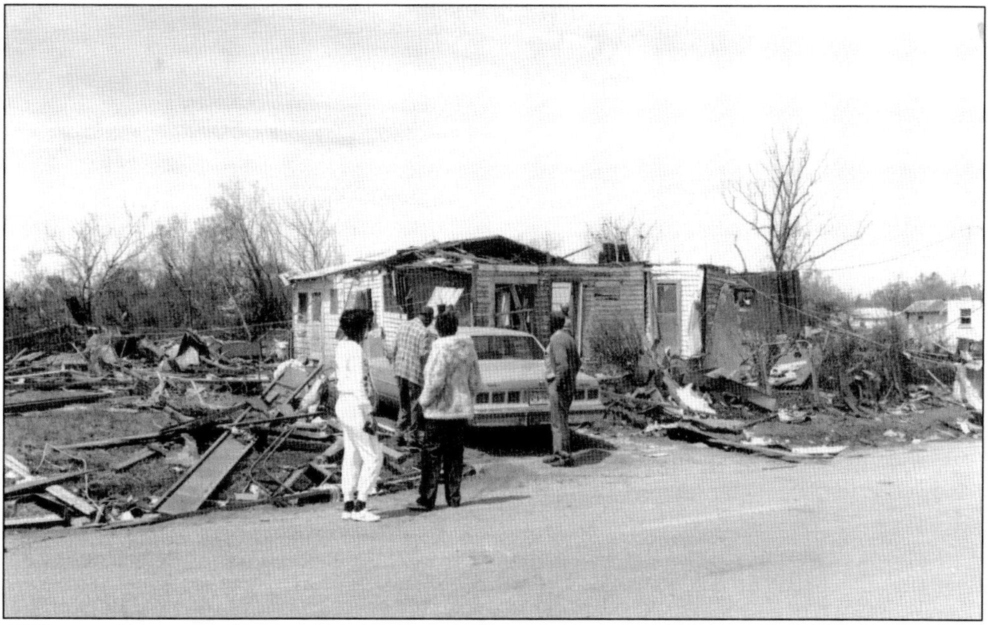

A HEAVILY DAMAGED HOME IN PARIS. Grayson County, just west of Lamar County, was struck by a tornado that destroyed eight homes and killed one person. These early tornados dissipated but reformed in the vicinity of Campbell Road and Loop 286 in Paris. (Courtesy of the *Paris News*.)

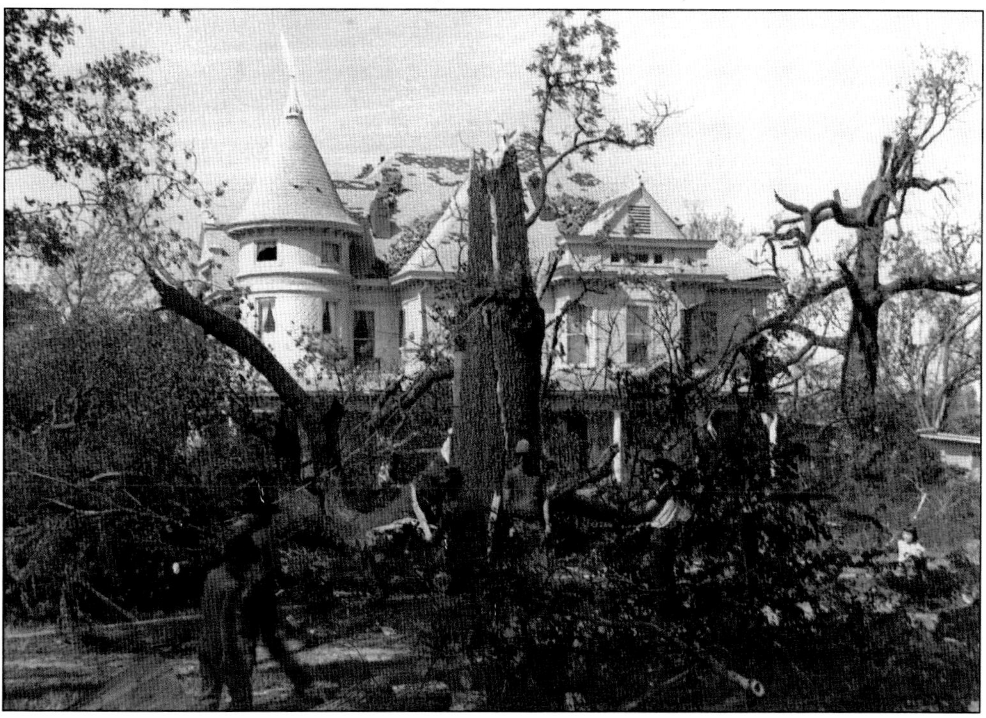

A BADLY DAMAGED HOME IN PARIS. The tornado plowed through Paris leaving, according to the National Weather Service, a path of destruction 200 to 300 yards wide. Winds within this tornado are estimated to have reached up to 260 miles per hour. The shattered trees in this photograph testify to the fury of the winds that day. (Courtesy of the *Paris News*.)

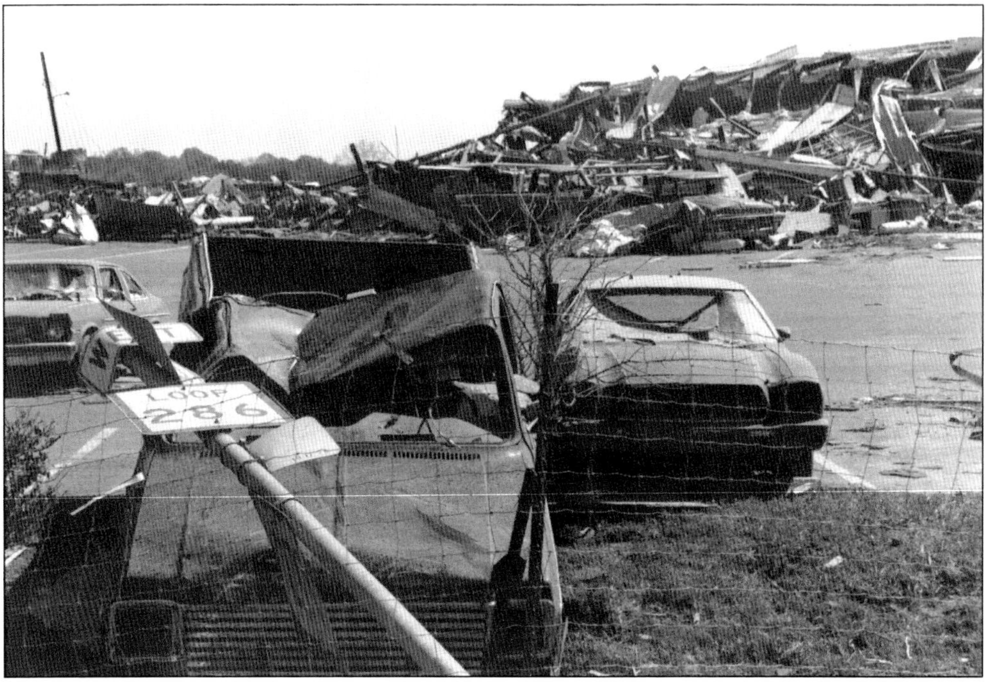

LOOP 286 AFTER THE TORNADO. After striking Paris, the tornado went on to strike both Reno and Blossom. All told, 10 people were killed, 170 injured, and 1,000 left homeless in the wake of the Paris tornado. It is believed that the death toll would have been much higher but for the warnings provided by Paris Police and Fire Departments as well as local radio stations. (Courtesy of the *Paris News*.)

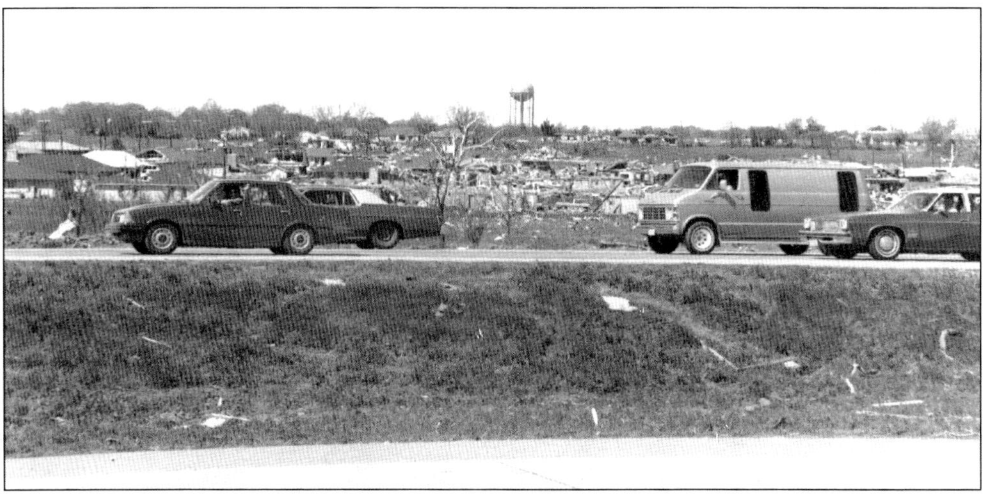

A FLATTENED NEIGHBORHOOD. According to the National Weather Service, 465 places of residence were damaged or destroyed. Damage has been estimated at $50 million. The police and fire departments gave Parisians about 30 minutes of warning before the tornado struck. There was no public siren system in Paris at the time. What warning residents received was from police cars and fire trucks driving through the city with sirens sounding as the tornado bore down upon Paris. (Courtesy of the *Paris News*.)

Three

Health Care and Education

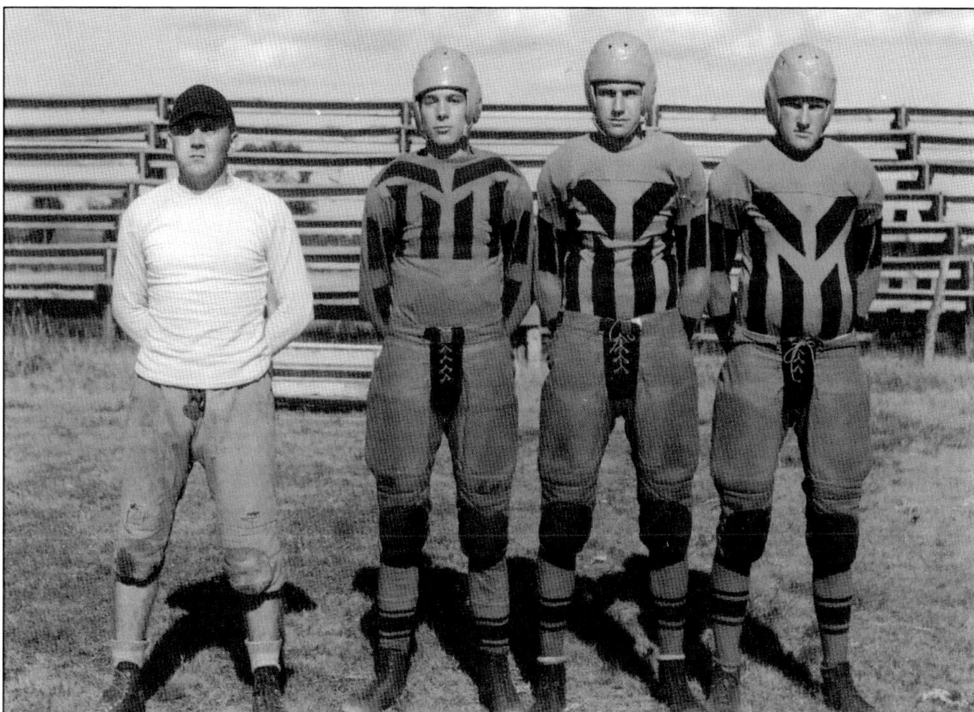

Members of an Early Paris Football Squad. The primary function of schools is to impart knowledge and foster critical thinking. Still, athletics have always been an integral component of a well-rounded education. It has been said that football is followed with a near religious fervor in Texas. Paris, like other parts of the nation, embraced sports as a part of education. These determined-looking young men are perhaps modeling proposed new protective gear in the 1920s.

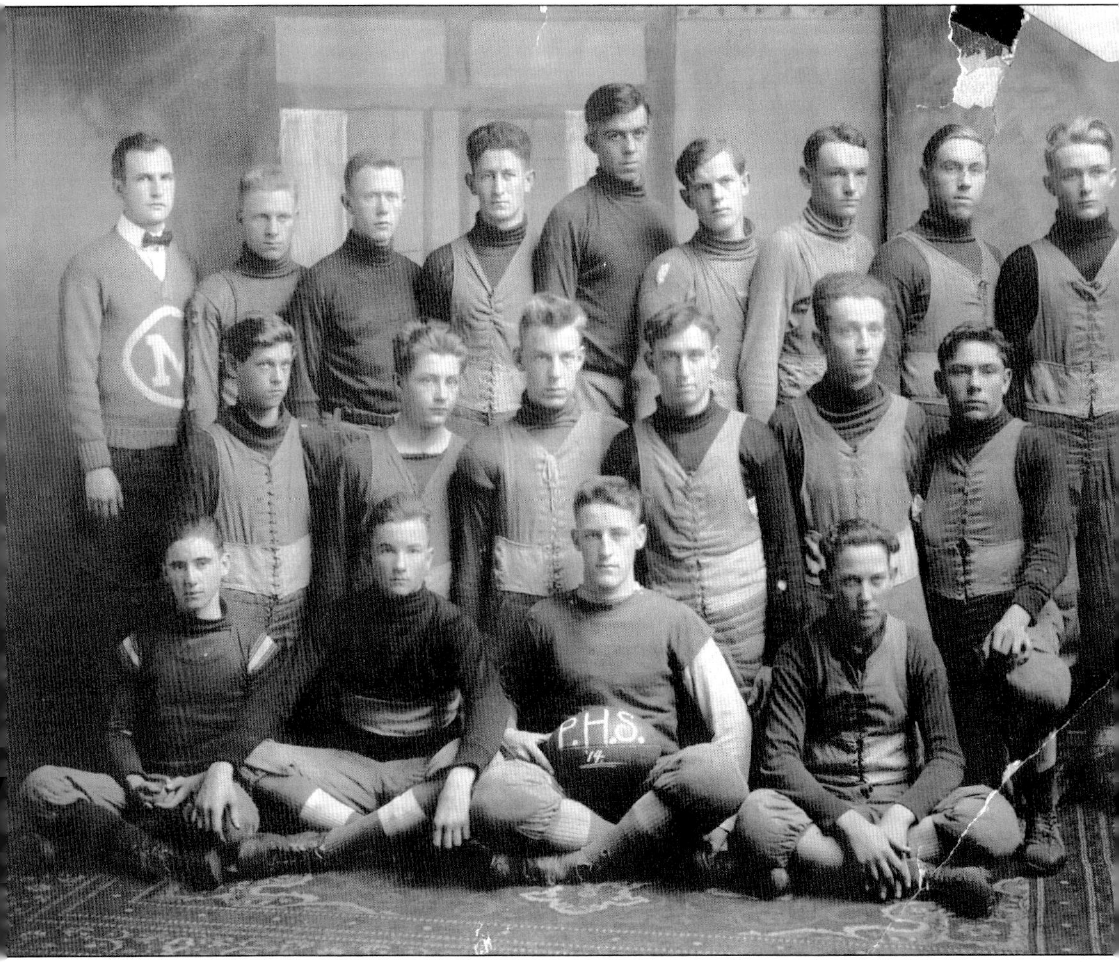

Paris High School Football Team in 1914. The Paris High School football team pictured here is notable for possessing almost no protective padding; the team boasted a 5-3 season that year. The Paris High School football team played its first game during the 1908 season. The first coach of the team was Ray Johnson, who led the squad to a 1-3 record that year.

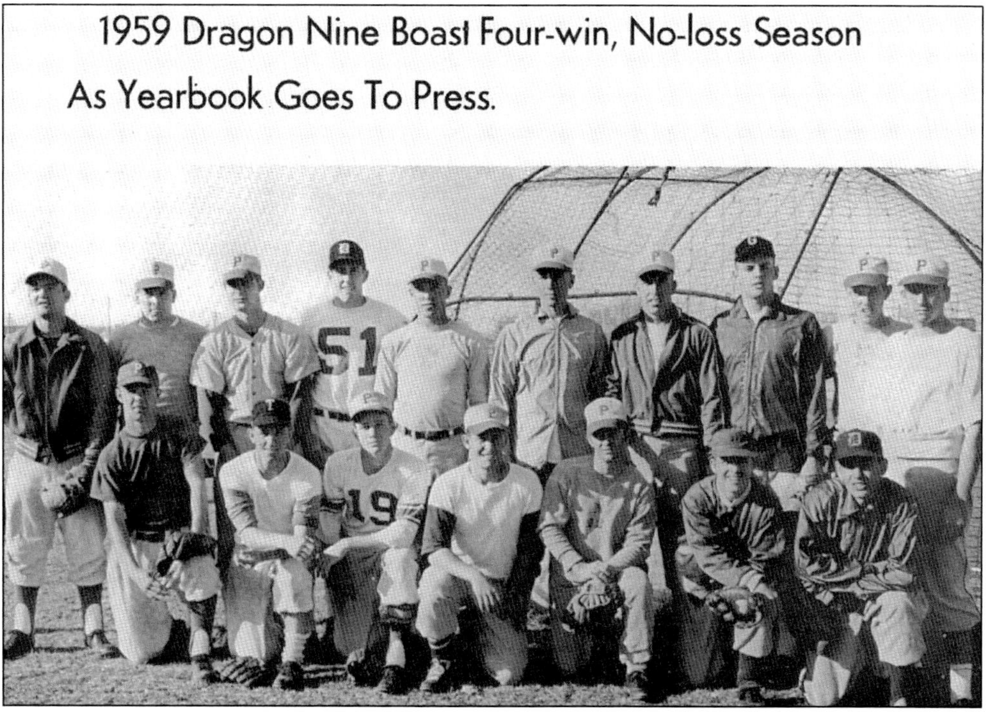

Two Images of Paris Junior College Dragons Baseball Teams. The Paris Junior College baseball team has a winning tradition, and the Dragons had an outstanding season in 1959. That year, the team rose to the occasion against tough opposition and won the National Junior College Tournament championship held in Colorado. Baseball coach James Self led the Dragons to the national championship that year. Self was inducted into the Dragon's Hall of Fame for his outstanding efforts. The date of the photograph below is unknown. The hairstyles suggest that this picture of the Paris Junior College baseball team was taken in the 1970s.

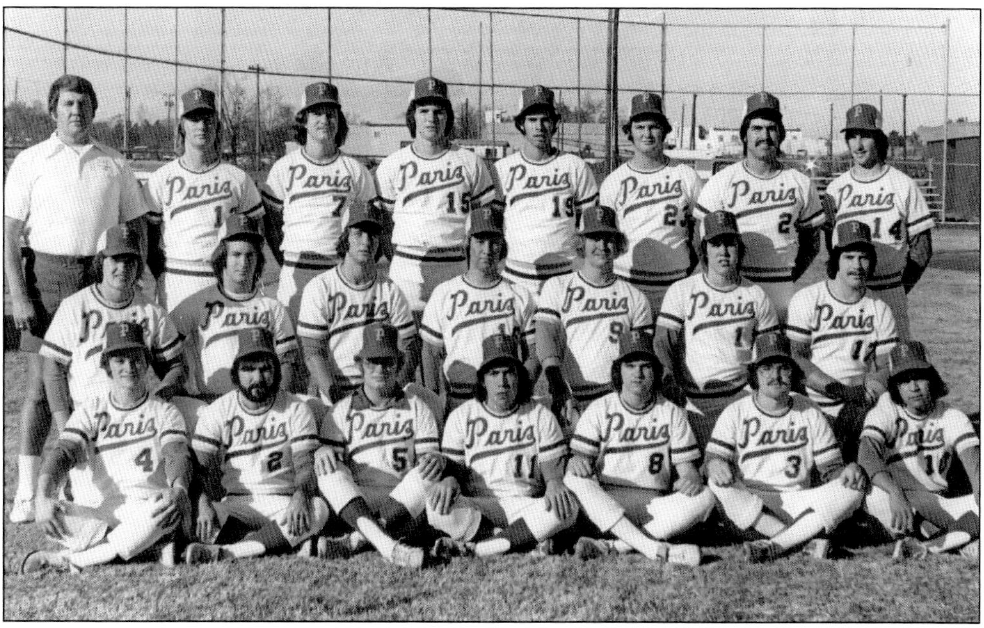

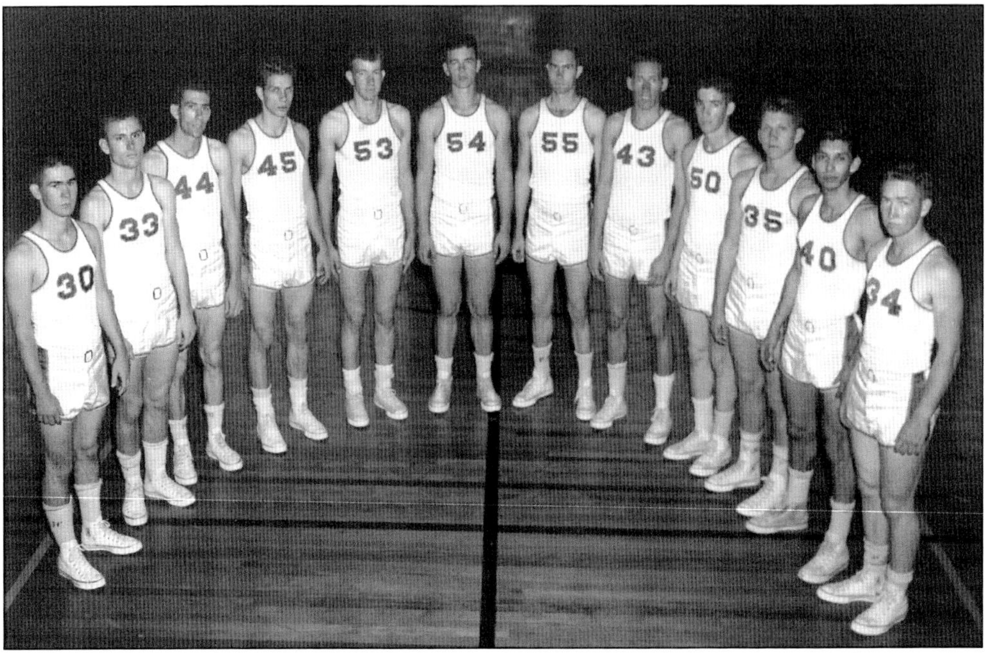

THE PARIS JUNIOR COLLEGE BASKETBALL TEAM. Paris Junior College basketball has had much success. Coach Bill Foy led the team to the National Junior College Athletic Association championship in the 2004–2005 season. The exact date of this photograph is unknown. Based upon the hairstyles and uniforms, it is possible that this image was taken around 1960.

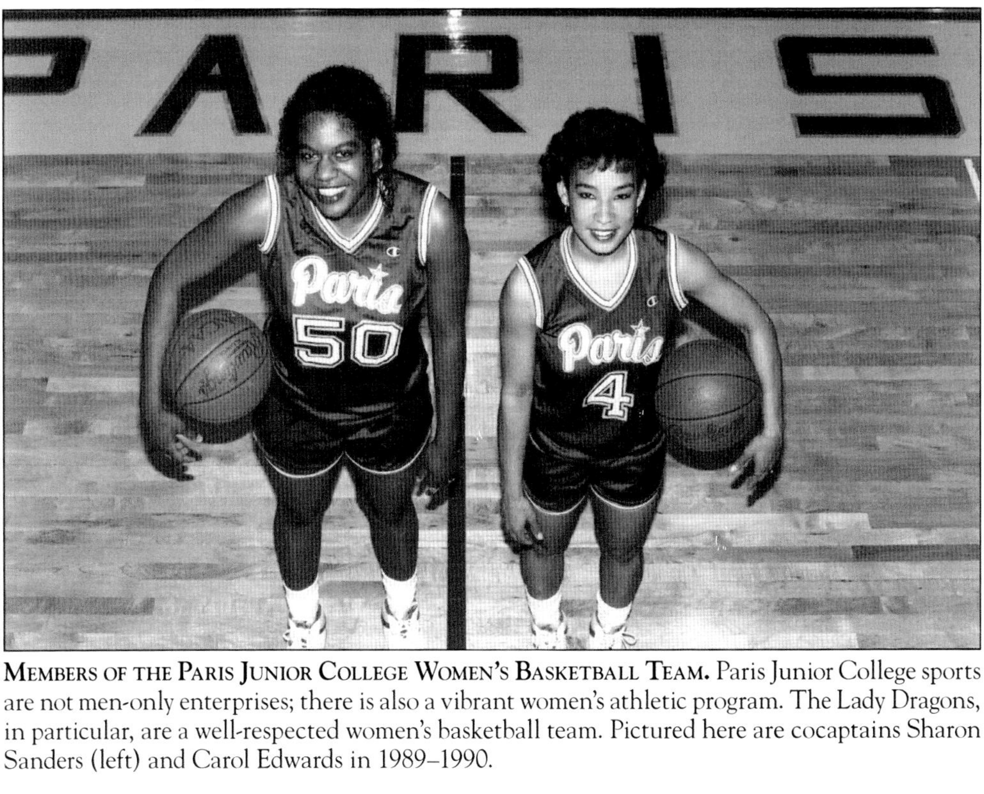

MEMBERS OF THE PARIS JUNIOR COLLEGE WOMEN'S BASKETBALL TEAM. Paris Junior College sports are not men-only enterprises; there is also a vibrant women's athletic program. The Lady Dragons, in particular, are a well-respected women's basketball team. Pictured here are cocaptains Sharon Sanders (left) and Carol Edwards in 1989–1990.

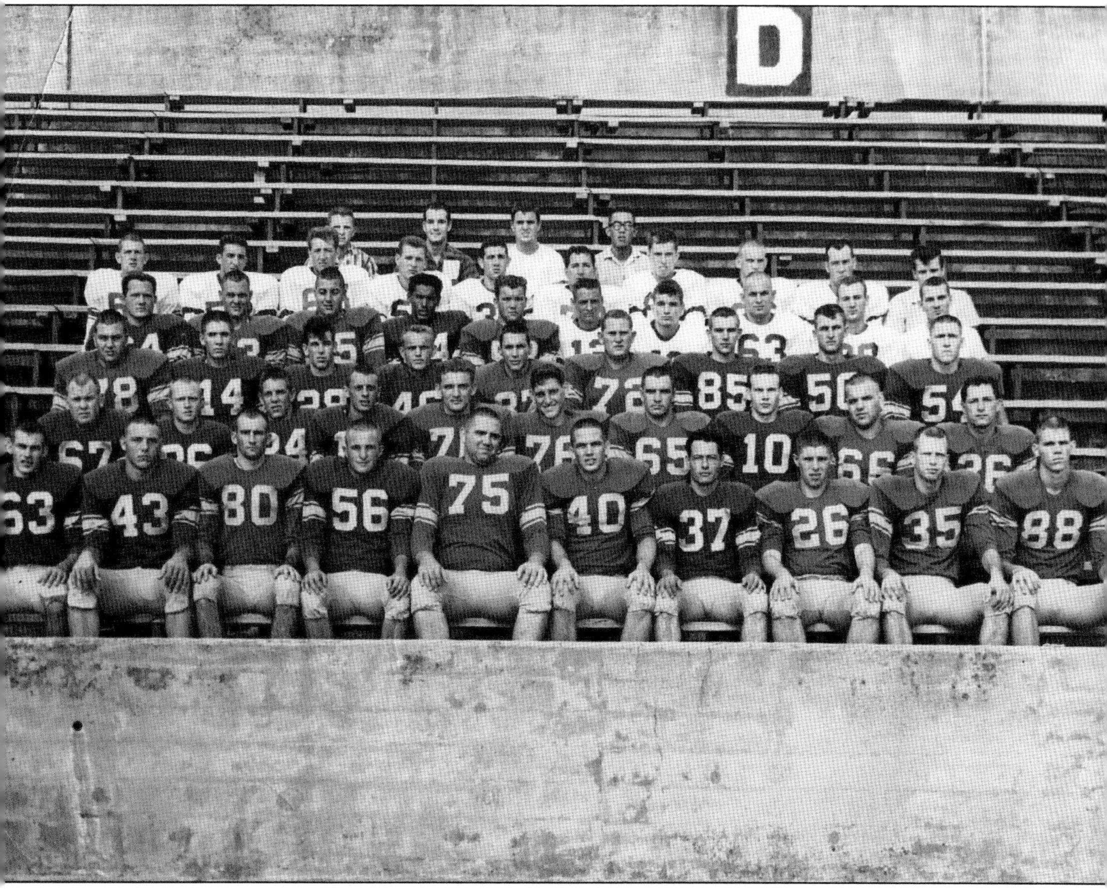

The 1960–1961 Paris Junior College Football Team. Unfortunately, Paris Junior College no longer fields a football team today. Indeed, Paris Junior College discontinued football in 1961. Therefore, this is an image of the last football squad for the Dragons. H.L. "Hub" Hollis is perhaps the best-remembered football coach of the Dragons. Hollis was the football coach when he was selected as the first athletic director in 1925. His name now graces the baseball complex on campus.

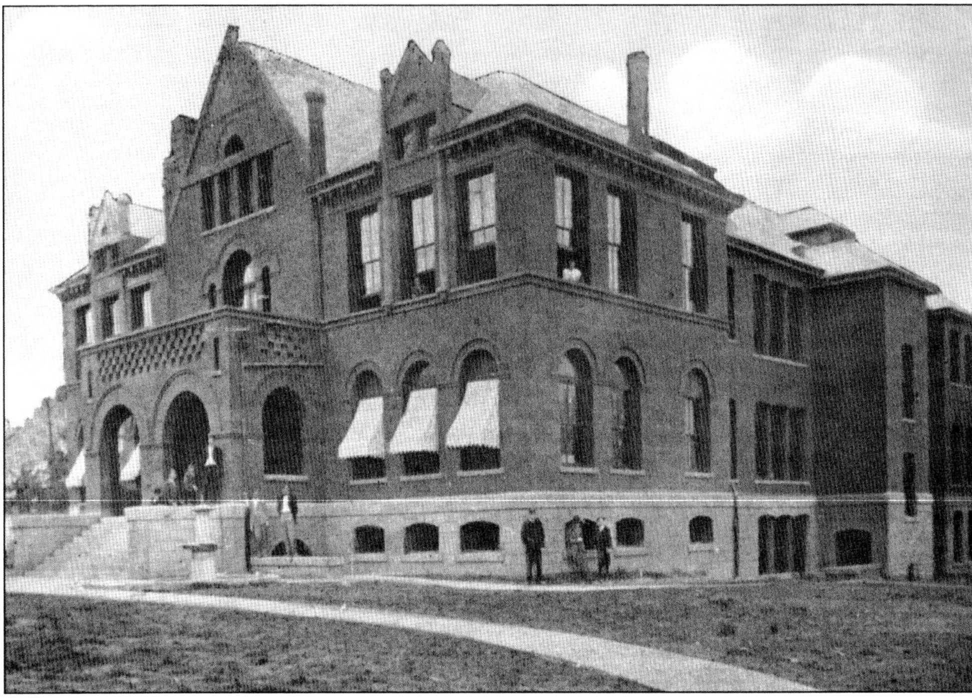

PARIS HIGH SCHOOL. Public education was a top priority for Paris during the late 19th and early 20th centuries. This commitment can be seen in the large and well-built Paris High School structure in 1906 (the year of its construction). Like so many other fine, old buildings, this structure was destroyed in the great fire of 1916.

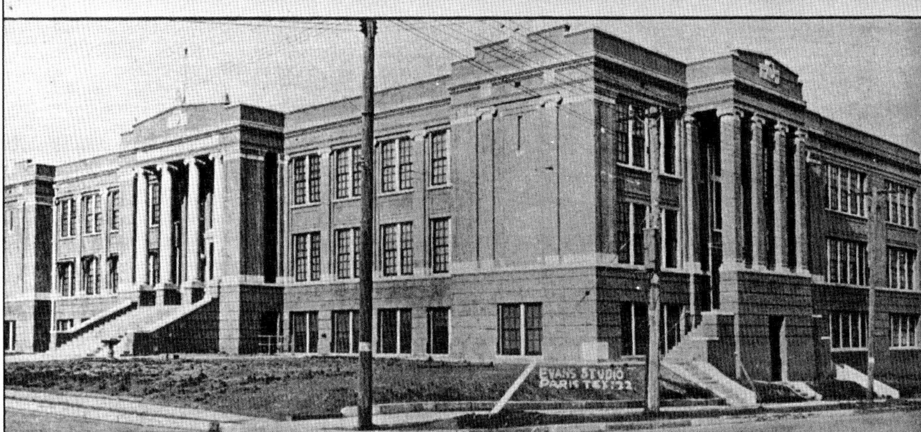

THE PARIS HIGH SCHOOL

PARIS HIGH SCHOOL IN 1922. This nice looking building is a testament to the importance of education in Paris. In Lamar County, there were 10 public school districts in operation in 1867; in some ways, this number of schools was unusual in the South at this time. In 1880, the city council ordered compulsory public education to be instituted.

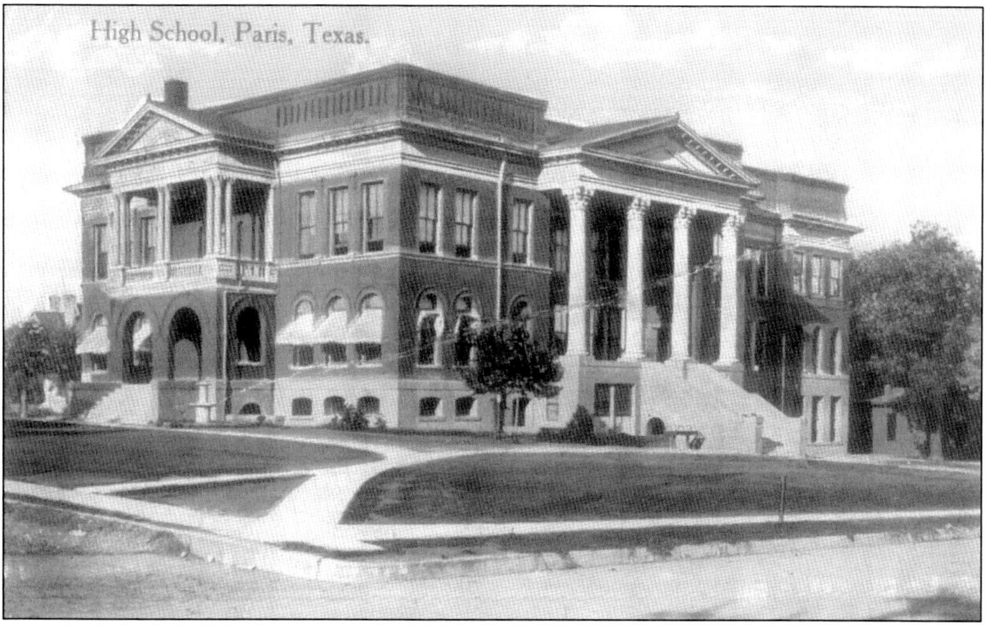

The High School Building in the 1930s. While this is a fine building, it pales in comparison to the new (2010) Paris High School. The Paris Independent School District, as it is now known, was established in 1884. Prof. J.C. Brooks was the man most responsible for putting together all the "nuts and bolts" of the 1884 consolidation. Brooks served as superintendent of the school district for two years. (Courtesy of the Lamar County Historical Society Museum.)

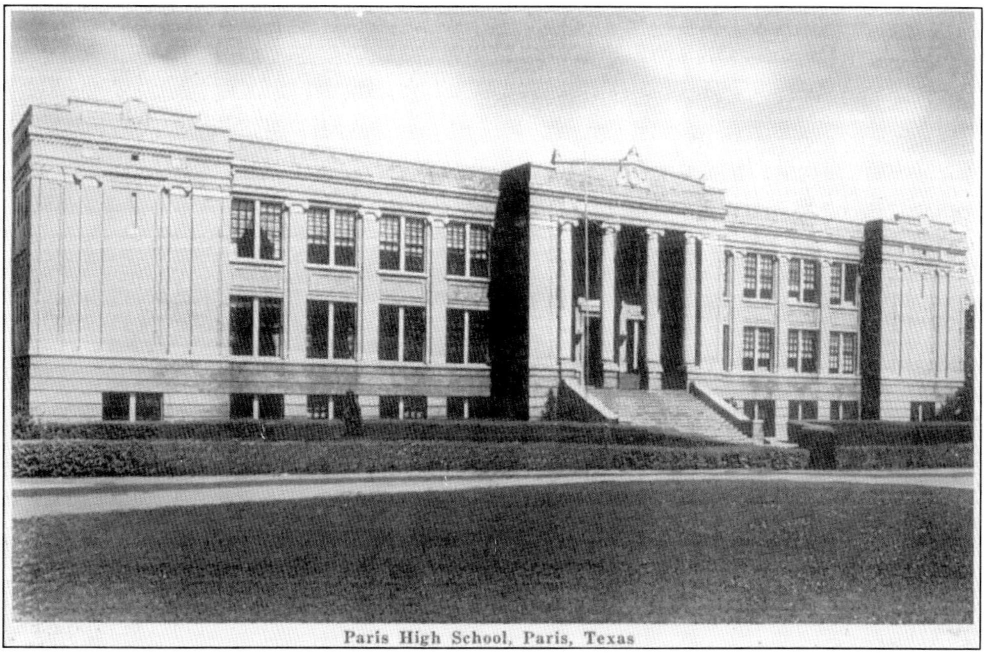

Another View of the Paris High School Building. The new Paris High School of 2010 was constructed at a cost of $54 million. It, too, is a testament to how education is viewed in Paris. As a comparison, the 1906 high school cost $200,000 to be built. (Courtesy of the Lamar County Historical Society Museum.)

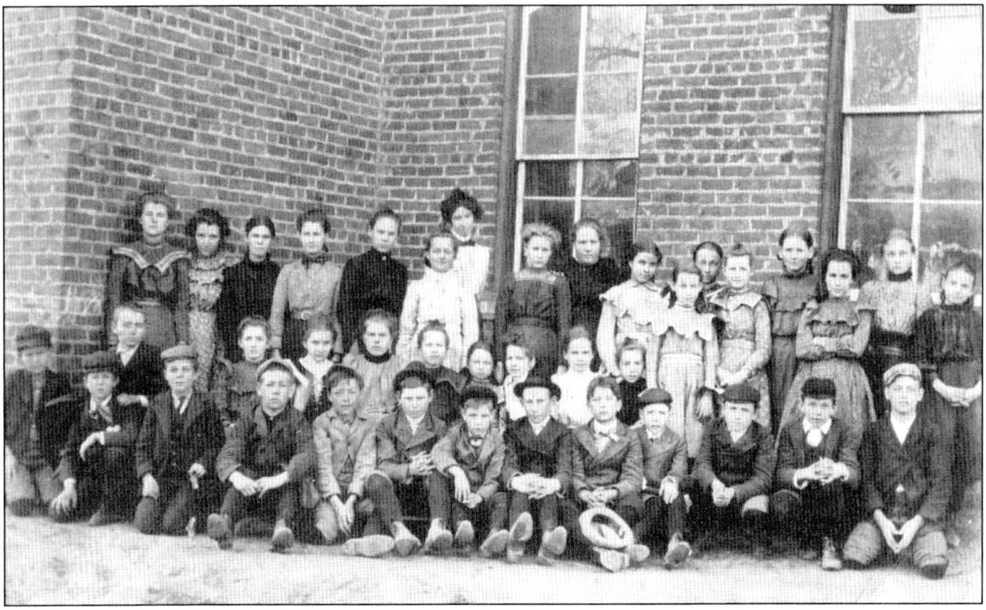

Graham School and Students. Graham School students in 1901 are shown above, most likely for a class photograph. There are 24 girls and only 14 boys pictured here along with the teacher. Graham School was originally established in 1853; at that time, it was known as Paris Female Institute. The image below was taken at about the same time. The structure itself was built and occupied in 1890. Graham School, Third Ward, and "the Negro School," as it was called, made up the original Paris School District in 1884. The first so-called "Negro School" was established in Paris in 1884.

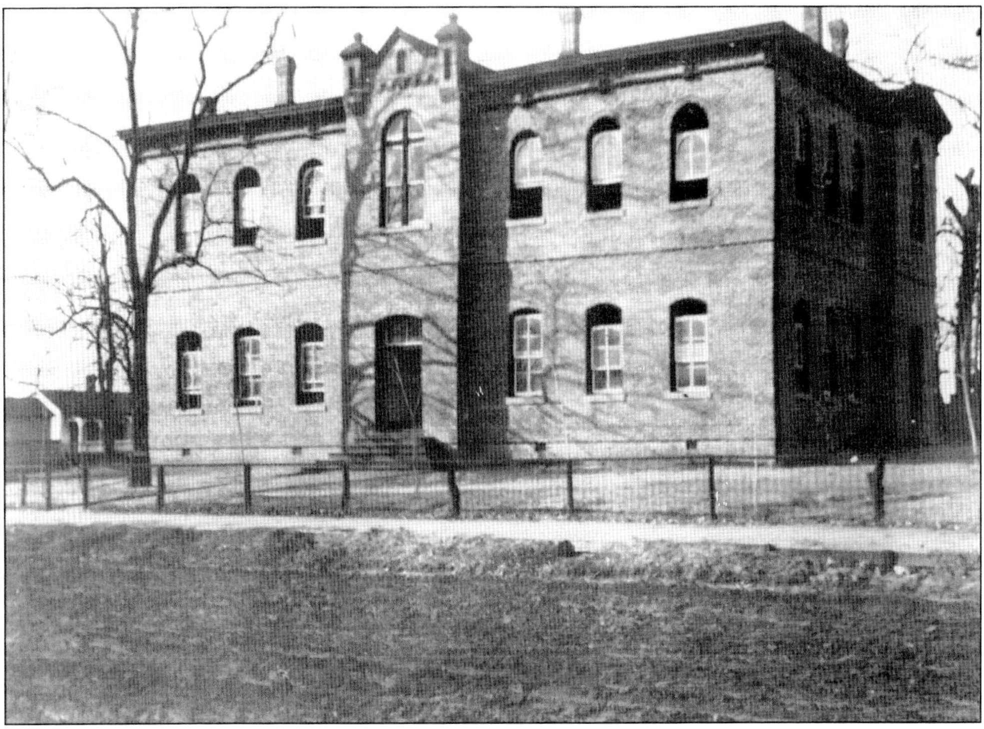

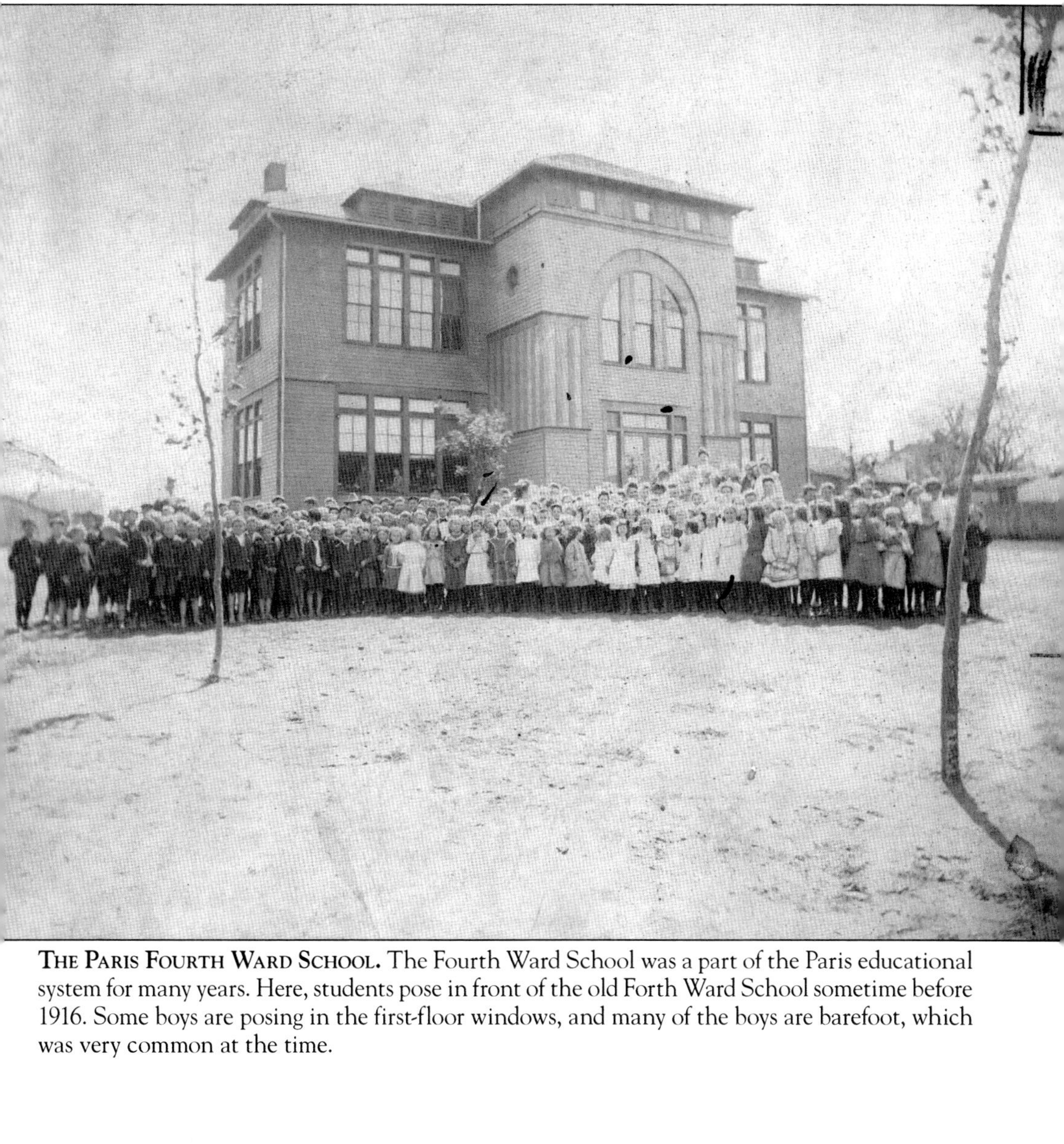

The Paris Fourth Ward School. The Fourth Ward School was a part of the Paris educational system for many years. Here, students pose in front of the old Forth Ward School sometime before 1916. Some boys are posing in the first-floor windows, and many of the boys are barefoot, which was very common at the time.

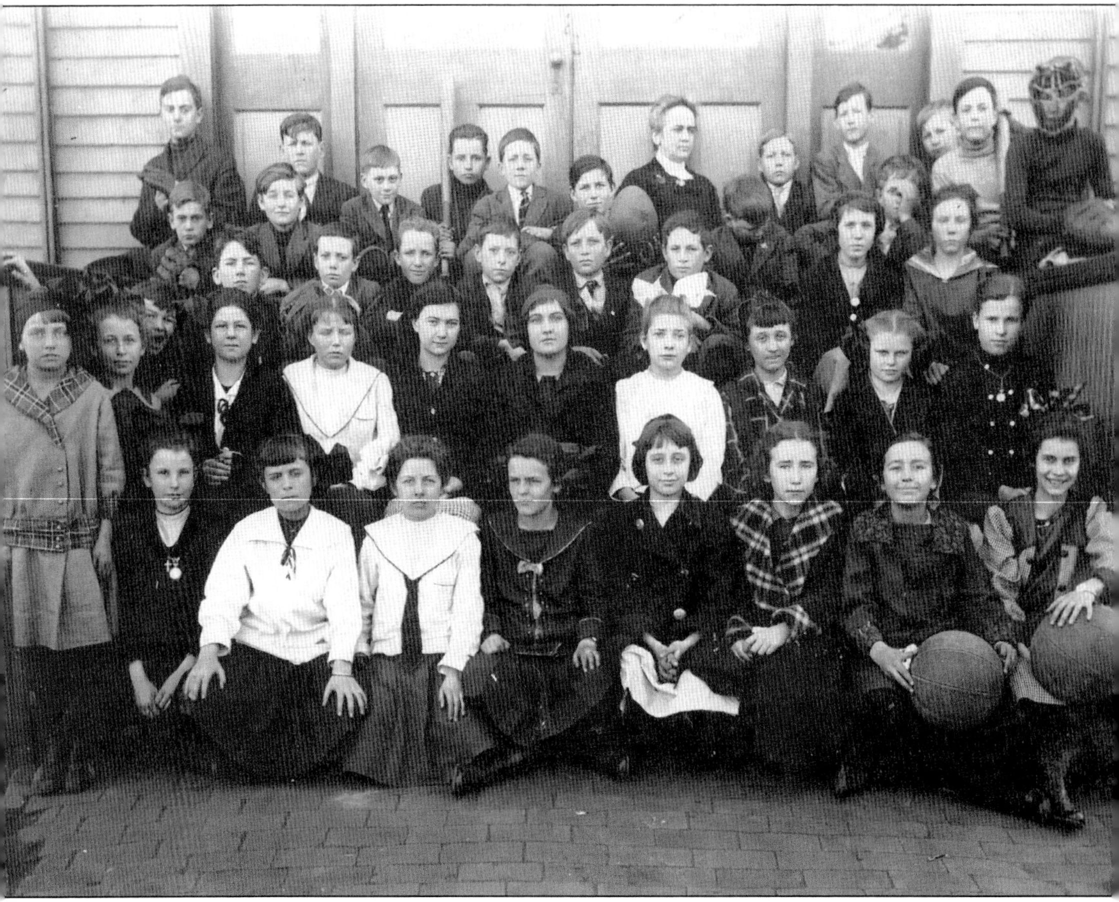

FOURTH WARD STUDENTS. The significance of sports as part of the educational process is clearly demonstrated in this photograph. A close examination of the photograph reveals that the two girls in the lower right are holding basketballs, a boy in the upper row has a football, two boys in the upper left are wearing baseball gloves, and the boy in the upper right is wearing a catcher's mitt as well as a mask. Interestingly, while most of the children are solemnly posing, the boy at the far left of the third row is mugging for the camera. This picture is of sixth- and seventh-grade students of the Fourth Ward School in 1913 or 1914.

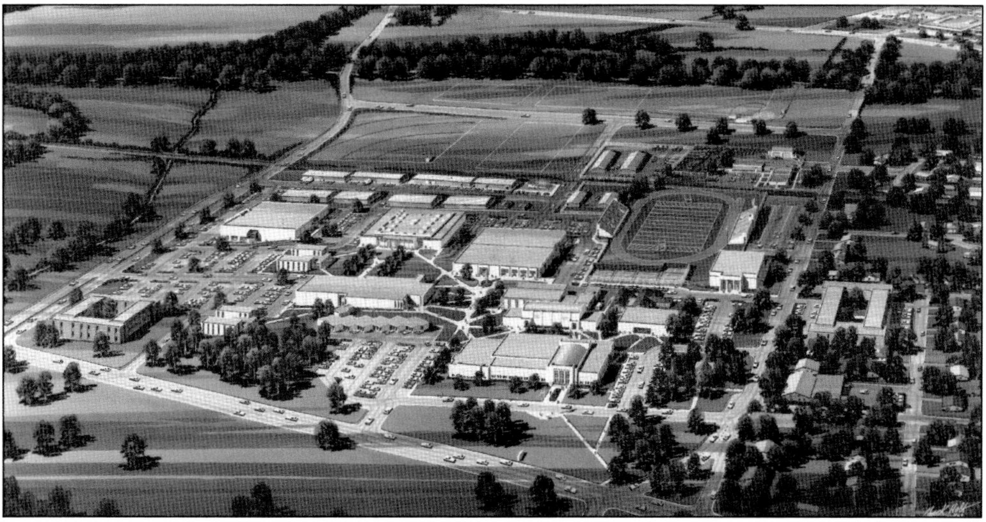

ARTIST'S RENDERING OF PARIS JUNIOR COLLEGE. As well as providing students with an affordable education, Paris Junior College injects millions of dollars per year into the Paris economy. The college was founded in 1924 and is a well-regarded institution that plays host to a number of outstanding academic and vocational programs. In addition, Paris Junior College offers vocational training programs to include air-conditioning technology, agriculture, computer-aided design, and welding.

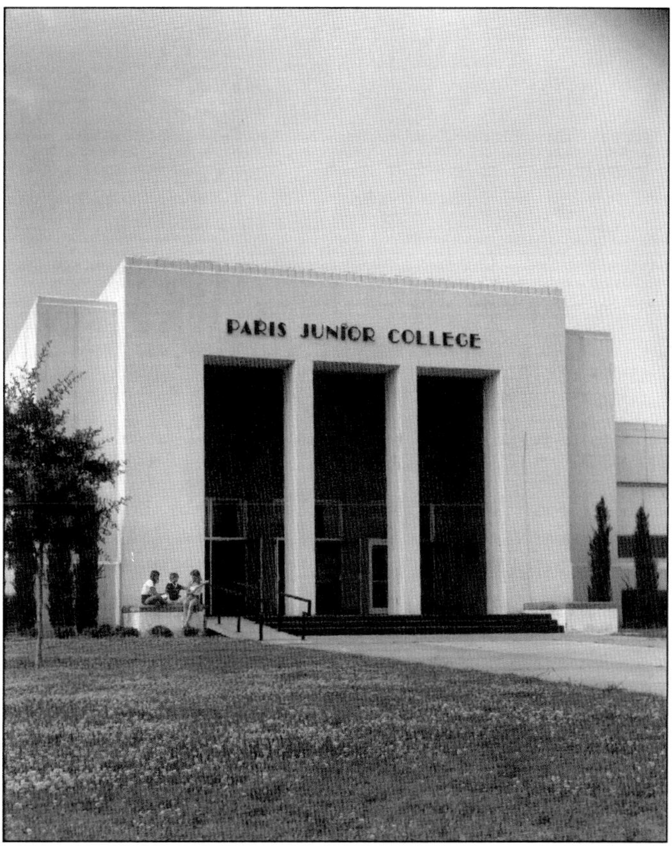

THE PARIS JUNIOR COLLEGE ADMINISTRATION BUILDING IN THE 1970S. Perhaps the best-known vocational program at Paris Junior College is the Texas Institute of Jewelry Technology. This vocational program was established on campus in 1942. This internationally recognized course of study offers students training in horology (watchmaking) and gemology.

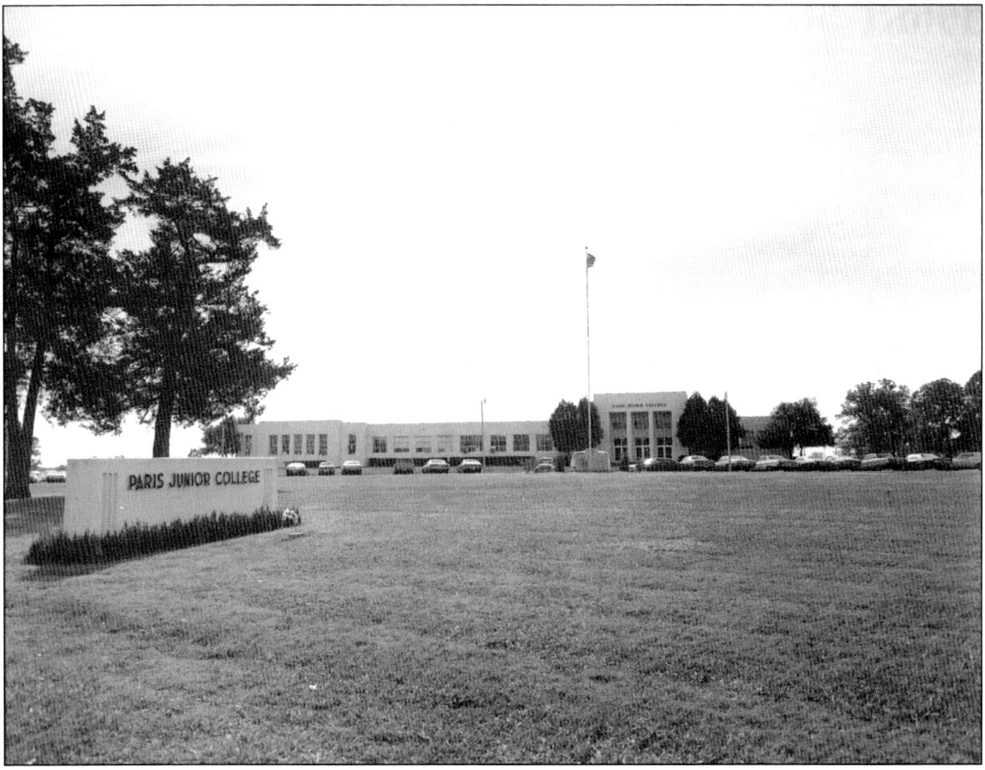

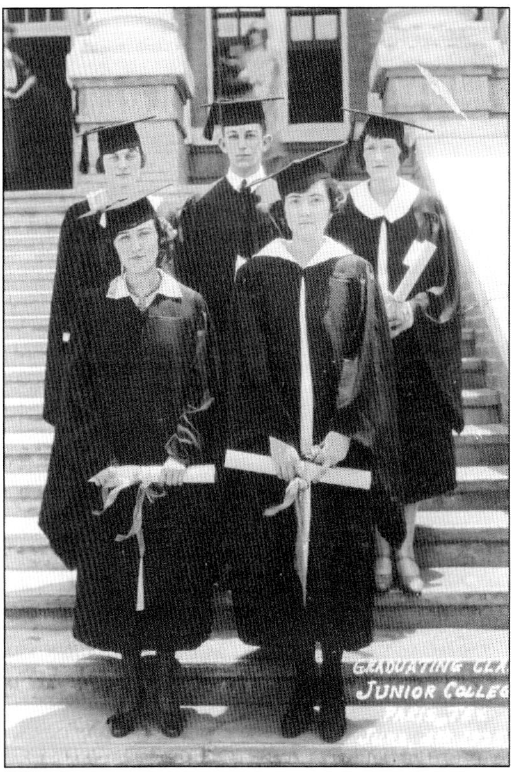

View of Paris Junior College from Clarksville Street. At Paris Junior College, students can chose between several excellent academic programs to include a fine arts course of study that includes theater arts. Not to be forgotten is the school's two-year nursing program. It is also the home of the A.M. & Welma Aikin Jr. Regional Archives. This photograph of the administration building was taken in 1972.

Paris Junior College Graduates in 1925. The first commencement exercise at Paris Junior College was held in 1925. There were only five graduates. This graduating class is notable in that there was only one male graduate at a time when men vastly outnumbered women in colleges and universities.

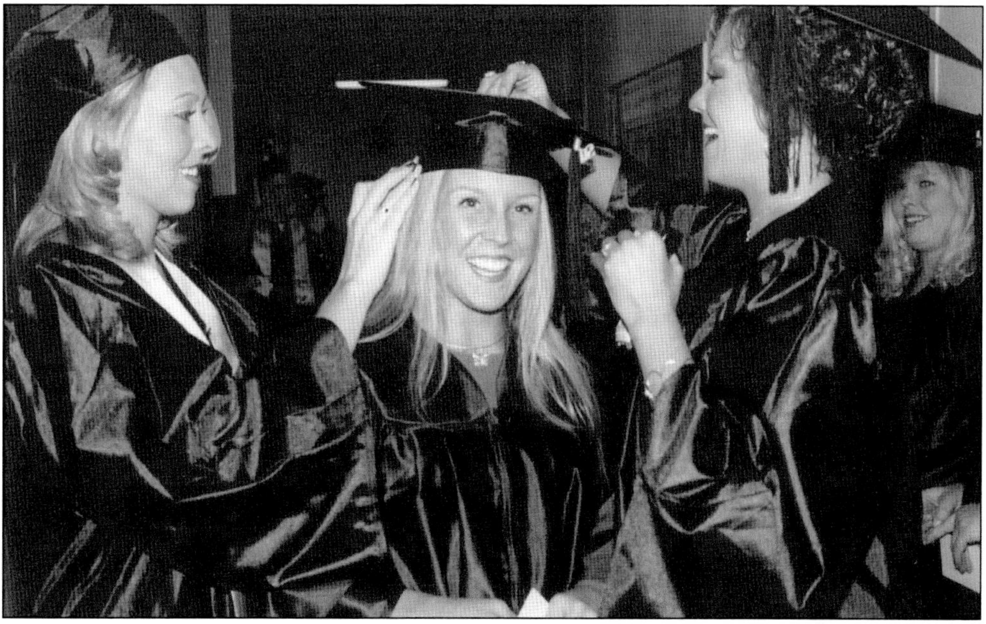

PARIS JUNIOR COLLEGE STUDENTS PREPARING FOR GRADUATION. The Paris Junior College cosmetology program is a well-known and respected program of study. Preparing for their cosmetology graduation on May 19, 2002, are, from left to right, Christina Wiggins, Carle Dupree, and Whitney Rogers. To obtain a cosmetology license in Texas, people are required to complete 1,500 hours of instruction.

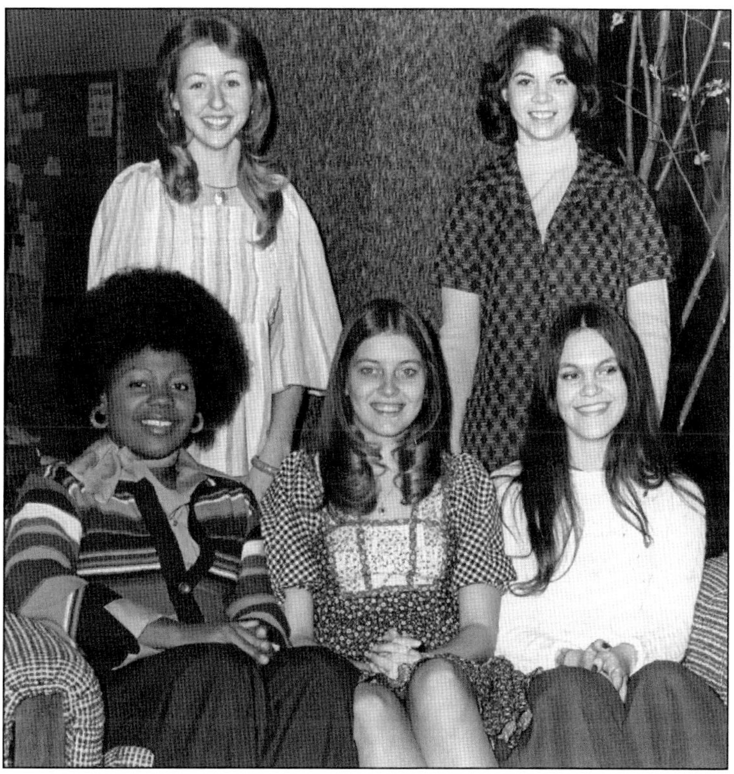

NOMINEES FOR PARIS JUNIOR COLLEGE HOMECOMING QUEEN IN THE 1970S. Paris Junior College has been celebrating homecoming since 1925. Homecomings are generally associated with high school football. These celebrations probably originated in the first decade of the 20th century. By the 1920s, homecomings were common across the United States.

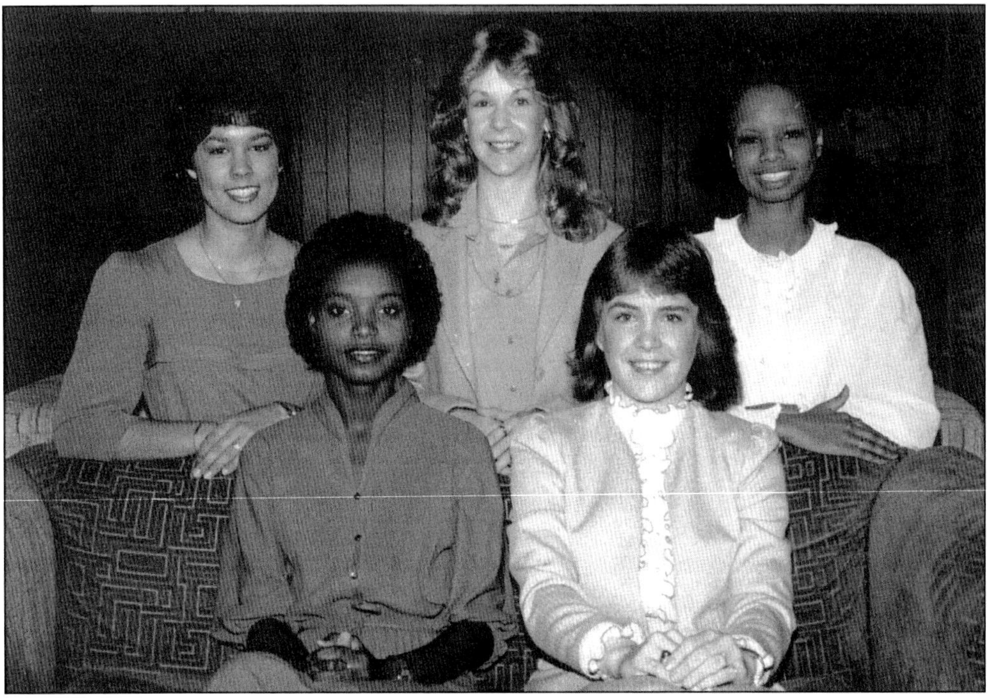

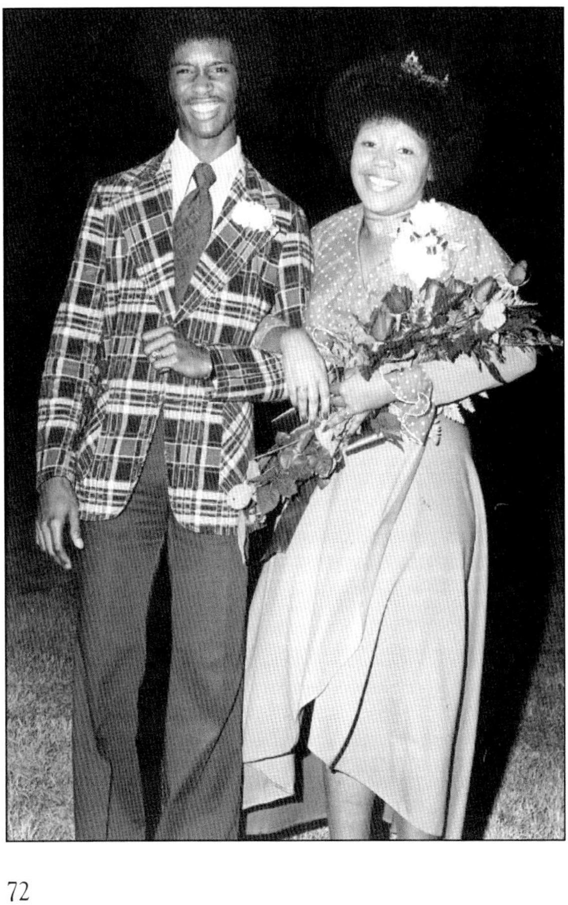

NOMINEES FOR HOMECOMING QUEEN. Homecoming at Paris Junior College is a major event. Here are the nominees for Paris Junior College homecoming queen in 1984. Those pictured are, from left to right, (first row) Victoria Dillahunty and Wendy Jettson; (second row) Vickie Coursey, Renee Rivers, and Stephanie English.

HOMECOMING KING AND QUEEN IN THE 1970S. The hair and clothing styles strongly suggest that this photograph was taken in the 1970s, which were notorious for the rather garish clothing that people were attracted to at the time. Indeed, today, the notion of the leisure suit is something that is almost comical.

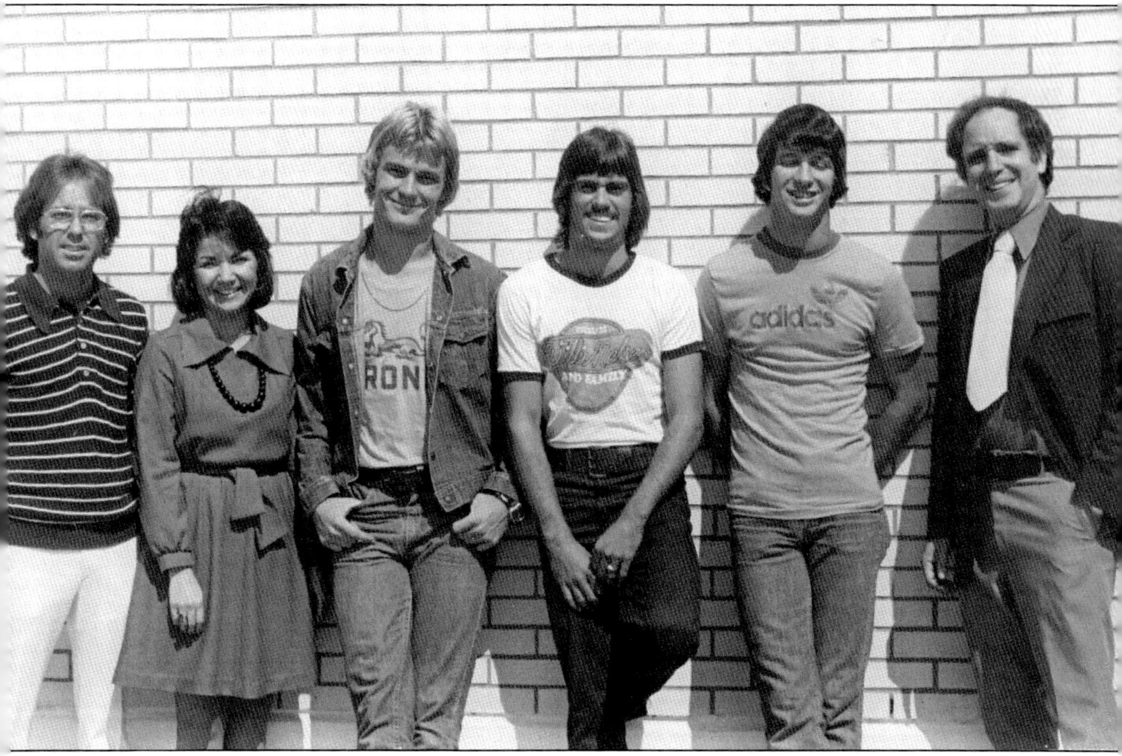

PROFESSORS AND STUDENTS AT PARIS JUNIOR COLLEGE. Robert Thornborough (far right) taught sociology at Paris Junior College for many years. Here, Thornborough poses with a colleague (far left) and students. Thornborough now works as a volunteer at the A.M. & Welma Aikin Jr. Regional Archives. Today, the college employs two full-time professors to teach sociology on campus.

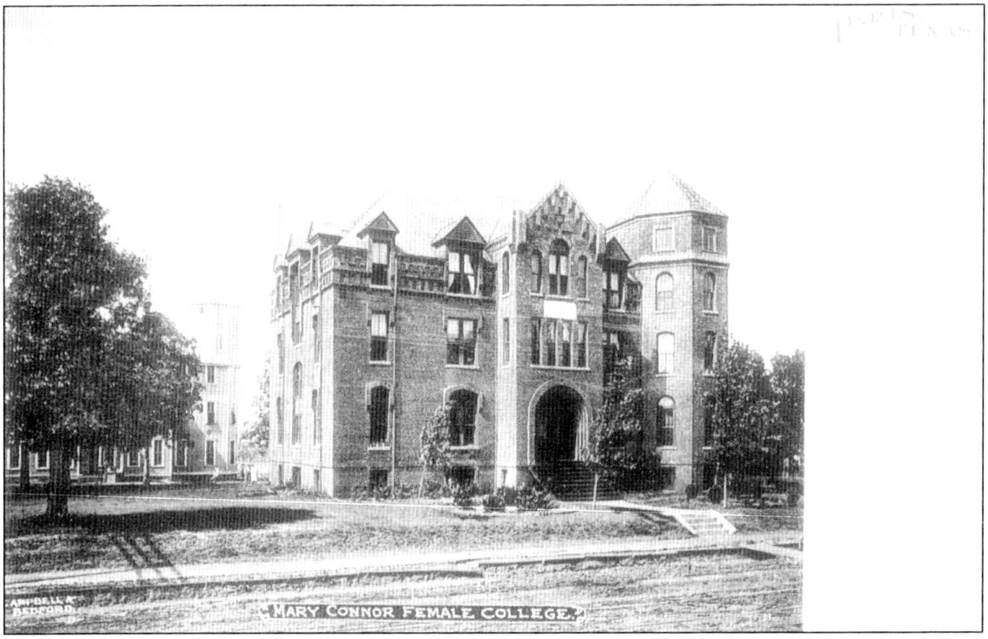

MARY CONNOR COLLEGE AND ALUMNAE. Above is Mary Connor College before the fire of 1916 destroyed it. Mary Connor College was a women's college in Paris, originally known as the Paris Female College. The photograph below is of a reunion of Mary Connor alumnae in 1964. The destruction of Mary Connor College and the failure of the Aikin institute led directly to the formation of Paris Junior College. Still, the alumnae were always proud of their school, as is evident in this image. The tradition of all-women colleges in the United States traces its roots to Mount Holyoke Female Seminary in 1837.

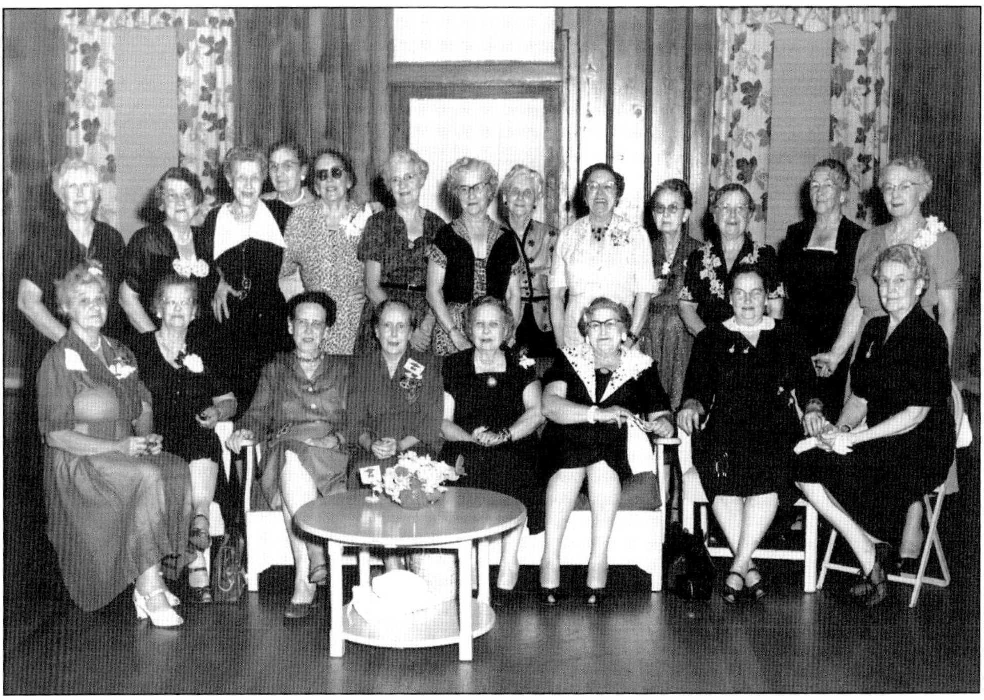

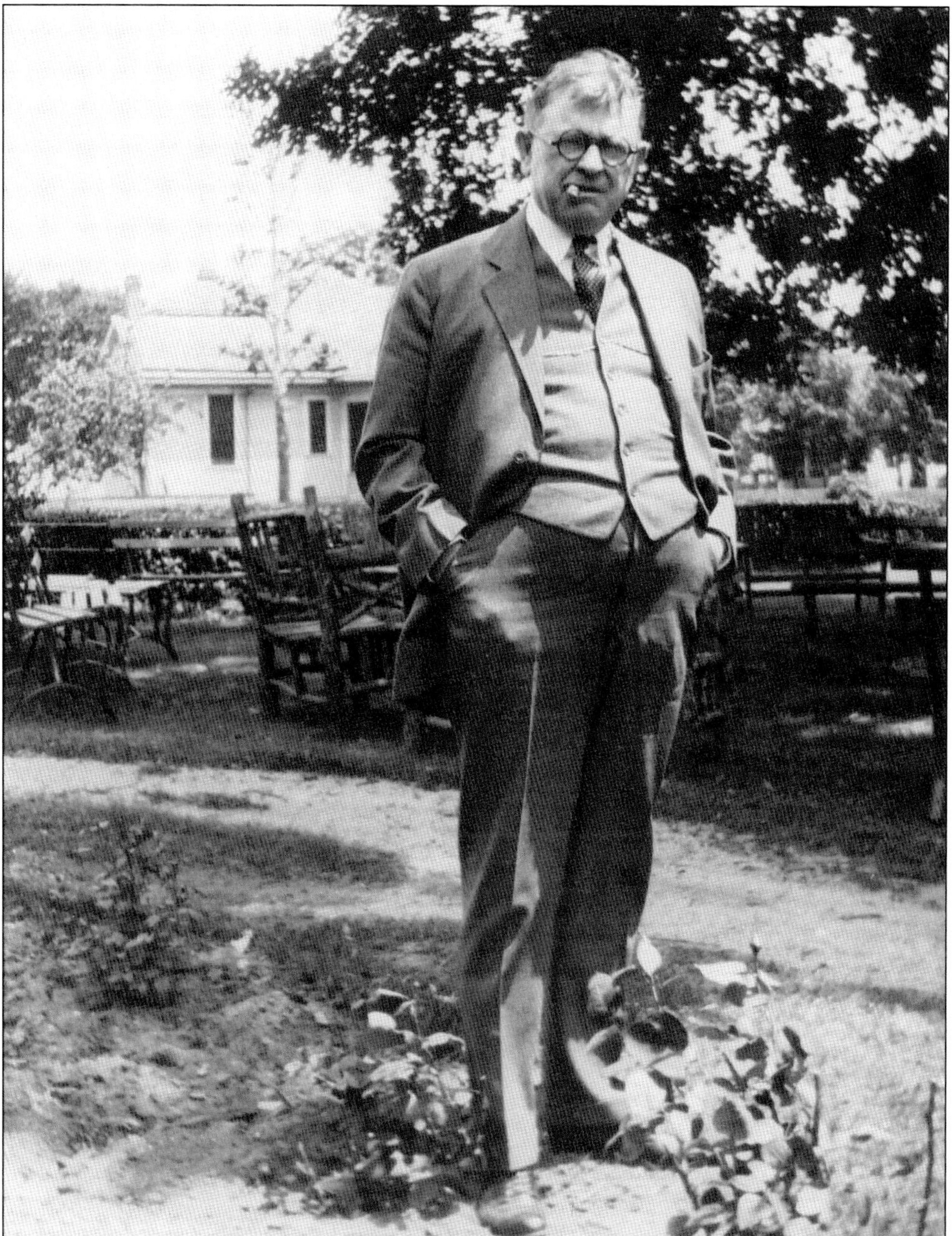

DR. L.P. MCCUISTION. The first hospital to be established in Paris was the Good Samaritan Hospital in 1892. This facility was later moved and renamed the Aikin Hospital in 1907 when the Catholic nuns of Our Lady of Mercy Convent transformed their failing school into Aikin Hospital. The Aikin Hospital was closed that same year, but the Sisters of Charity of the Incarnate Word acquired the property. In October 1910, the sisters opened St. Joseph's Infirmary, and soon thereafter, Dr. L.P. McCuistion became medical director. The facility included 70 beds and 14 bassinets for newborns.

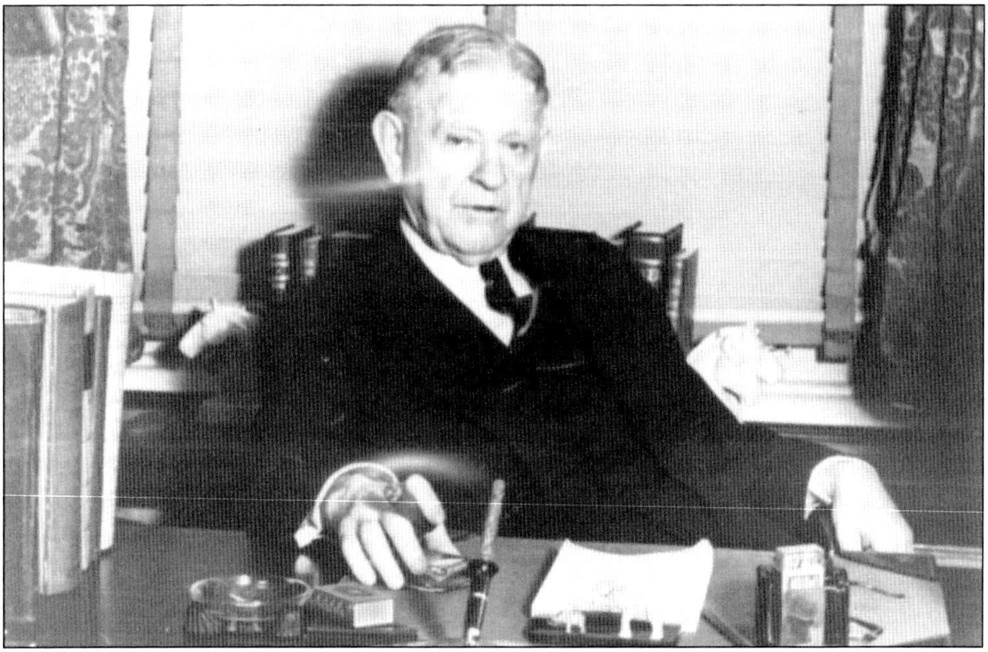

Dr. McCuistion in His Office. In many ways, Dr. L.P McCuistion (1869–1947) can be considered "the father of Paris health care." McCuistion's home is a local landmark. It was built in 1858. Today, McCuistion's home operates as the Fry-Gibbs Funeral Home. McCuistion's old home was recorded as a Texas Historic Landmark in 1965.

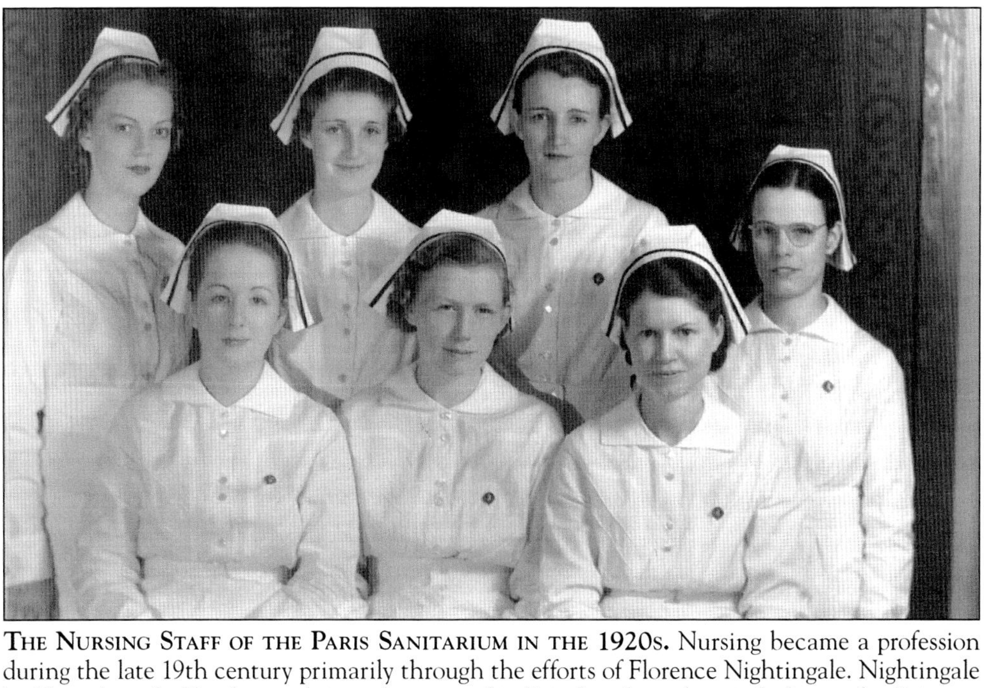

The Nursing Staff of the Paris Sanitarium in the 1920s. Nursing became a profession during the late 19th century primarily through the efforts of Florence Nightingale. Nightingale had been horrified by the conditions that existed in British military hospitals during the Crimean War. Nurses are much more than simply "the doctor's assistant," and from the time the sanitarium was founded in 1914, nurses were critical to the operations of the facility.

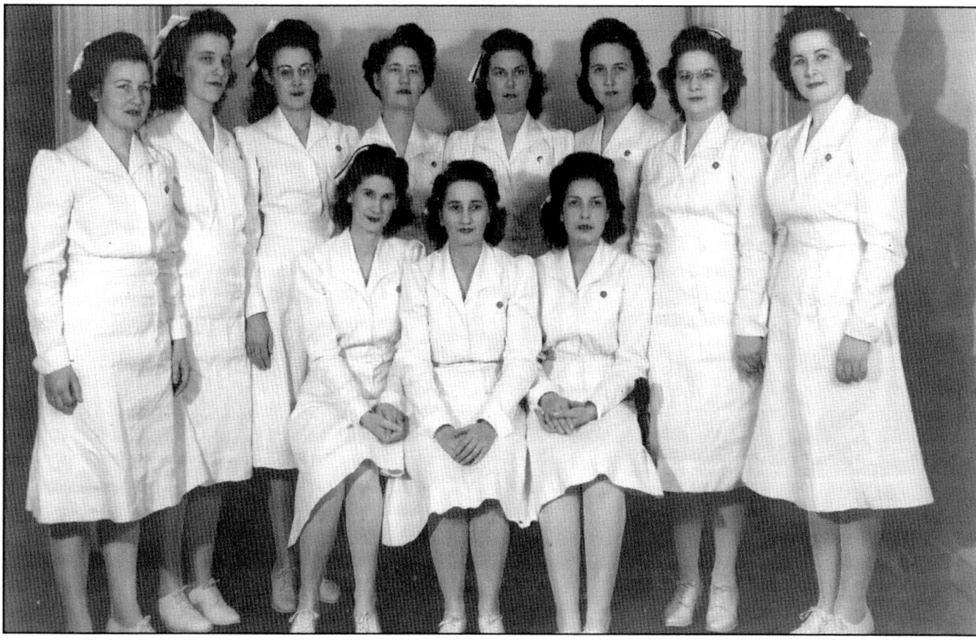

The Paris Sanitarium's Nurses in the 1940s. Registered nurses are highly trained professionals. They undergo rigorous training and have their own code of professional ethics. Today, registered nurses can receive their professional qualifications in one of two ways: either through a two-year or four-year program of study. It is said that the two-year programs are more "hands on" than four-year programs. Whatever the case, all nursing programs are highly selective.

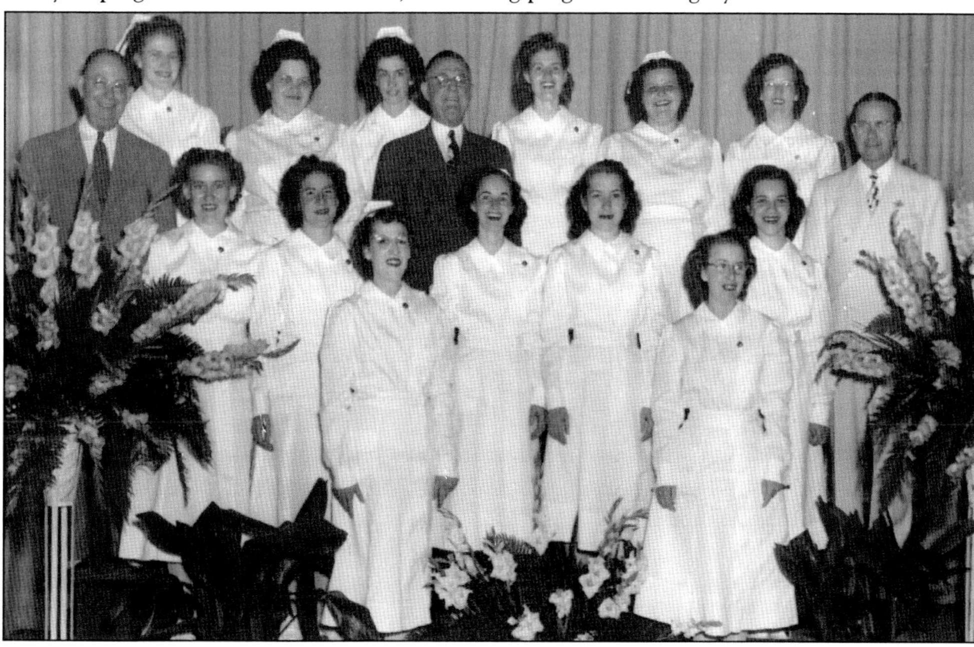

Graduate Nurses. Individuals must undergo a rigorous practical and academic course of instruction in order to become a registered nurse. Pictured here is the last graduating class of the Sanitarium of Paris Nursing College in 1948. Individuals enrolled in nursing training at the sanitarium underwent a three-year course of instruction.

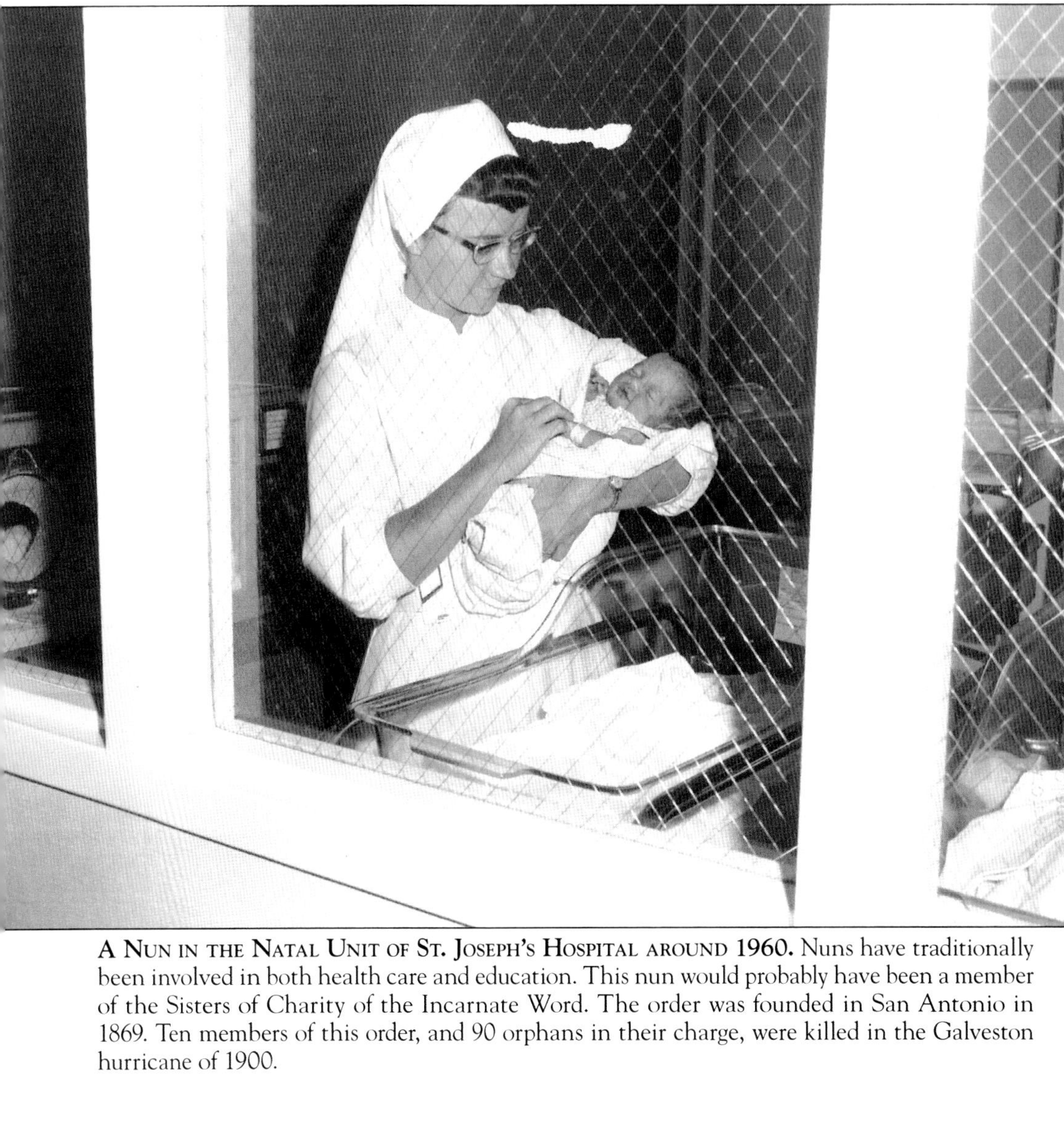

A NUN IN THE NATAL UNIT OF ST. JOSEPH'S HOSPITAL AROUND 1960. Nuns have traditionally been involved in both health care and education. This nun would probably have been a member of the Sisters of Charity of the Incarnate Word. The order was founded in San Antonio in 1869. Ten members of this order, and 90 orphans in their charge, were killed in the Galveston hurricane of 1900.

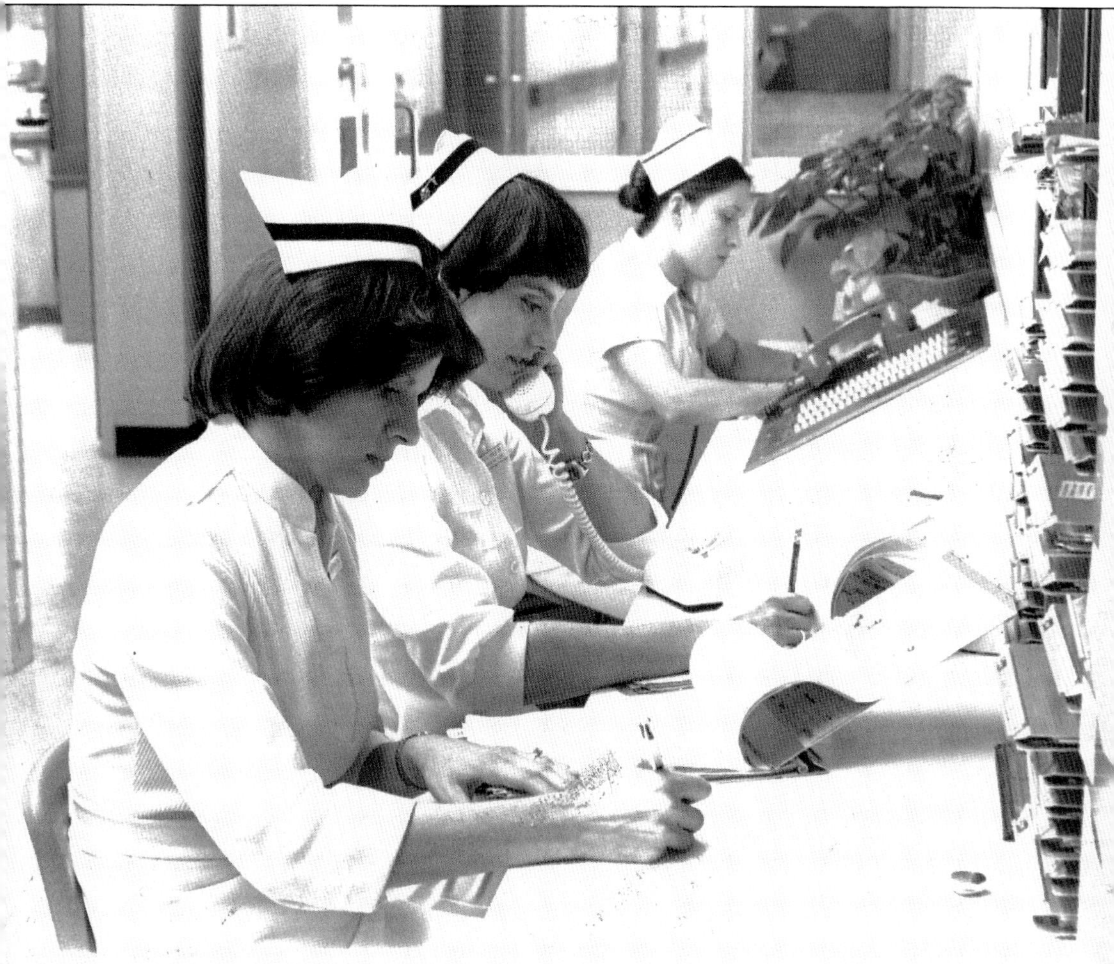

REGISTERED NURSES AT WORK IN ST. JOSEPH'S HOSPITAL IN THE 1970S. Nursing stations, such as this one, are the nerve center for medical operations in clinics and hospitals. Nurses do more than provide primary care for patients. In many ways, nurses are the frontline administrators and record keepers for any health-care system. The absence of computers, which are integral to health care today, is clearly seen in this photograph.

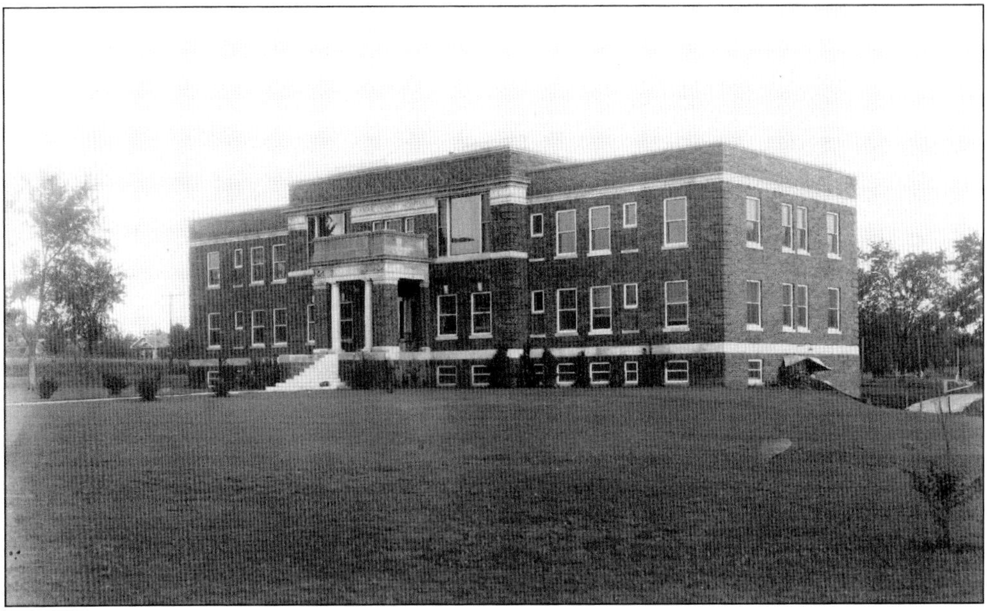

LAMAR COUNTY HOSPITAL IN THE 1920s. The Lamar County Hospital was built in the Classical Revival style. It was completed and went into operation in 1926. The hospital was located at 625 West Washington Street. This facility was a charity hospital that provided medical care to the poor of Lamar County. In the days before federally administered programs, such as Medicaid, the poor had to rely on facilities such as this for medical care. The photograph below is of the same facility but with a different name, the Lamar County Medical Center. The date of the photograph below is unknown.

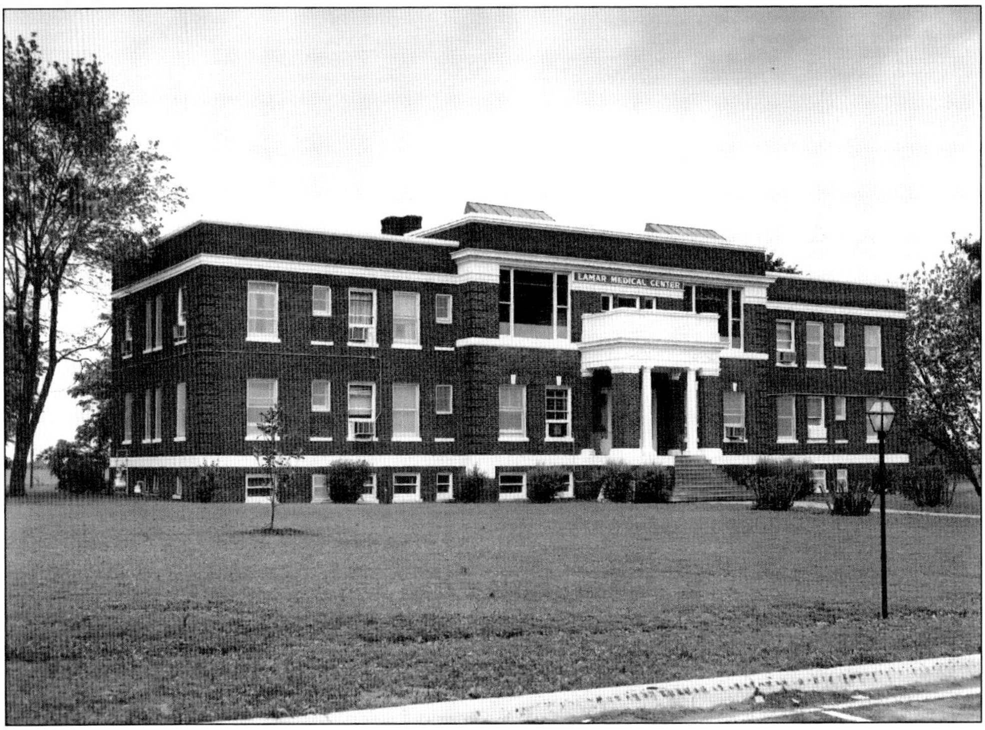

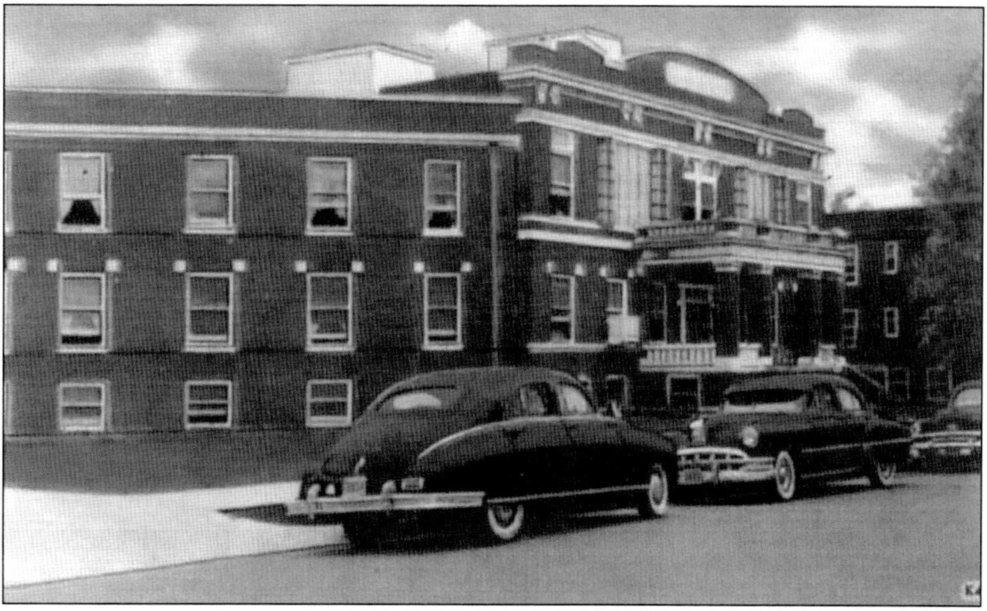

The Sanitarium of Paris in the 1950s. The sanitarium was an important part of what might be called the Lamar County Health Care System. Dr. McCuistion, who taught ethics and surgery at the Paris Training School for Nurses located in the St. Joseph's Hospital, was the founder the sanitarium in 1914. (Courtesy of the Lamar County Historical Society Museum.)

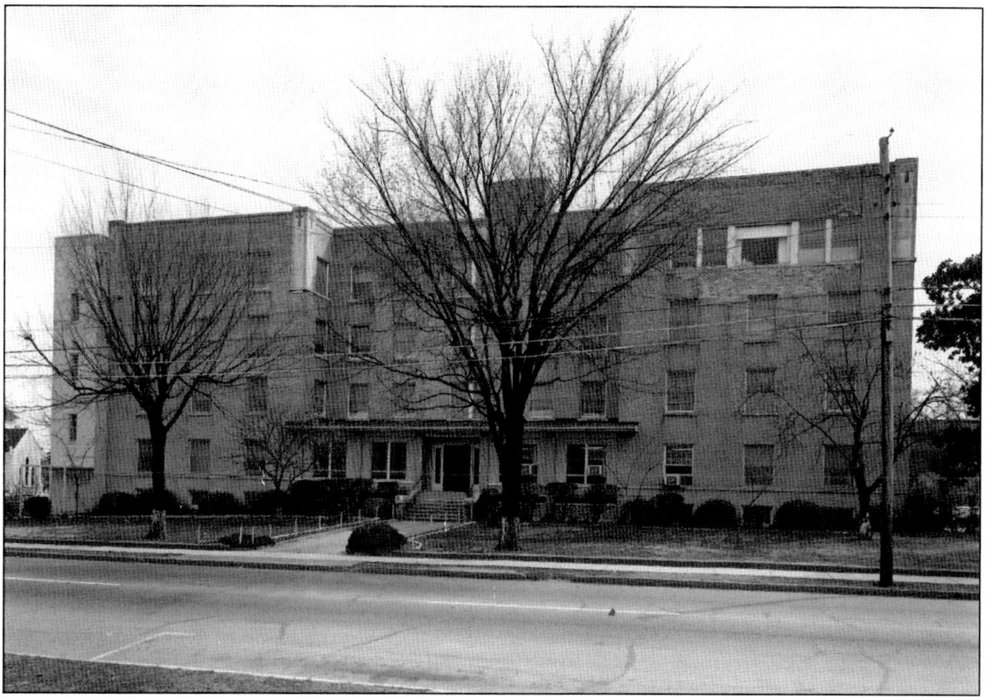

St. Joseph's Hospital in 1950. St. Joseph's Hospital is now known as the Paris Regional Medical Center, South Campus. For many years, it was St. Joseph's Hospital, with its nuns, its excellent health care, and its central location on Clarksville Street, which was the symbol of health care in Paris, Texas.

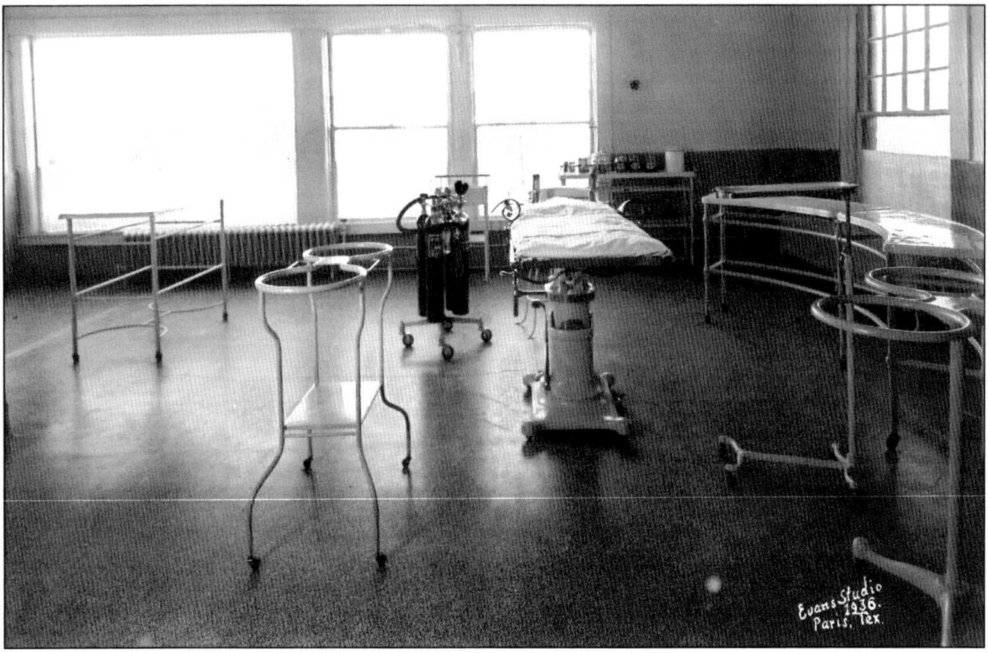

A Surgical Operating Room in 1936. Any operating room from this period stands in stark contrast to early-21st-century operating theaters. Before modern anesthetics, surgical equipment, and medical advances, "routine" surgery of today was a desperate and often life-threatening roll of the dice in the early 20th century.

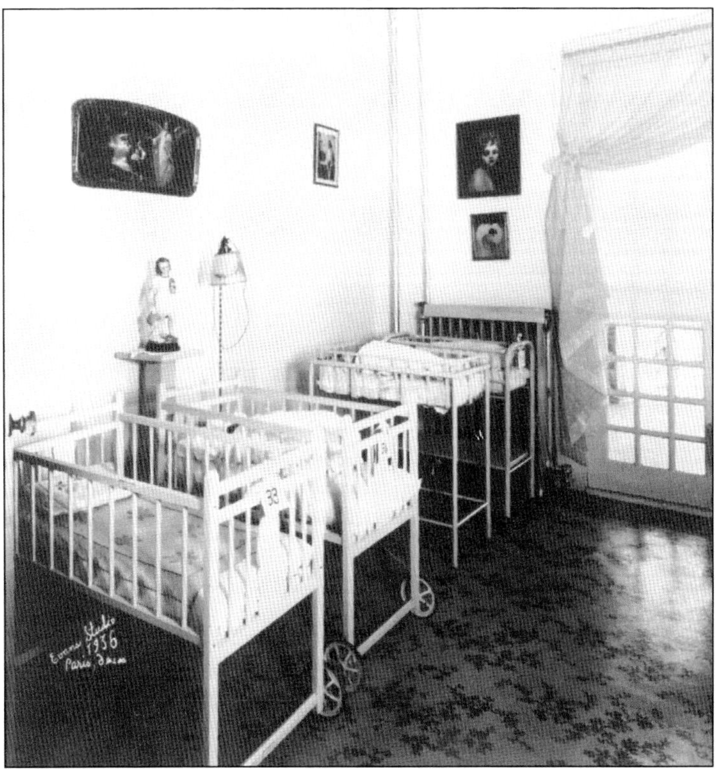

A Newborn Unit in 1936. Good care for newly born infants is critical. It is easily forgotten that, before the 20th century, babies and their mothers stood in significant risk of dying depending on circumstances. In the absence of modern prenatal care, infants could, and were, born with all manner of medical issues.

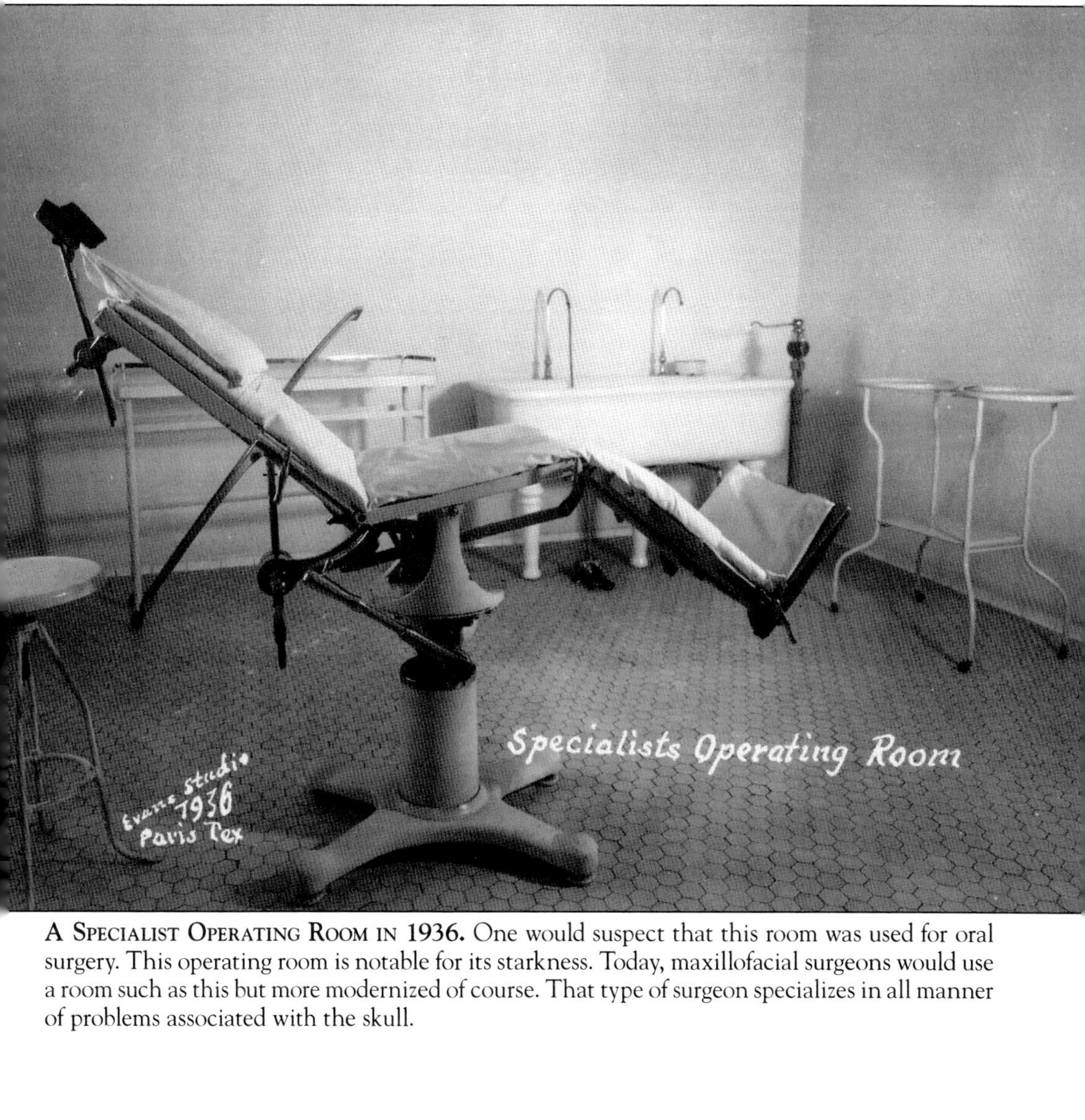

A SPECIALIST OPERATING ROOM IN 1936. One would suspect that this room was used for oral surgery. This operating room is notable for its starkness. Today, maxillofacial surgeons would use a room such as this but more modernized of course. That type of surgeon specializes in all manner of problems associated with the skull.

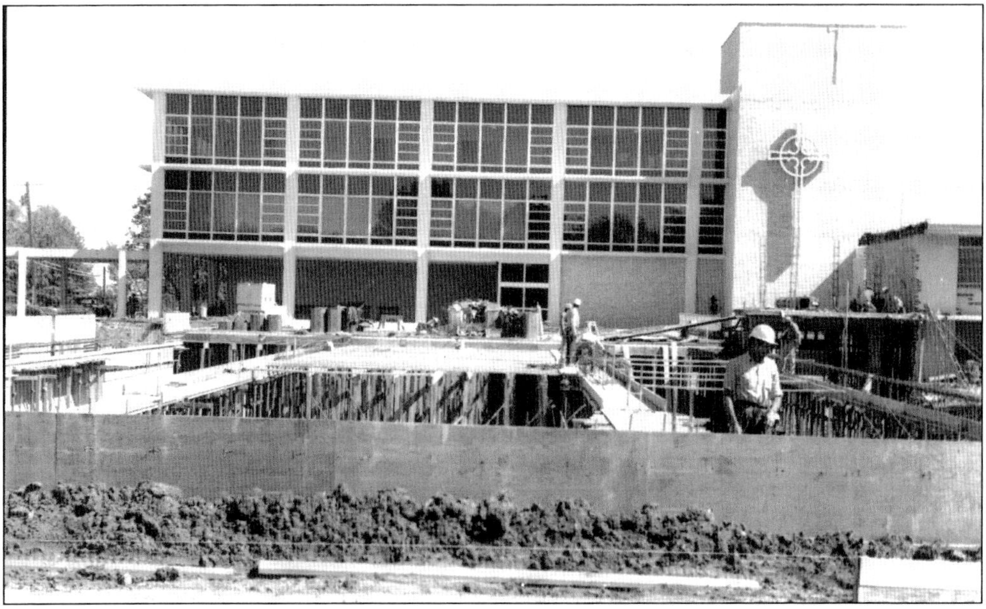

THE "NEW" ST. JOSEPH'S HOSPITAL UNDER CONSTRUCTION AND THE COMPLETED STRUCTURE ABOUT 1970. Today, as a part of the Paris Regional Medical Center (PRMC), this hospital provides a variety of services to the Lamar County community. Prior to becoming a part of PRMC, St. Joseph's Hospital was a part of the Christus Health System (*Christus* is Latin for "Christ"), which is a Catholic-related health system that operates more than 40 hospitals in Texas, Arkansas, Louisiana, Oklahoma, and Mexico. Visible in the photograph above is the St. Joseph's distinctive logo, the Celtic cross. The below image is of the completed St. Joseph's in 1970.

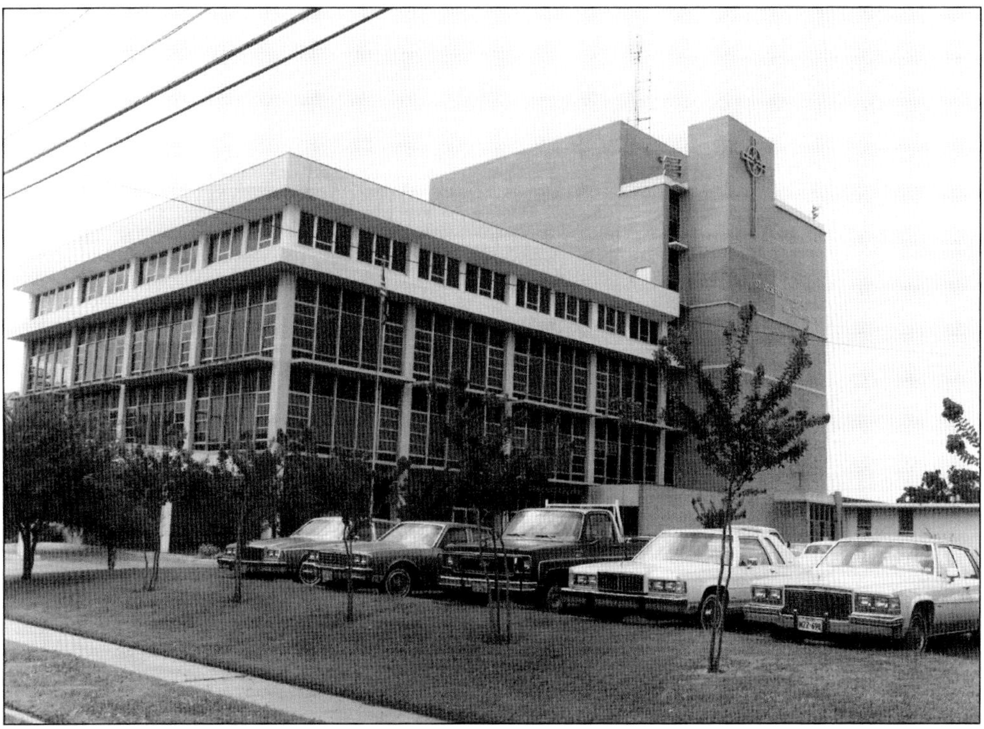

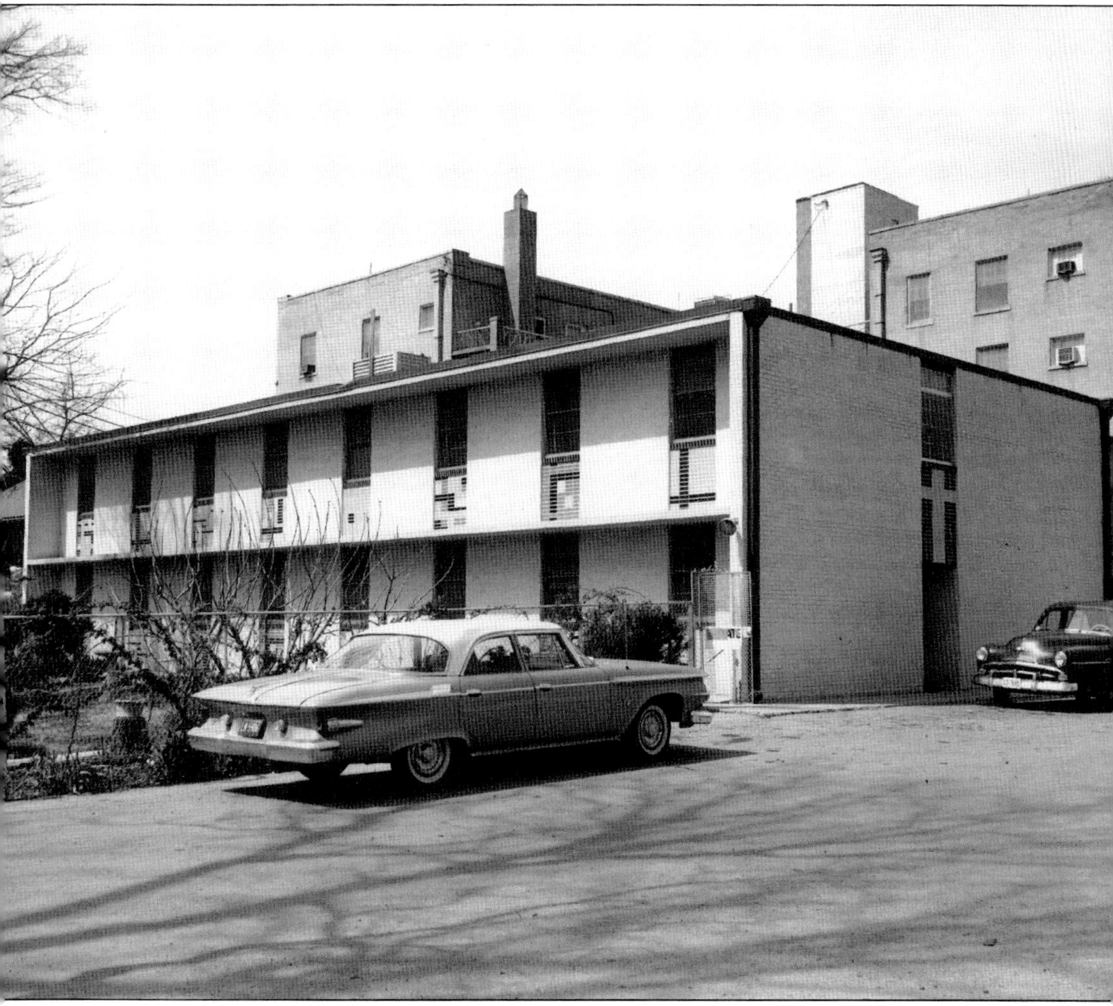

AN ANNEX TO ST. JOSEPH'S HOSPITAL IN PARIS. This photograph was taken, perhaps, in 1962. Annexes, such as this, could house doctor's offices, equipment storage, or be where medical records were stored. It is possible that this annex provided housing for hospital employees; this was common practice at the time.

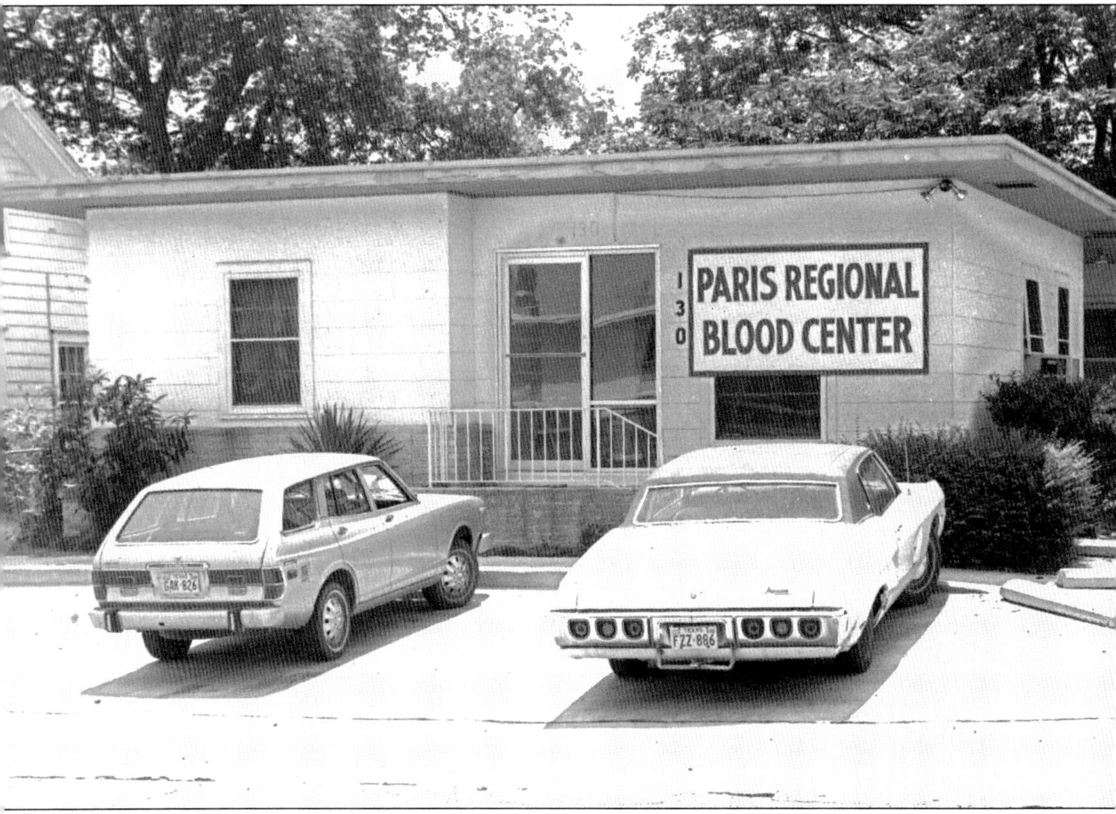

The Paris Regional Blood Center in 1982. Whole blood cannot be synthesized, nor can it be stored for long. The sick and injured rely on voluntary blood donations to provide the blood that they need. Whole blood can only be stored for a maximum of 35 days. Because of this, hospitals rely on a constant supply of donated blood to meet the needs of their patients.

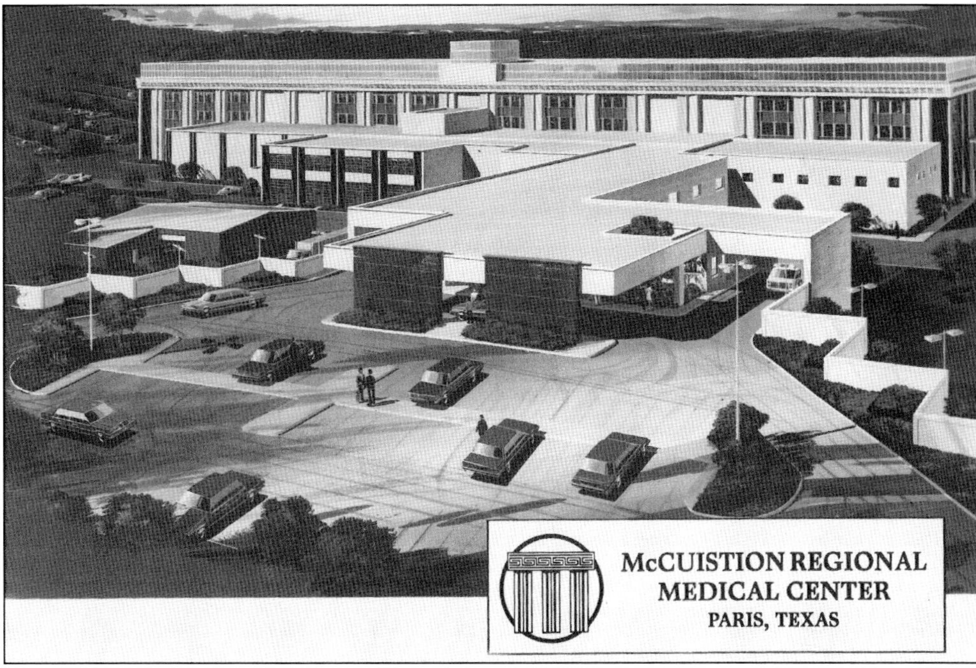

McCuistion Regional Medical Center. Above is an architect's rendering of the proposed new McCuistion Hospital, located on Loop 286. The photograph below is the brand-new McCuistion Regional Medical Center in 1968. Today, McCuistion is known as the Paris Regional Medical Center, North Campus. The McCuistion Medical Center, North Campus, boasts 198 beds and a staff of 105 registered nurses as well as a highly respected team of medical doctors and surgeons. If patients need care above and beyond what is available in Paris, critical patients are flown via Careflight to an appropriate specialist center in Dallas.

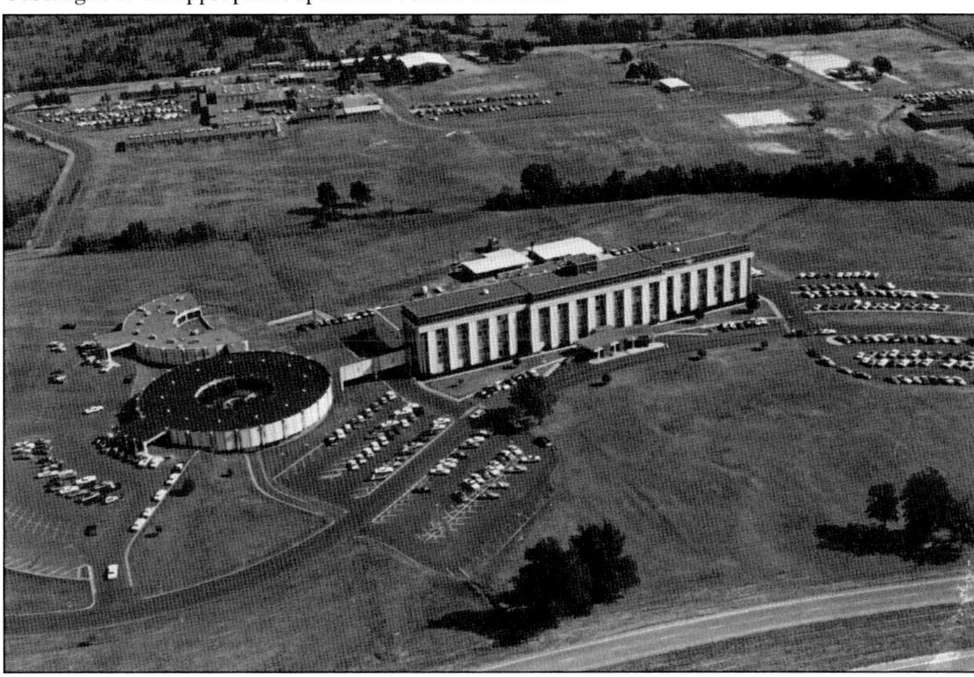

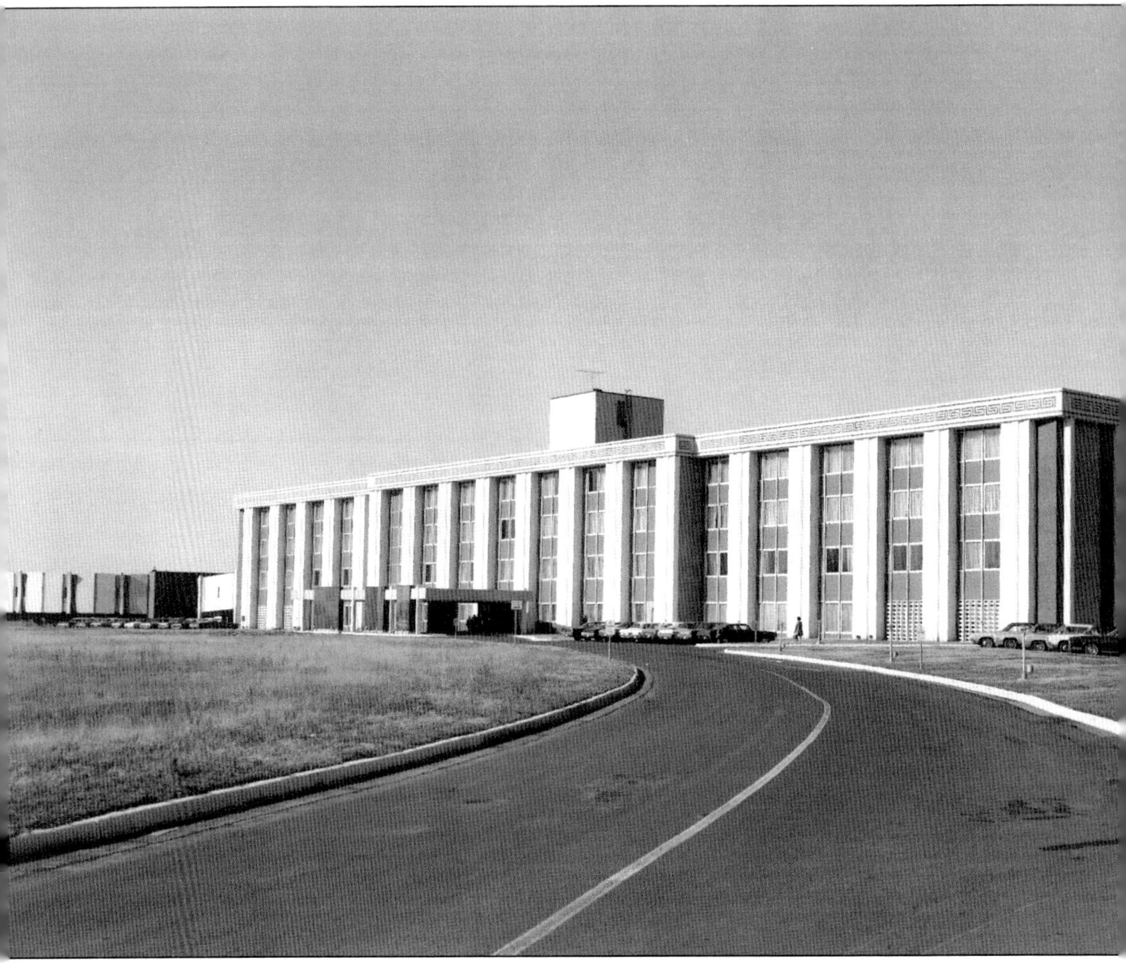

Another View of the Newly Opened McCuistion Medical Center. This hospital is classified as a short-term, acute-care hospital. Essent owns McCuistion as a part of the Paris Regional Medical Center. Within the unified Paris Regional Medical Center, all acute care has been consolidated at the North Campus on Loop 286.

Four

SERVING THE COMMUNITY

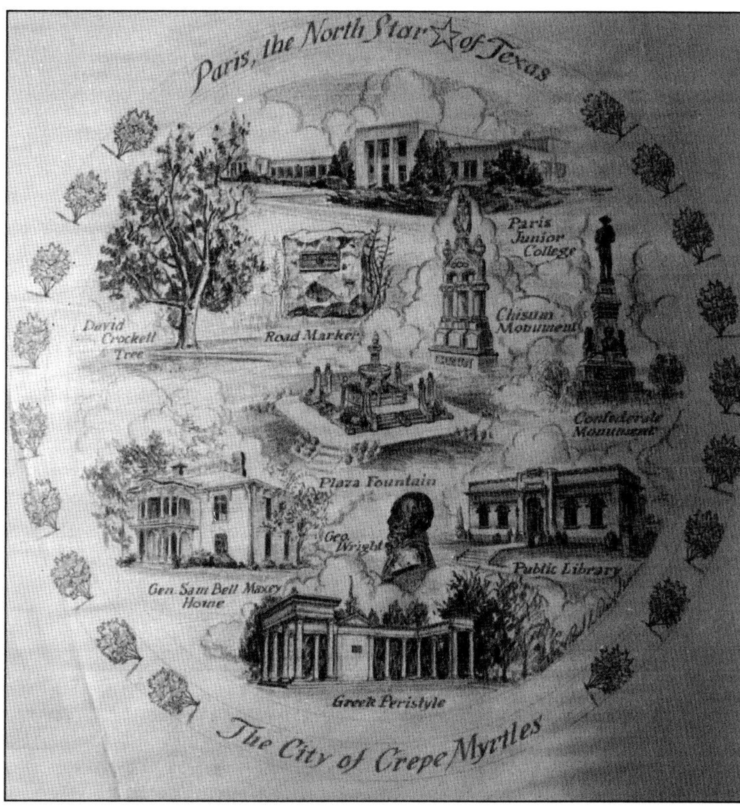

THE CONCEPT OF COMMUNITY. A community can be defined by a variety of selected attributes. Further, symbols assist in identifying and strengthening the bonds of community. The image here is interesting in that it attempts to define the Paris community in a number of ways; it identifies the city's two nicknames as well as significant architectural features of the area.

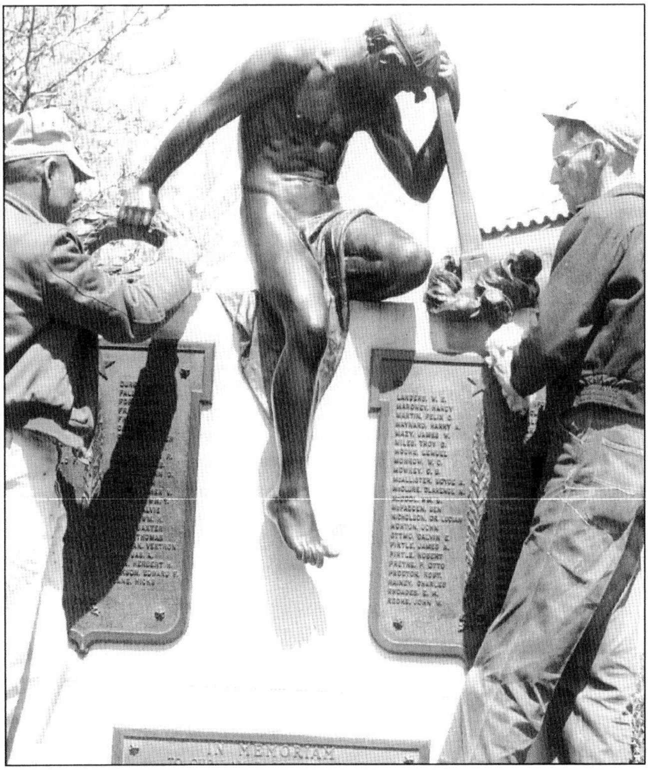

THE LAMAR COUNTY WORLD WAR I MEMORIAL BEING REPAIRED. This is a good shot of the World War I memorial undergoing routine repairs. Approximately 340 men from Lamar County served in the military during World War I. Eleven of these men gave their lives during that conflict. J.L. Wees designed this monument.

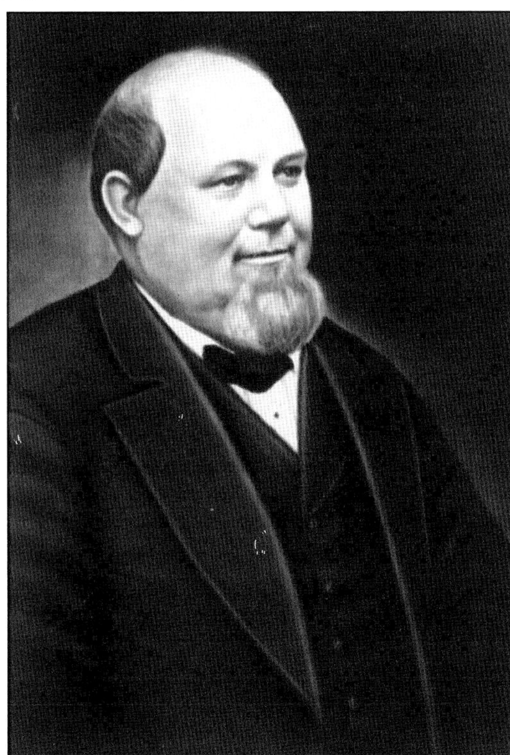

WILLET BABCOCK. Willet Babcock was born in New York in 1828. He and his wife moved to Paris in 1859. Babcock became a successful businessman; he owned and operated the Babcock Furniture Manufacturing Plant as well as an opera house. Most notably, Babcock helped organize the first volunteer fire department in Paris, the Phoenix Fire Company, and served as its first fire chief. Babcock died in 1881. His grave marker, with its "Jesus with Cowboy boots" in Evergreen Cemetery, is known worldwide.

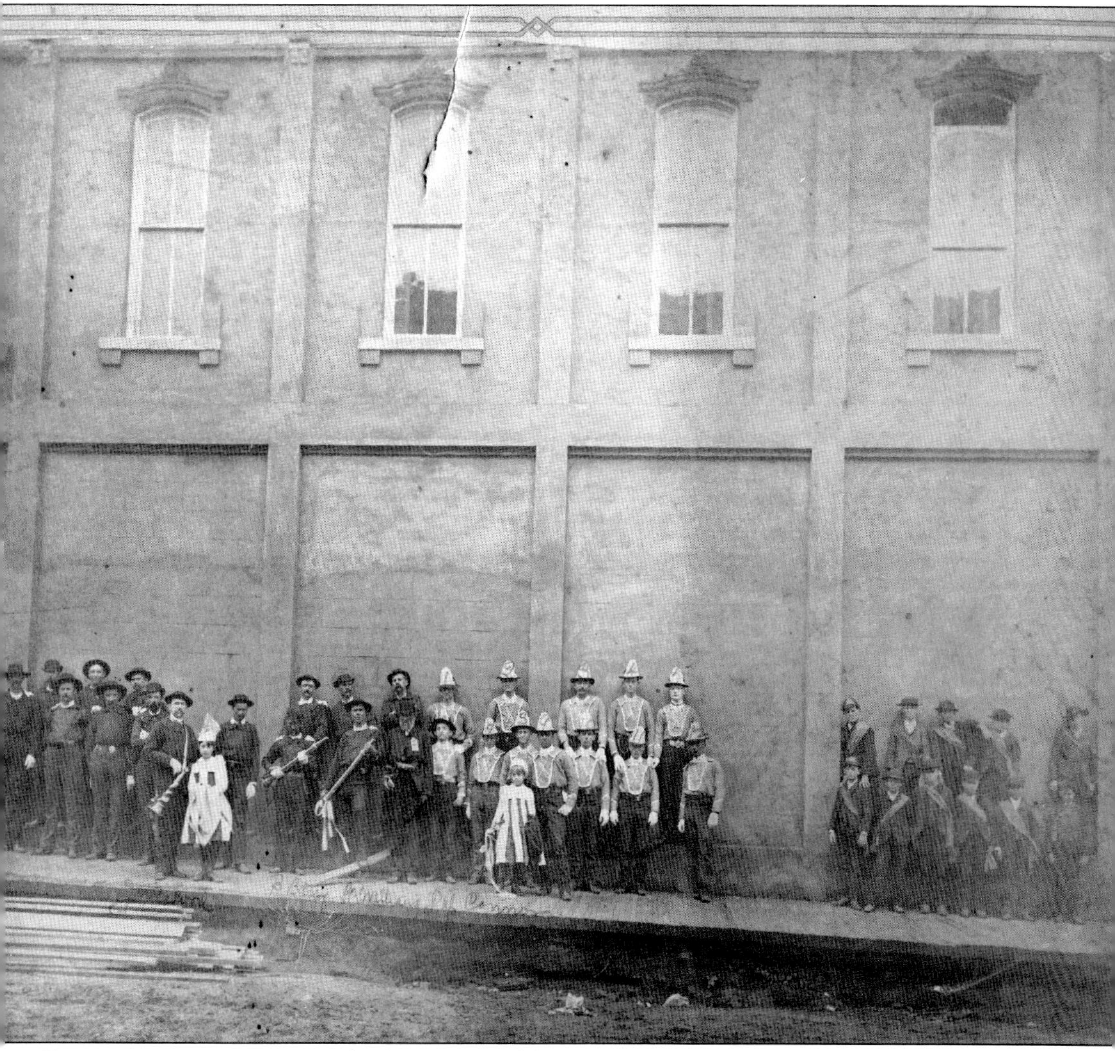

Paris Volunteer Firemen. The first organized fire protection in Paris was formed in 1872–1873, under the guidance of Willet T. Babcock (1828–1881). Although this first organization was strictly composed of volunteers, it was chartered with the State of Texas in 1875. The organization grew and was apparently quite well trained. The early volunteers (known as the Phoenix Fire Company) were tested by the fire of August 31, 1877, and performed well by all accounts. This is perhaps the first photograph of the Phoenix Fire Company. A close examination of the image reveals that the firefighters are wearing a symbolic hook and ladder as an identifying decoration on their uniforms.

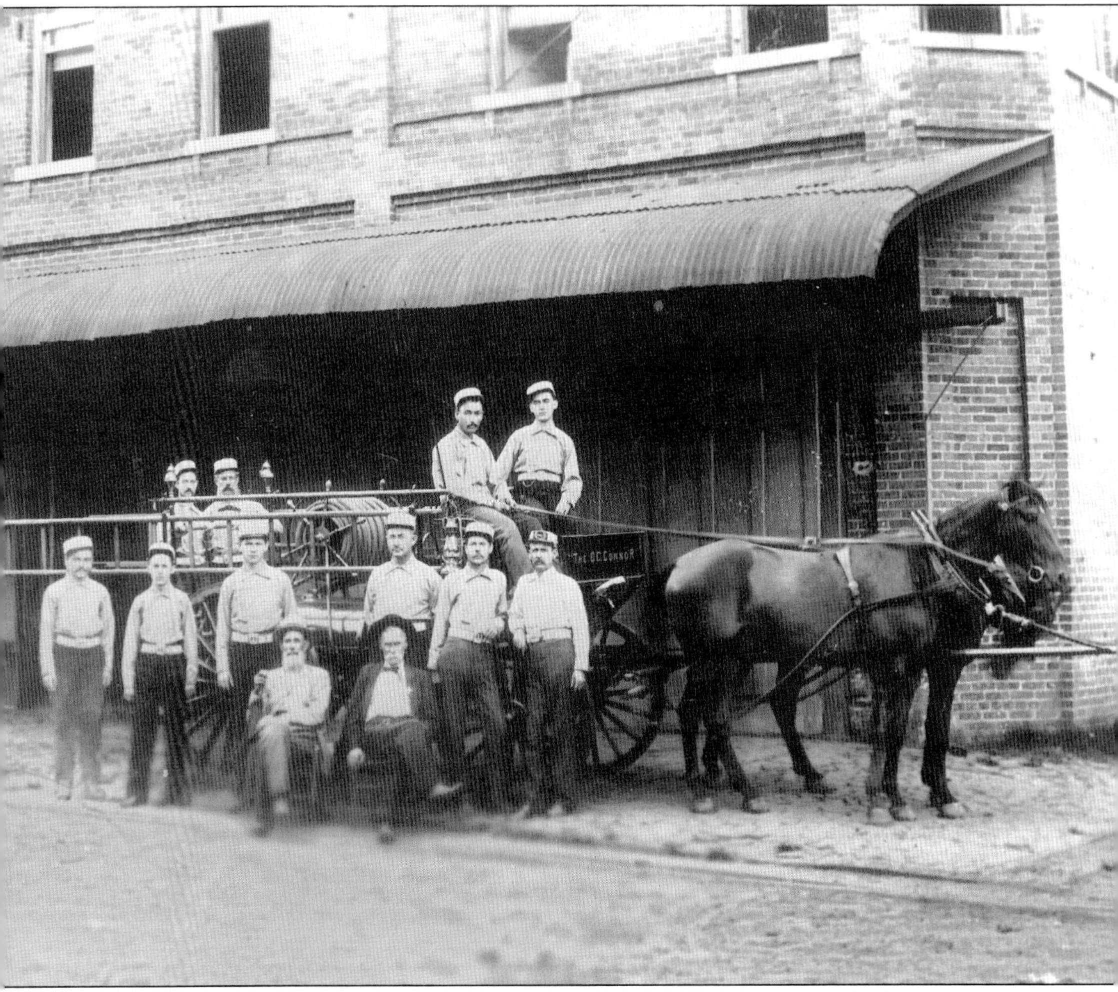

A Horse-Drawn Fire Wagon in the Late 19th Century. This particular fire wagon is named "The O.C. Connor." The Paris fire chief is standing at the right, nearest the horses. The older figures seated in the center cannot be identified, but one of them is wearing what seems to be a sheriff's star. In 1908, it was deemed that Paris needed a full-time, paid, city-controlled fire department. Thus, during the administration of Mayor Ed McCuistion, the Volunteer Phoenix Fire Company was disbanded and replaced with a paid force.

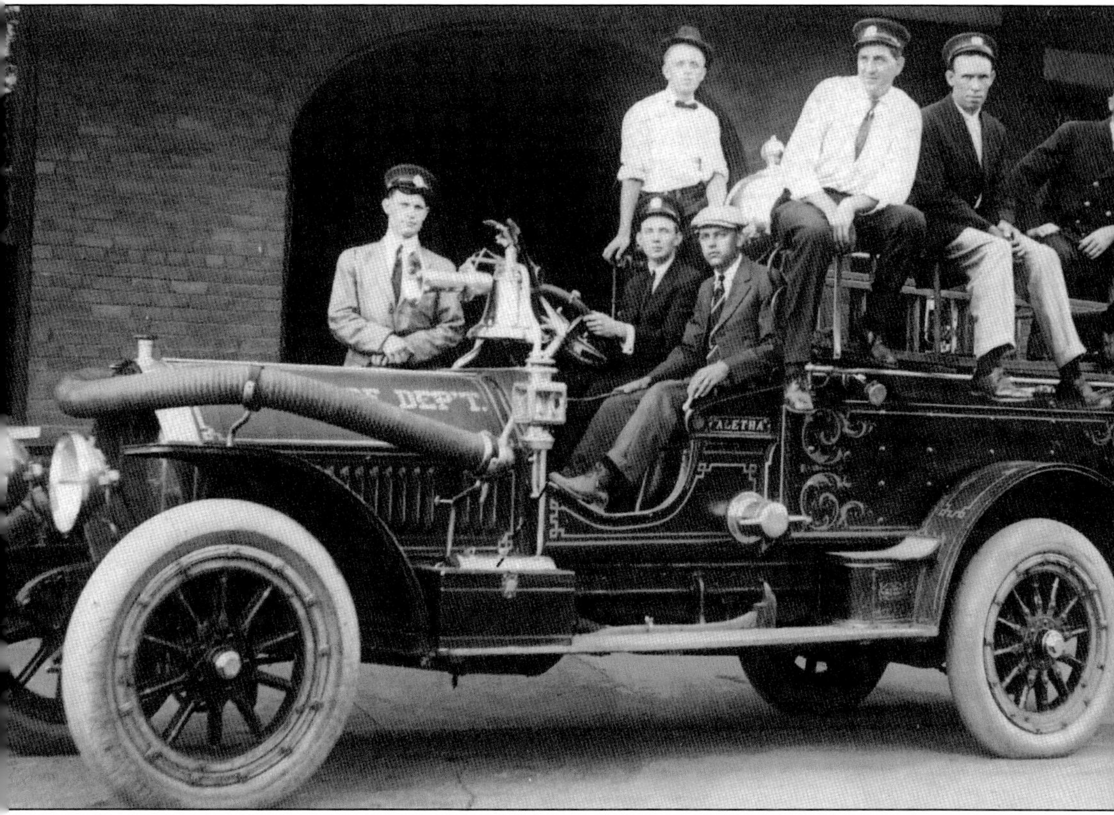

Paris Firefighters Posing with Newly Acquired Fire Engine. Fireman "Mutt" Cross is at the wheel. The Paris Fire Department served with remarkable bravery during the fire of 1916. They stood their ground. In one case, fireman Mutt Cross remained with his engine despite great personal danger. The fire overwhelmed his position, and Cross only survived by cutting a fire hose and taking shelter in a gutter, covered by the water, as the flames past over him.

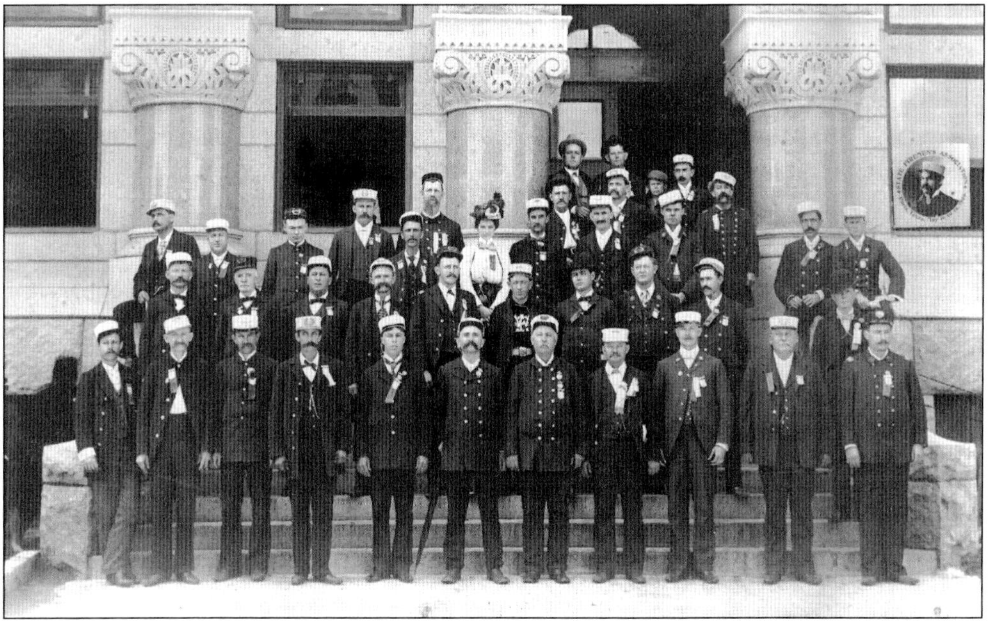

A MEETING OF VOLUNTEER FIRE CHIEFS IN PARIS. Although the early Paris Fire Department was composed of volunteers, it did not operate in isolation. The volunteers associated and trained with other volunteer departments in Texas. This is a photograph of visiting fire chiefs who attended the State Firemen's Association meeting in Paris on May 10–12, 1899. A badge worn by one of the attendees is in the possession of the Paris Fire Department to this day.

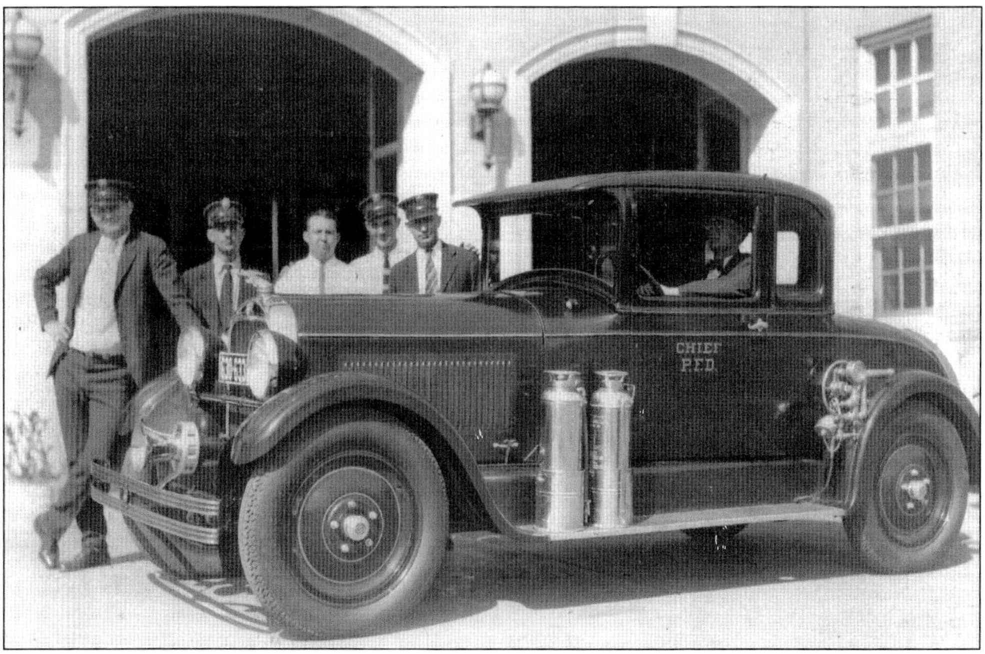

THE NEW CHIEF'S CAR. Even in the depths of the Great Depression, Paris was keen to invest in vital community services. Here, members of the Paris Fire Department show off their new chief's car about 1930. As of 2011, the fire department consists of 48 suppression personnel, three administrators (including the chief), and one secretary.

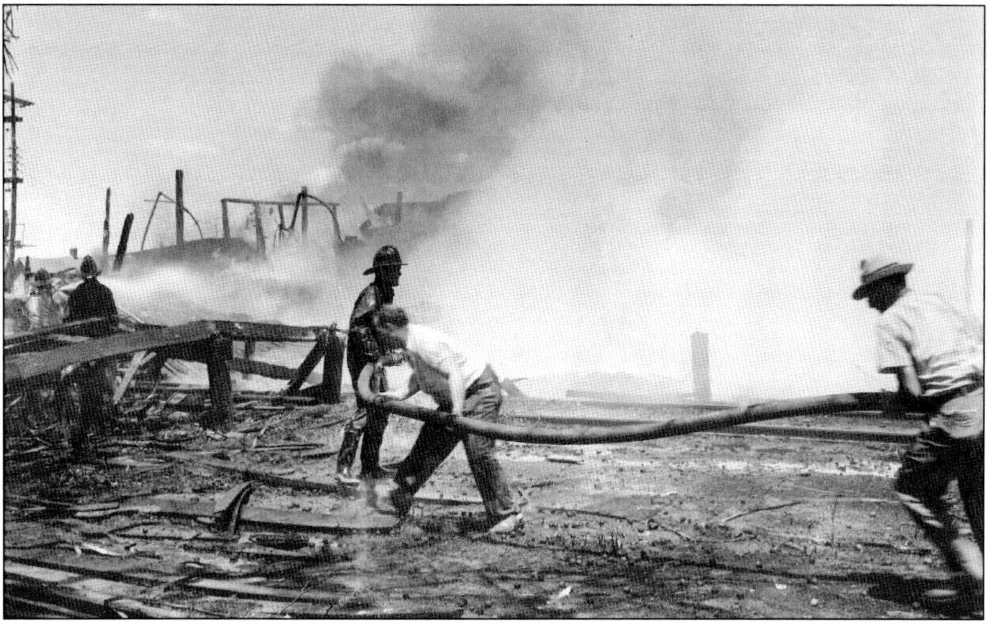

Fighting the Hammond Manufacturing Plant Fire. The fire at the Hammond Manufacturing Plant was a major conflagration in Paris that taxed the fire department's personnel. The fire was so fierce that day that local citizens lent a helping hand to the embattled firefighters. This is not a practice that is currently encouraged.

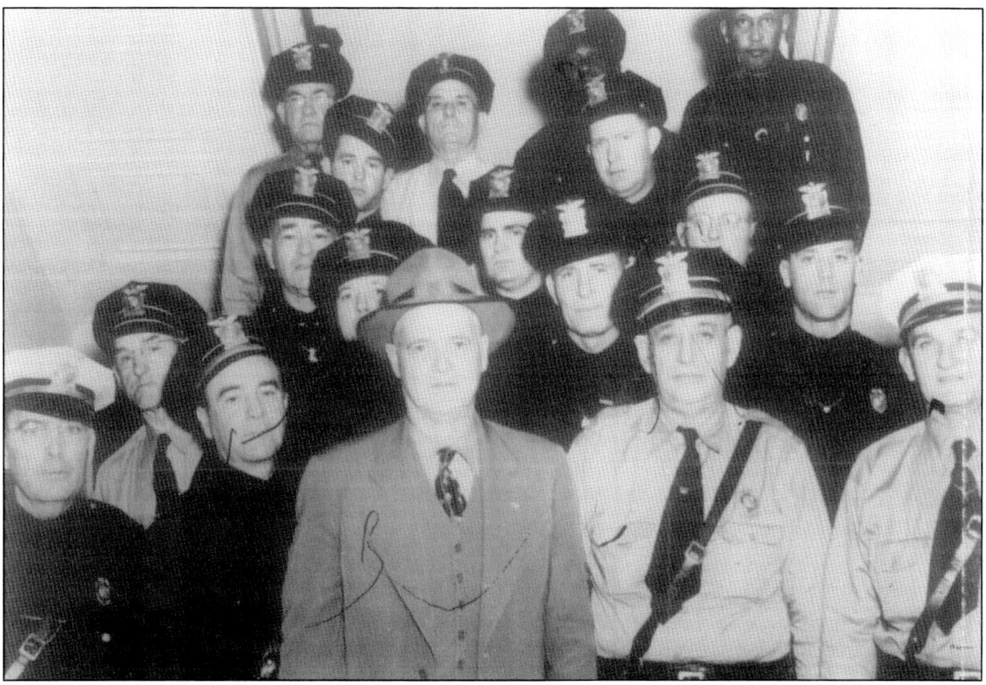

The Paris Police Department. Paris has possessed a professional police force since the late 19th century. The first uniformed Paris police officer was Larkin Hunt. The date of the photograph is uncertain, but one can see that the department was integrated the time. The figure in civilian clothes is presumably the chief of police.

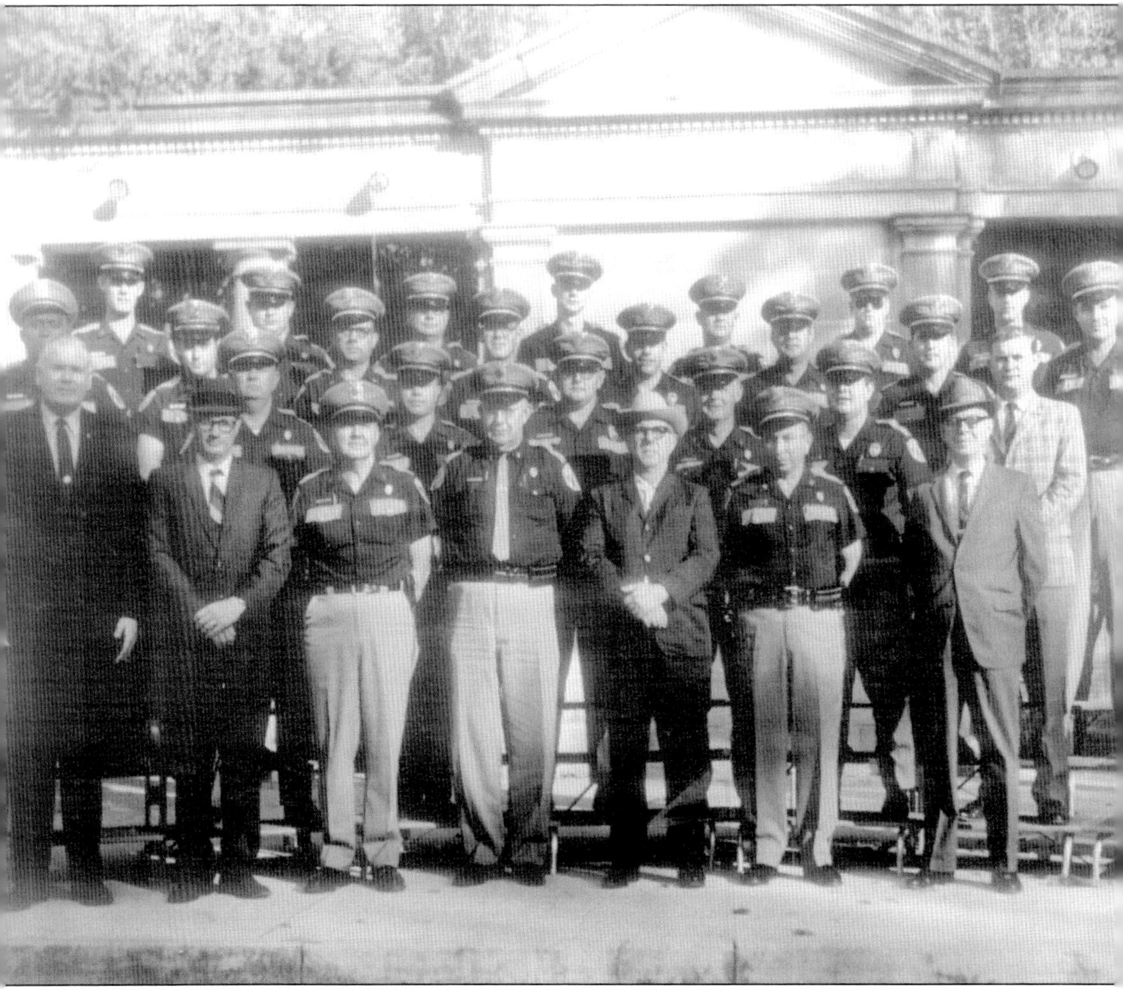

Members of the Police Department. The Paris Police Department has suffered four deaths in the line of duty: William Albright (1874), William Schultz (1904), Duaine Cross (1920), and David Roberts (1985). In this photograph, members of the Paris Police Department pose at the Peristyle in Bywaters Park. (Courtesy of Ruth Sparks.)

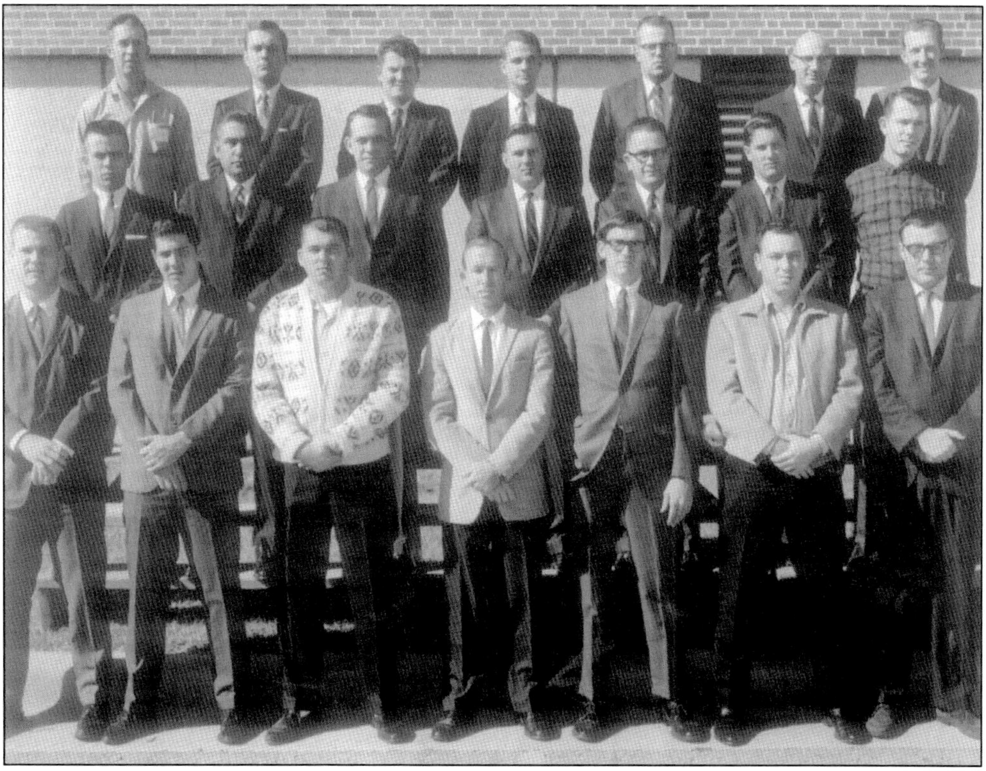

PLAINCLOTHES PARIS OFFICERS. Police departments are organized into various divisions based upon mission and community needs; the larger the force, the more complex the organization. Currently, the Paris Police Department is organized into three divisions: patrol, criminal investigation, and services. The department employs 61 police officers and the chief as of 2011. (Courtesy of Ruth Sparks.)

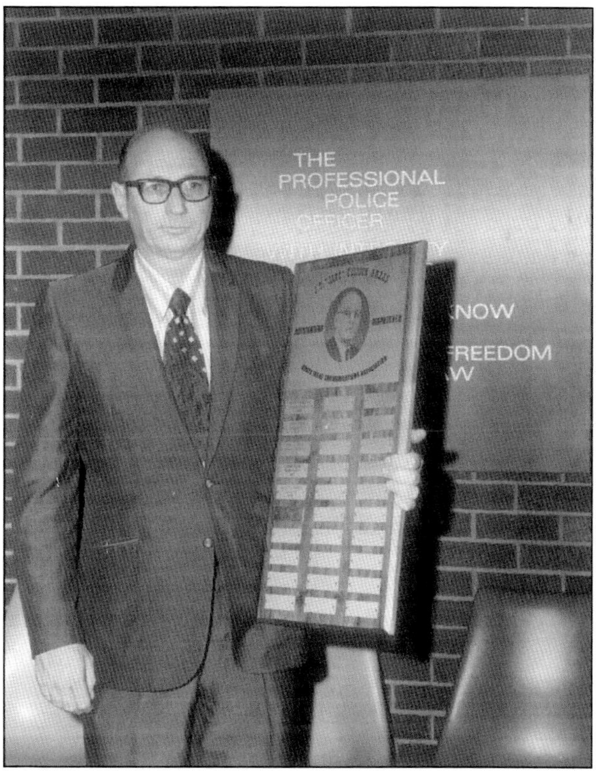

POLICE LIEUTENANT ARCHIE SPARKS RECEIVING AN AWARD FOR HIS SERVICE. Archie Sparks served as a member of the Paris Police Department between 1953 and 1986. At the time of his retirement, he was the lieutenant in charge of the service division. In this photograph, Sparks is receiving an award for his many years of service to the community. (Courtesy of Ruth Sparks.)

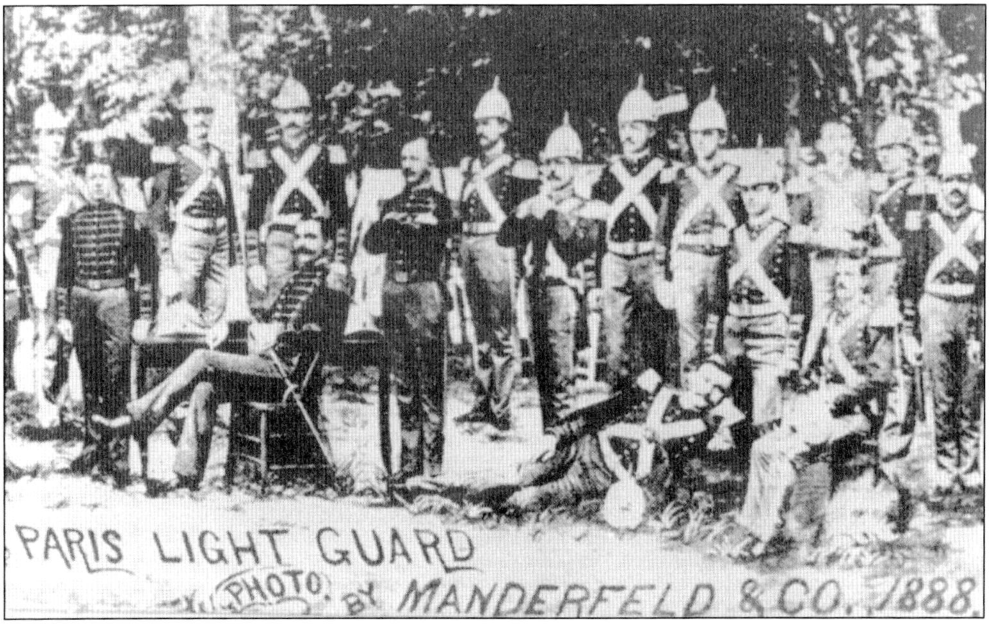

THE PARIS LIGHT GUARD IN 1888. Before the federal Militia Act of 1903, there was no real standardized militia or reserve force in the United States. Thus, up until 1903, one can find evidence of all manner of militia forces, sometimes fantastically uniformed, in towns across the nation. An example of this is the Paris Light Guard. The Paris Light Guard was organized in 1887, under the command of West Point graduate Captain Bailey.

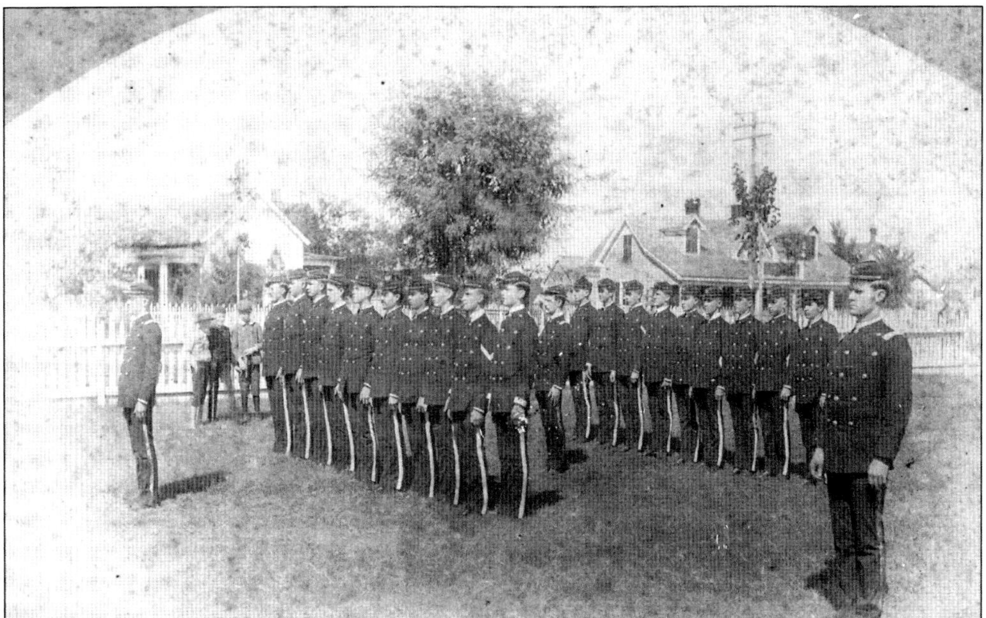

THE MAXEY RIFLES IN 1887. This 1887 Paris militia force, the Maxey Rifles, are a stark contrast to the Paris Light Guard in regards to uniform. This force was organized in 1887, under the command of Capt. E.S. Easley (far right, nearest to the camera). Easley had attended, but did not graduate from, West Point.

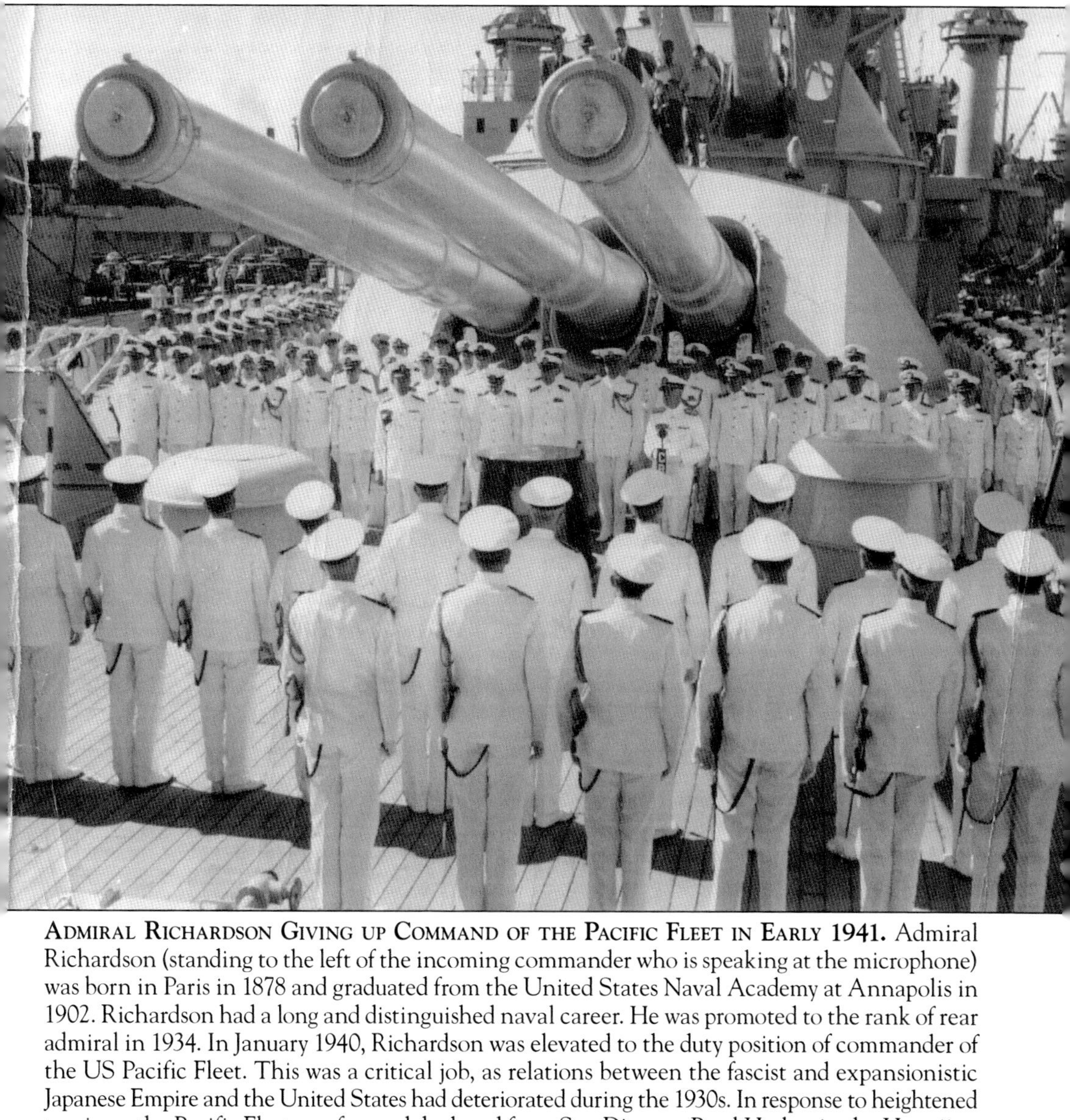

ADMIRAL RICHARDSON GIVING UP COMMAND OF THE PACIFIC FLEET IN EARLY 1941. Admiral Richardson (standing to the left of the incoming commander who is speaking at the microphone) was born in Paris in 1878 and graduated from the United States Naval Academy at Annapolis in 1902. Richardson had a long and distinguished naval career. He was promoted to the rank of rear admiral in 1934. In January 1940, Richardson was elevated to the duty position of commander of the US Pacific Fleet. This was a critical job, as relations between the fascist and expansionistic Japanese Empire and the United States had deteriorated during the 1930s. In response to heightened tensions, the Pacific Fleet was forward deployed from San Diego to Pearl Harbor in the Hawaiian Islands. Richardson did not agree with this move, as he believed stationing the fleet at Pearl Harbor degraded the fleet's readiness. Richardson left command of the Pacific Fleet in February 1941: only 10 months before the Japanese attack on Pearl Harbor. Admiral Richardson retired from naval service in 1942. He passed away in 1974 at the age of 96.

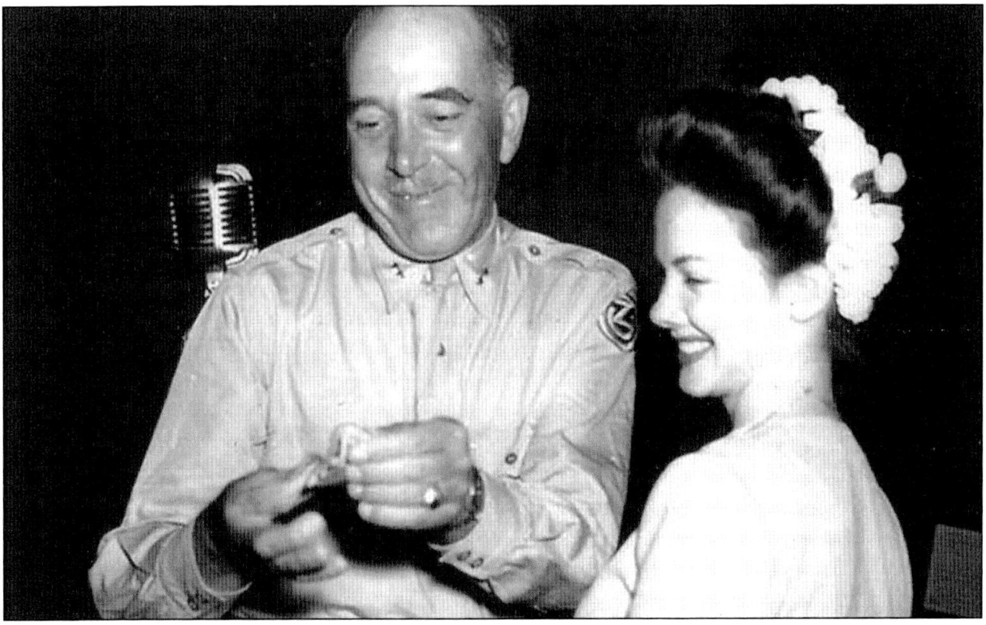

General Anderson at Camp Maxey. Camp Maxey, just north of Paris, was established as an infantry-division training center in July 1942. Two infantry divisions, the 102nd and 99th, were trained at Maxey before being shipped to fight in Europe. In addition, Camp Maxey served as a prisoner of war camp for captured German soldiers. This photograph shows the commander of the 102nd, Maj. Gen. John B. Anderson, interacting with a USO singer at Camp Maxey.

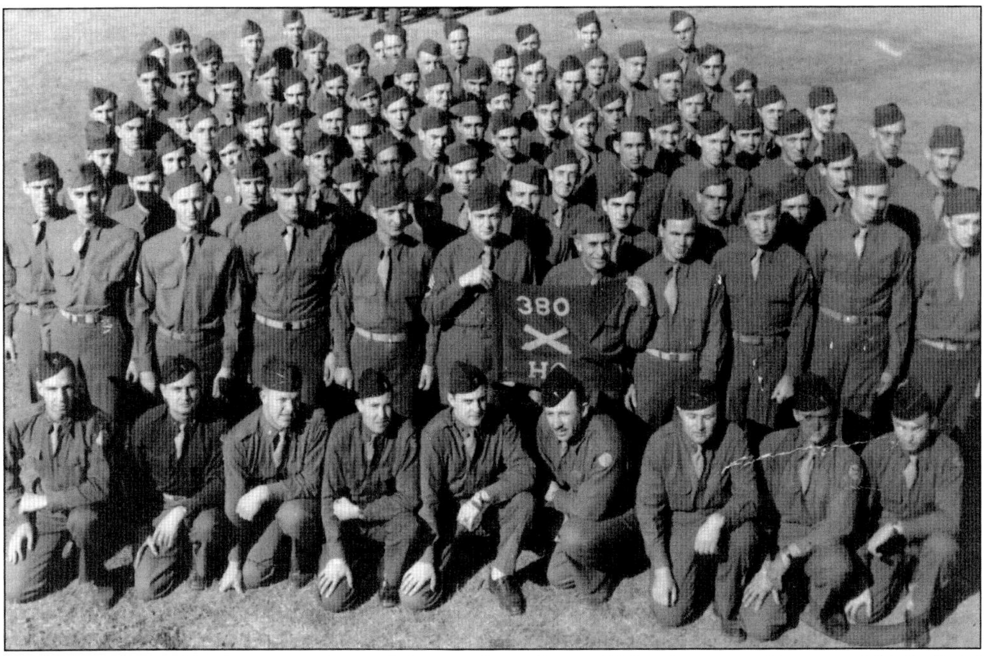

World War II Soldiers at Camp Maxey. Members of Headquarters Battery, 380th Field Artillery Battalion, 102nd Infantry Division, pose for the camera at Camp Maxey. The 102nd entered combat in Europe in late October 1944. All told, the division suffered 8,825 casualties (62.6 percent of its authorized strength) during its service in Europe.

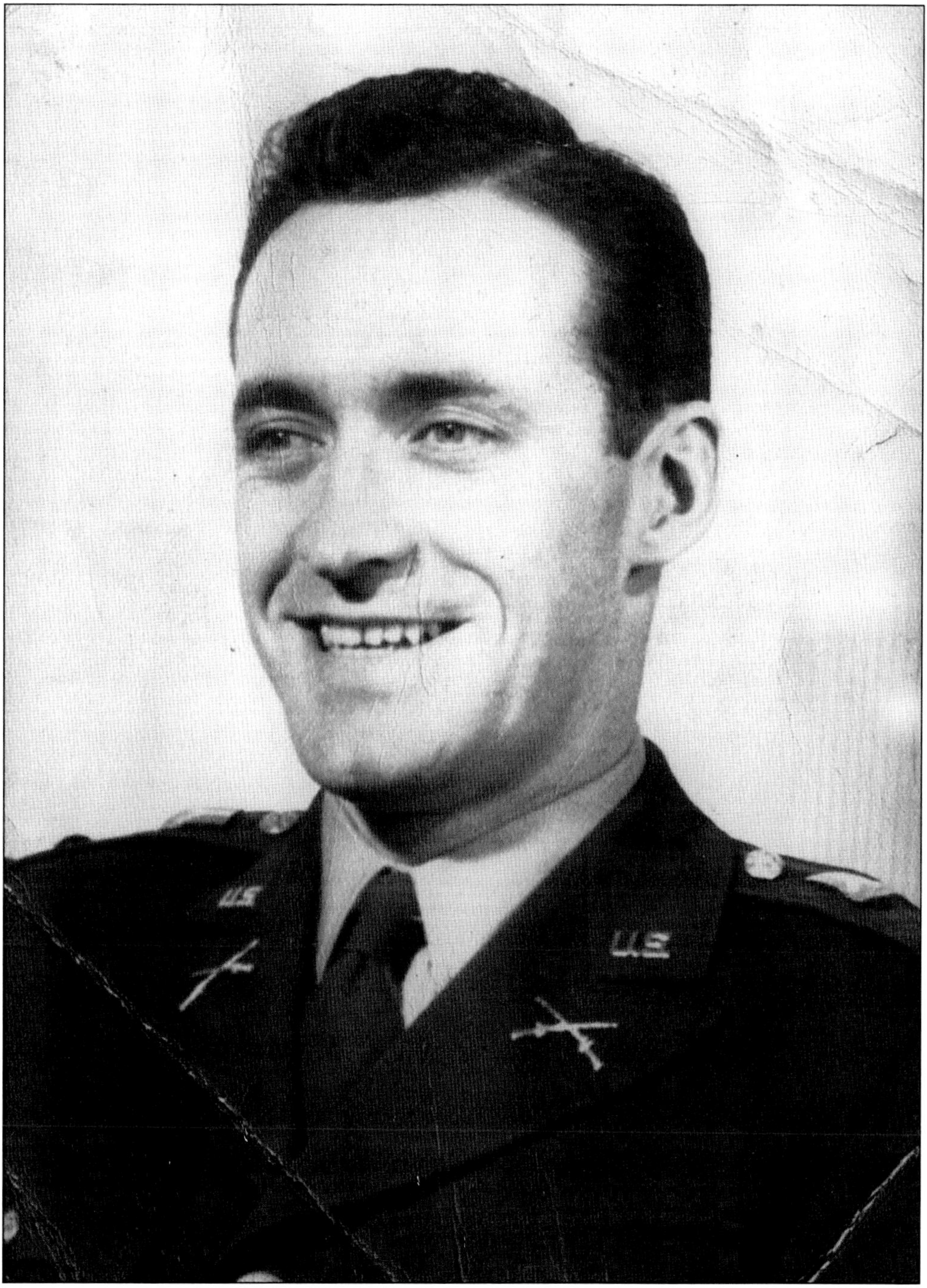

Nathan James Bell III. Nathan Bell was born in Virginia and served with the 99th Infantry Division in Europe during World War II. While training with the 99th at Camp Maxey, Bell met and married Margie Wilson of Paris. The 99th Infantry entered combat in early November 1944 and was engaged in significant combat during the Battle of the Bulge. The division suffered a total of 11,987 casualties (85.1 percent of its authorized strength) during the war. After the war, Nathan Bell moved to Paris and founded Nathan Bell Realtors. Bell was elected mayor of Paris in 1948.

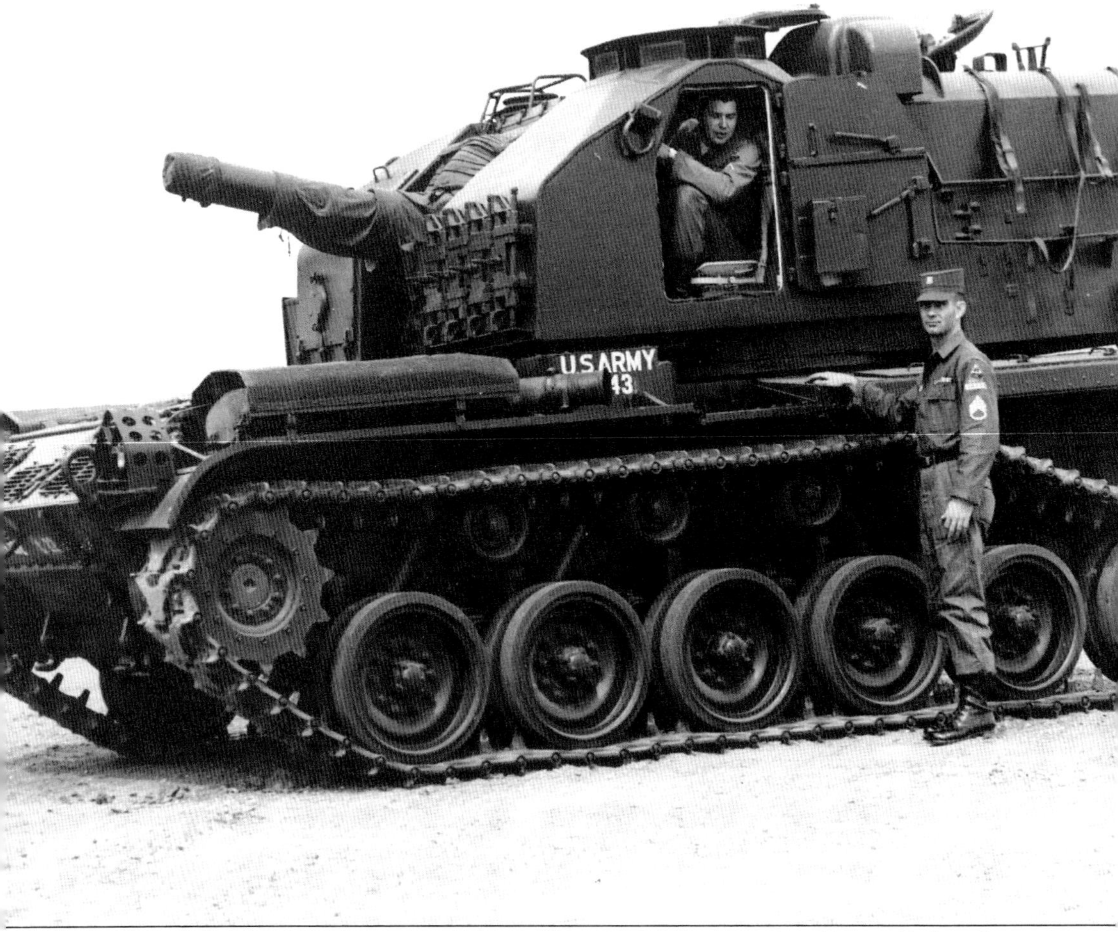

A SERGEANT OF THE 49TH ARMORED DIVISION. This is an image of a self-propelled artillery piece of the 49th Armored Division at Camp Maxey in 1962. The 49th (Lone Star) Armored Division was formed in 1947 and was a component of the Texas Army National Guard. The 49th Armored Division was formed from the famous 36th Infantry Division.

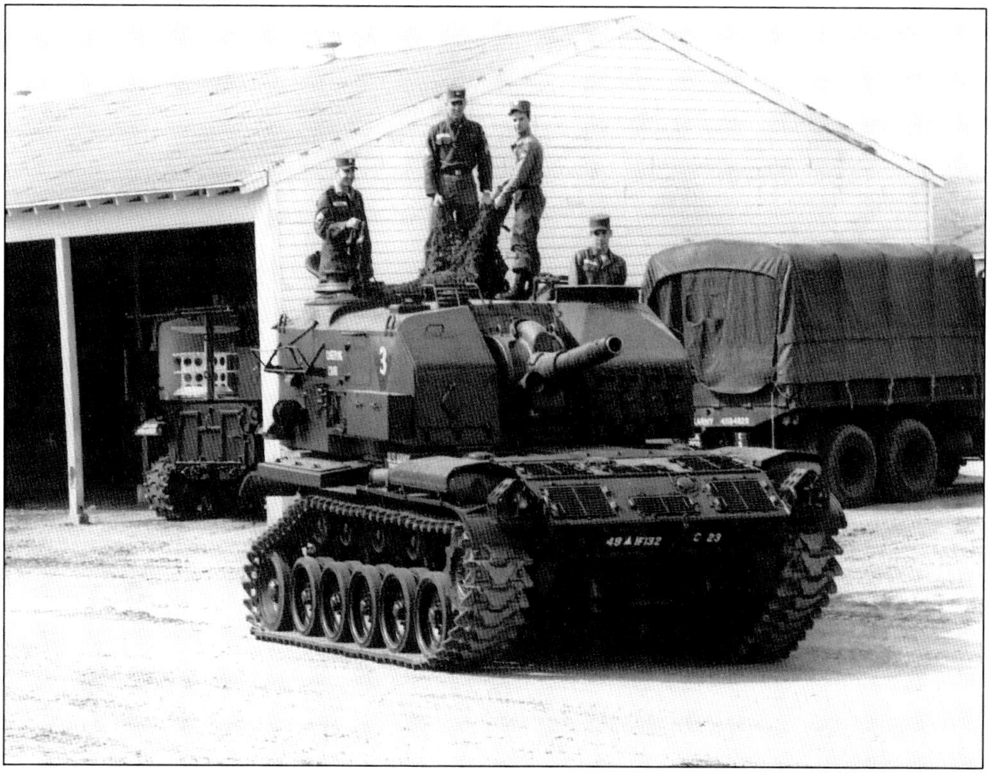

A Self-Propelled Artillery Piece at Camp Maxey. The vehicle pictured here belonged to C Battery, 1st Howitzer Battalion, 132nd Artillery of the 49th Armored Division. The crew has named this vehicle "the creeping crab." The 49th Armored served the nation between its activation in 1947 and deactivation in 1968. The division enjoyed another period of service between 1973 and 2004.

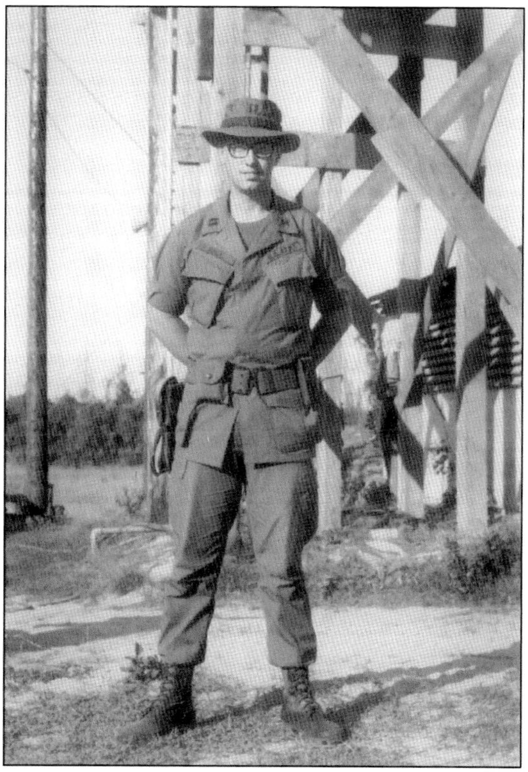

Jim Bell IV in Vietnam. Nathan James "Jim' Bell IV was born and raised in Paris. After graduating from the University of Texas at Austin, Bell served as a quartermaster officer with the American Division in South Vietnam throughout 1970. After exiting active military service, Bell earned his master's degree in 1983. Jim Bell's wife, Pat (née Sparks), worked for 23 years as director of the Small Business Development Center on the campus of Paris Junior College. Jim is a licensed Texas Realtor and co-owner of Nathan Bell Realtors in Paris. (Courtesy of Jim Bell.)

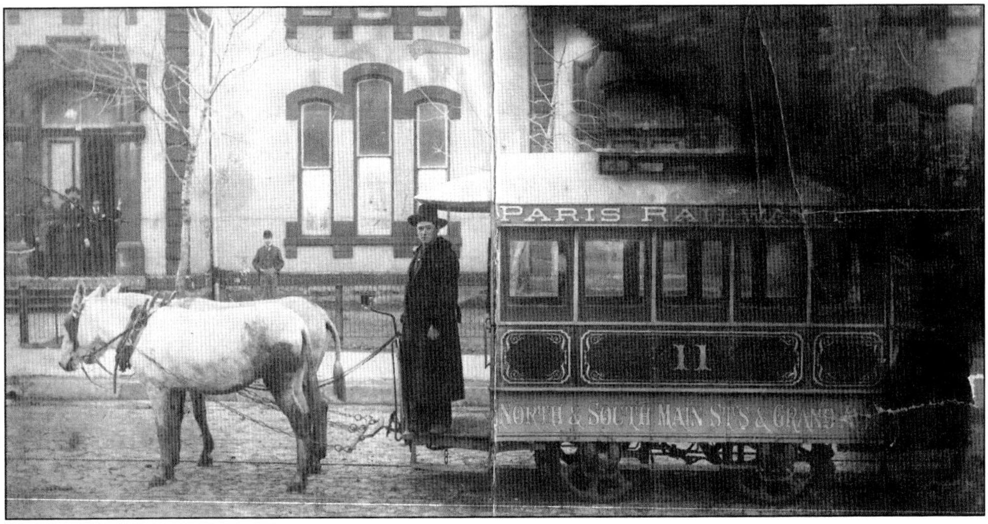

A Mule-Drawn Trolley Car in Paris. Although Texas is known as a state that is almost addicted to automobiles, a state that does not necessarily accept the idea of mass transit, 19th-century Paris embraced streetcars. The Paris Transit System began operations in late August 1878.

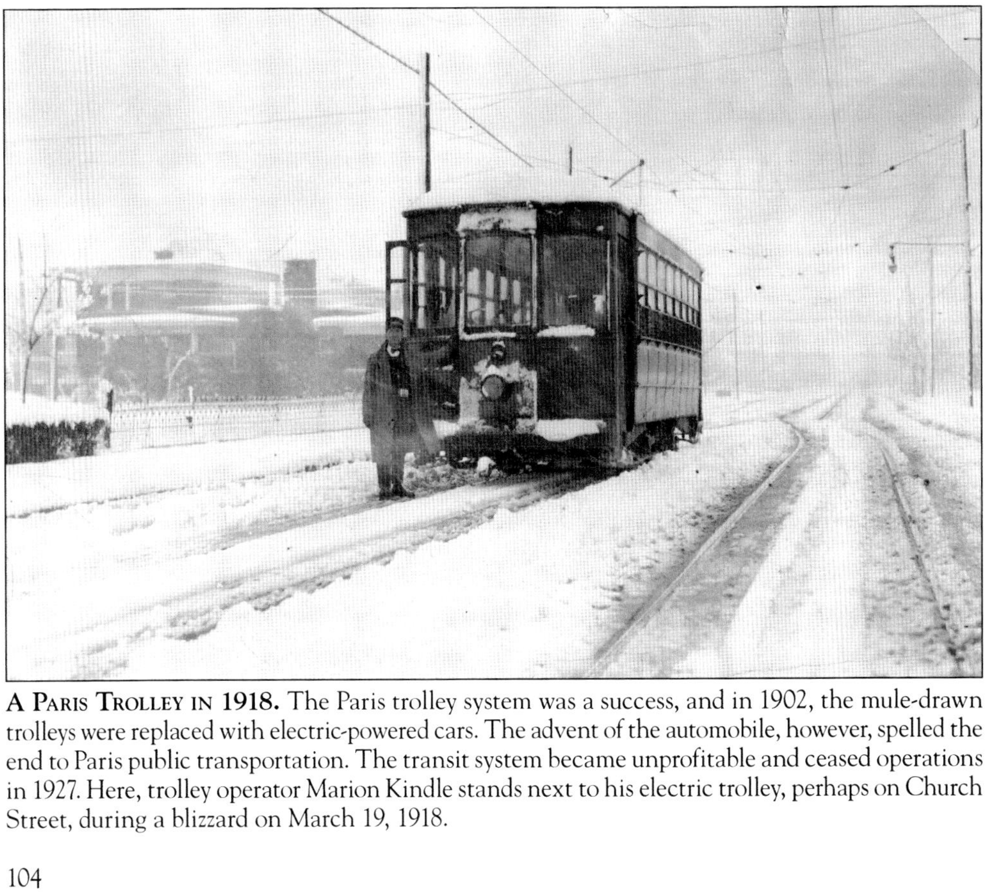

A Paris Trolley in 1918. The Paris trolley system was a success, and in 1902, the mule-drawn trolleys were replaced with electric-powered cars. The advent of the automobile, however, spelled the end to Paris public transportation. The transit system became unprofitable and ceased operations in 1927. Here, trolley operator Marion Kindle stands next to his electric trolley, perhaps on Church Street, during a blizzard on March 19, 1918.

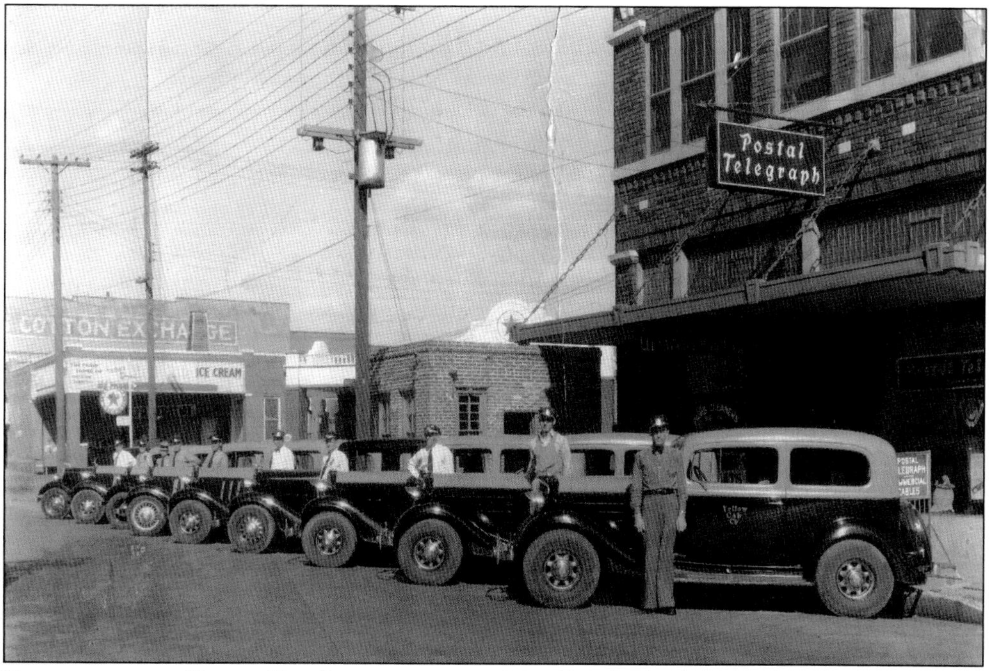

EMPLOYEES OF THE YELLOW CAB COMPANY IN THE 1940S. Paris had cab service for many years. Aaron Greiner founded Paris's first horse-drawn cab company about 1884. One can also see the telegraph office in this photograph. Paris was connected to the national telegraph system in 1874.

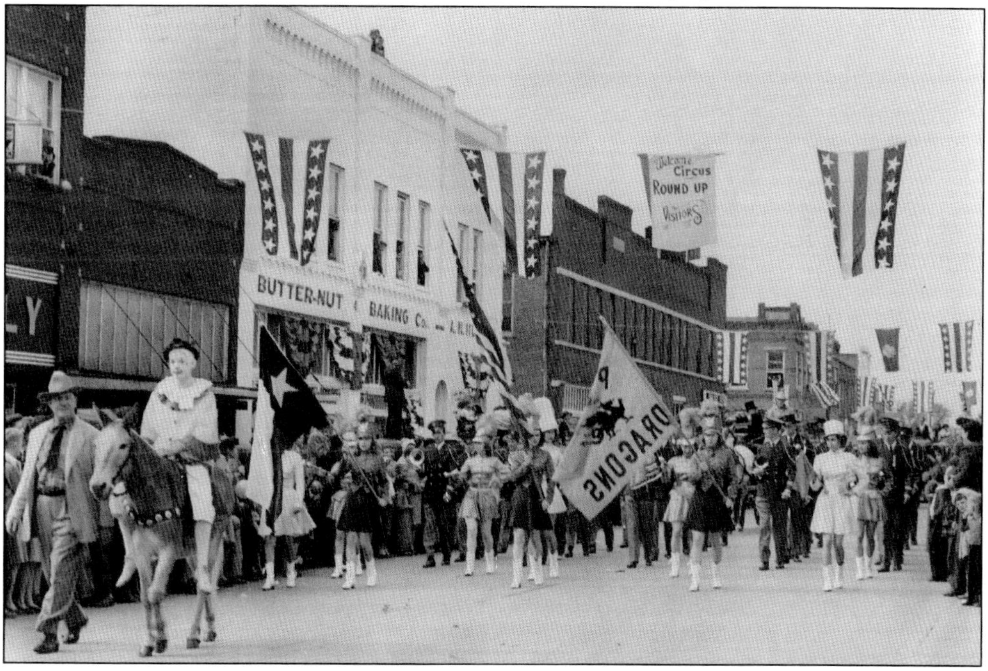

THE PARIS JUNIOR COLLEGE MARCHING BAND AT THE OPENING DAY OF A LOCAL CIRCUS. When the circus comes to town, it is a time for families to get out of the house and enjoy exciting, and sometimes exotic, entertainment. The phenomenon of communities coming together to enjoy a day of colorful entertainment goes back to before the days of the Roman Empire.

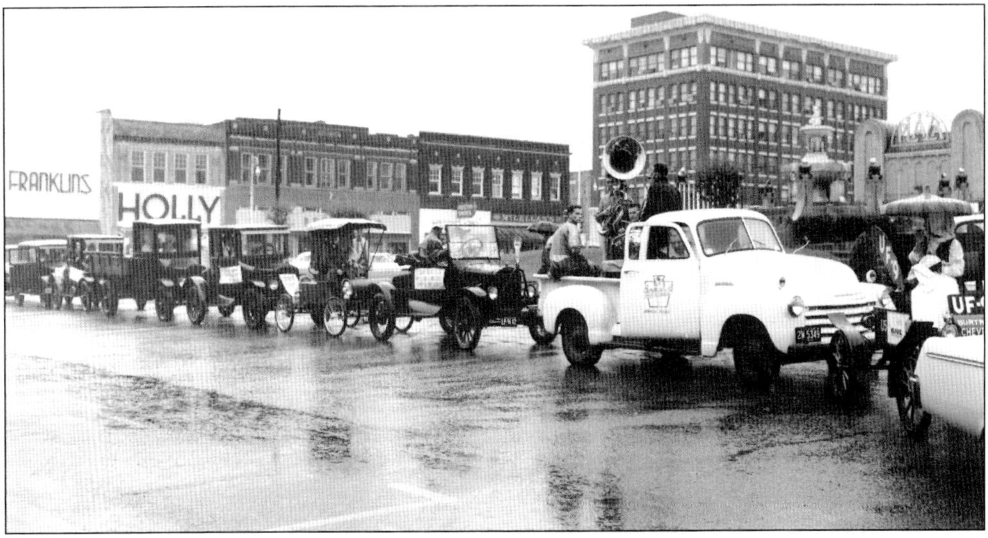

A RAINY DAY FOR A PARADE. Here is an interesting image of a local parade for charity in, perhaps, 1963. The white pickup truck is sponsored by the Paris chapter of the Boy's Club. The Negro Boy's Club sponsored the older vehicle immediately behind it. The Plaza Theater can be identified on the right.

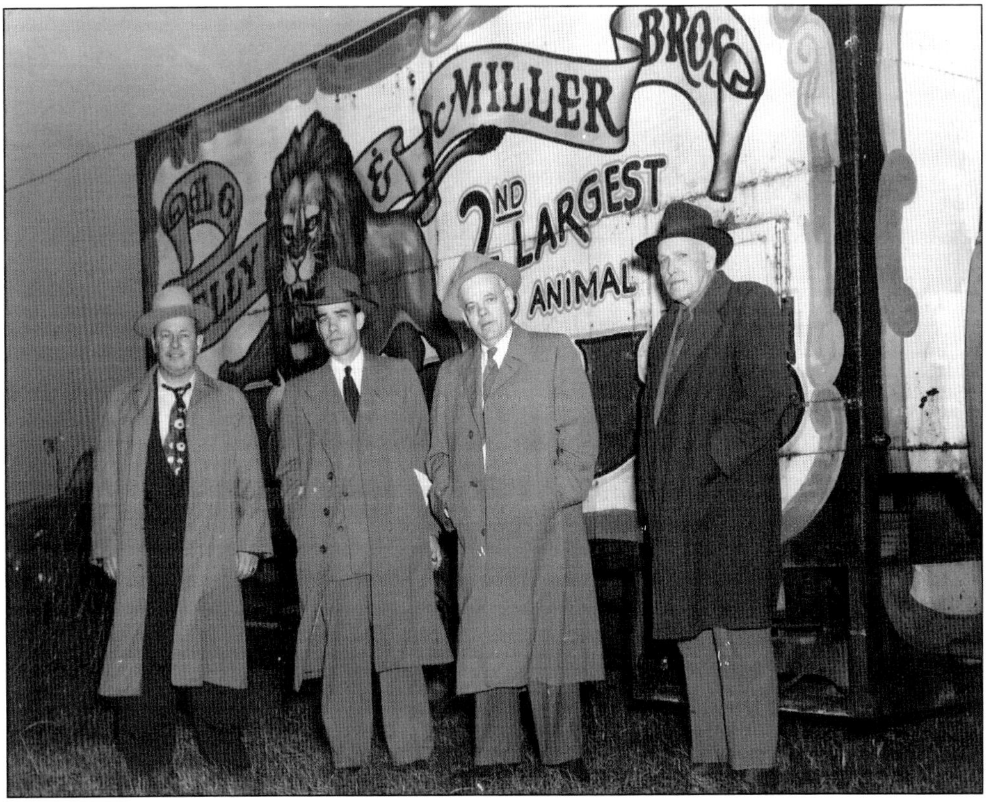

THE CIRCUS IN PARIS, TEXAS! Here, proprietors of the Kelley and Miller Brothers Circus pose for the camera in Paris. Paris has enjoyed circuses, and other similar events, since the 19th century. The Lamar County Fairgrounds are a favorite spot for circuses to set up operations.

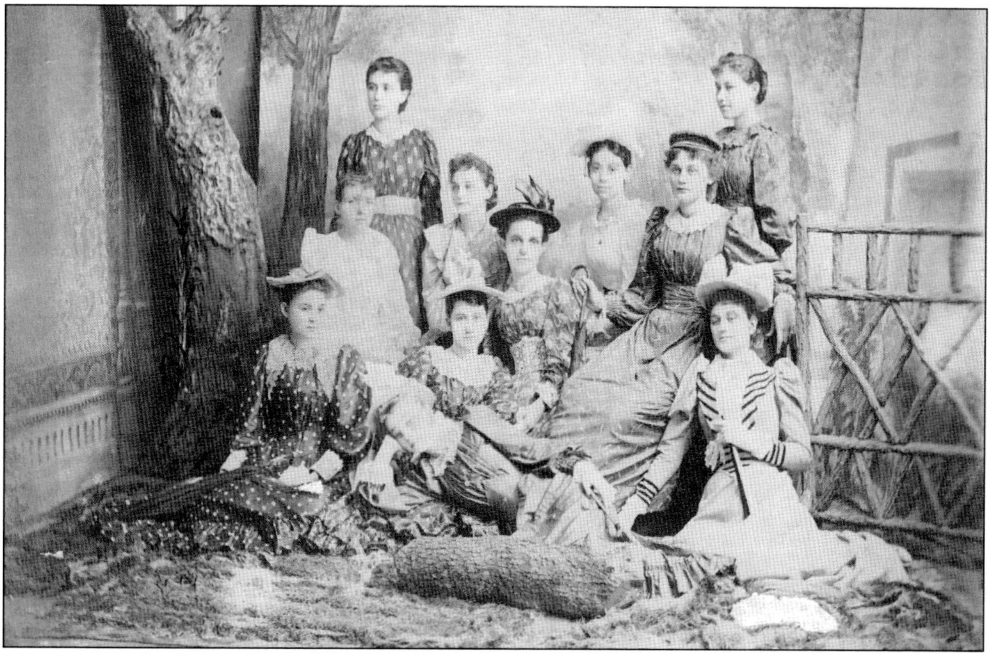

Members of the Paris Chapter of the King's Daughters. These members of the Paris chapter of the King's Daughters are wearing fashionable, yet subdued, outfits. Based upon the clothing styles worn, this photograph may have been taken in 1887. If that dating is correct, this image is of the original members of the organization.

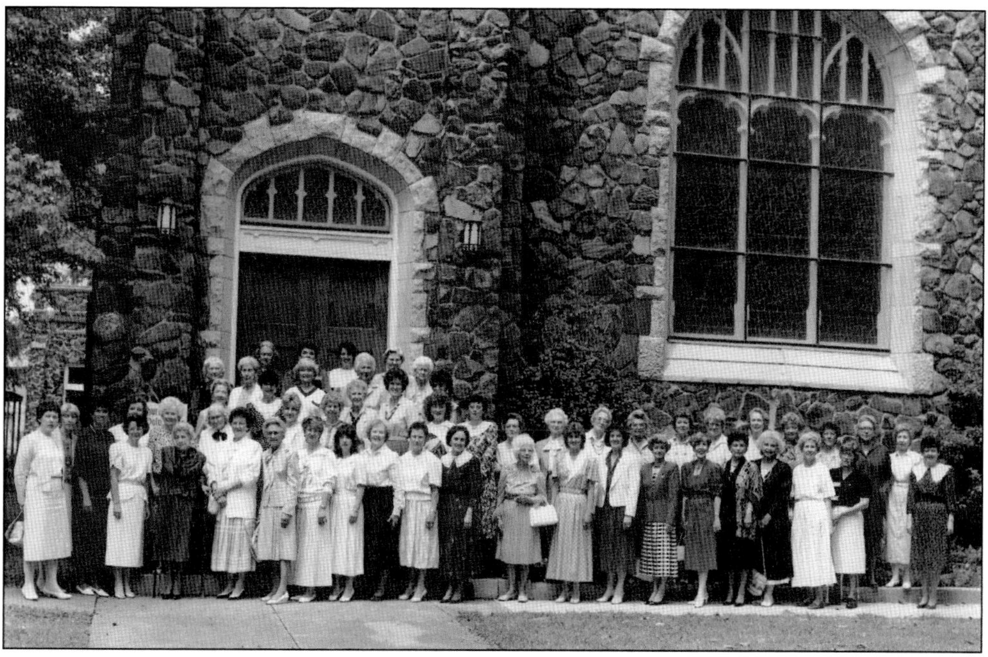

The King's Daughters in 1987. The King's Daughters were of vital importance during the Great Depression of the 1930s in getting aid to those made destitute by that financial catastrophe. This photograph memorializes members of the King's Daughters at Holy Cross Episcopal. They are celebrating their 100th jubilee on May 5, 1987.

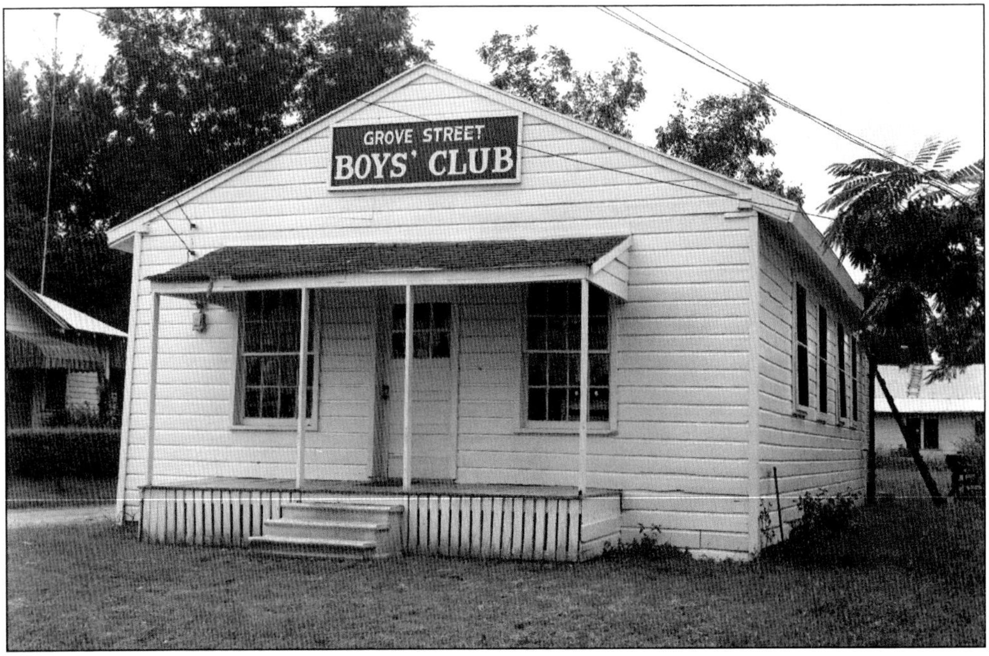

THE BOYS CLUB FACILITY IN THE 1930S. The Paris Boys Club was established in 1930. The Boys & Girls Clubs are a nationwide organization that seeks to foster citizenship and achievement among young people. The Boys Club of Paris is still active, as is the Boys & Girls Club of Red River Valley.

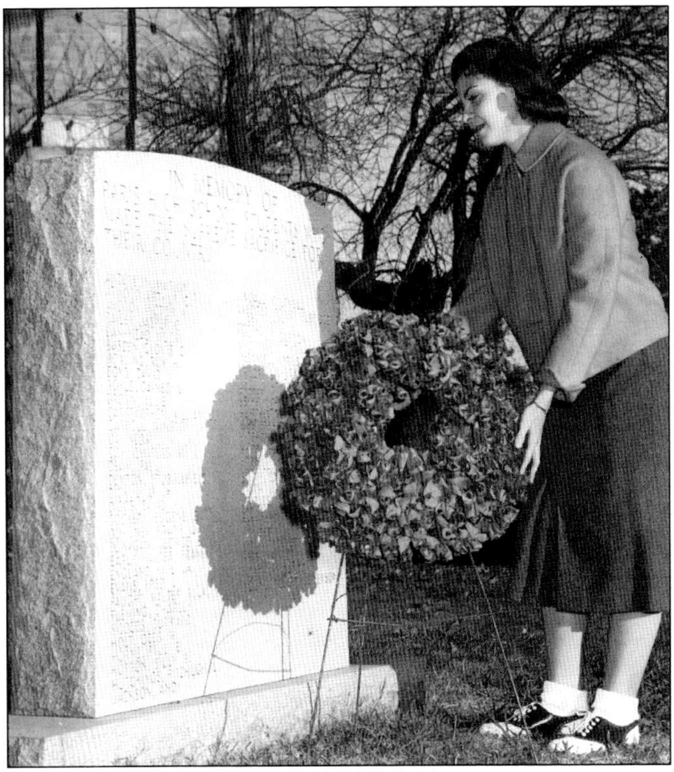

WREATH-LAYING CEREMONY IN 1957. Citizens of Paris have always sought to honor those who have sacrificed in the nation's service. Here, a student lays a wreath in 1957 at a monument honoring those Paris High School graduates who gave their lives for their country. At the time of this photograph, there were 60 names on the monument.

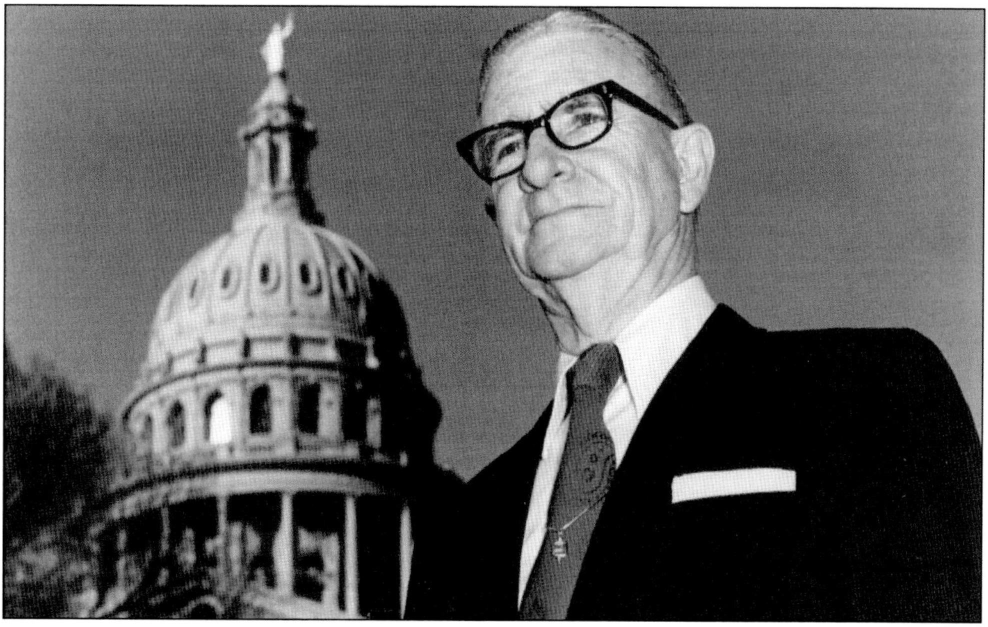

State Senator Aikin in Austin. Texas state senator A.M. Aikin Jr. was a Paris native and served in the Texas legislature for 46 years. He retired from politics in January 1979. Aikin was keenly interested in, and worked hard for, the cause of improving public education. Aikin died in 1981. Aikin's papers, and a reproduction of his Austin office, can be found at the A.M. & Welma Aikin Jr. Regional Archives on the campus of Paris Junior College.

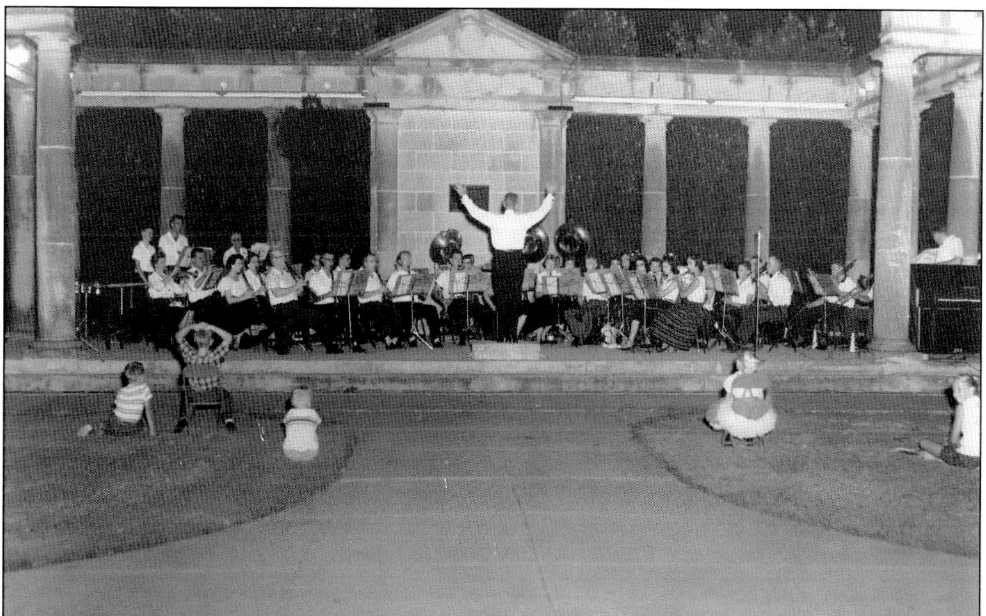

The Paris Municipal Band's Public Concert in 1958. The Paris Municipal Band was formed in 1923. The location of this particular concert is the Peristyle in Bywaters Park, located across from the Gibraltar Hotel. J.K. Bywaters donated the park to the city in 1914. The Peristyle was dedicated in 1931.

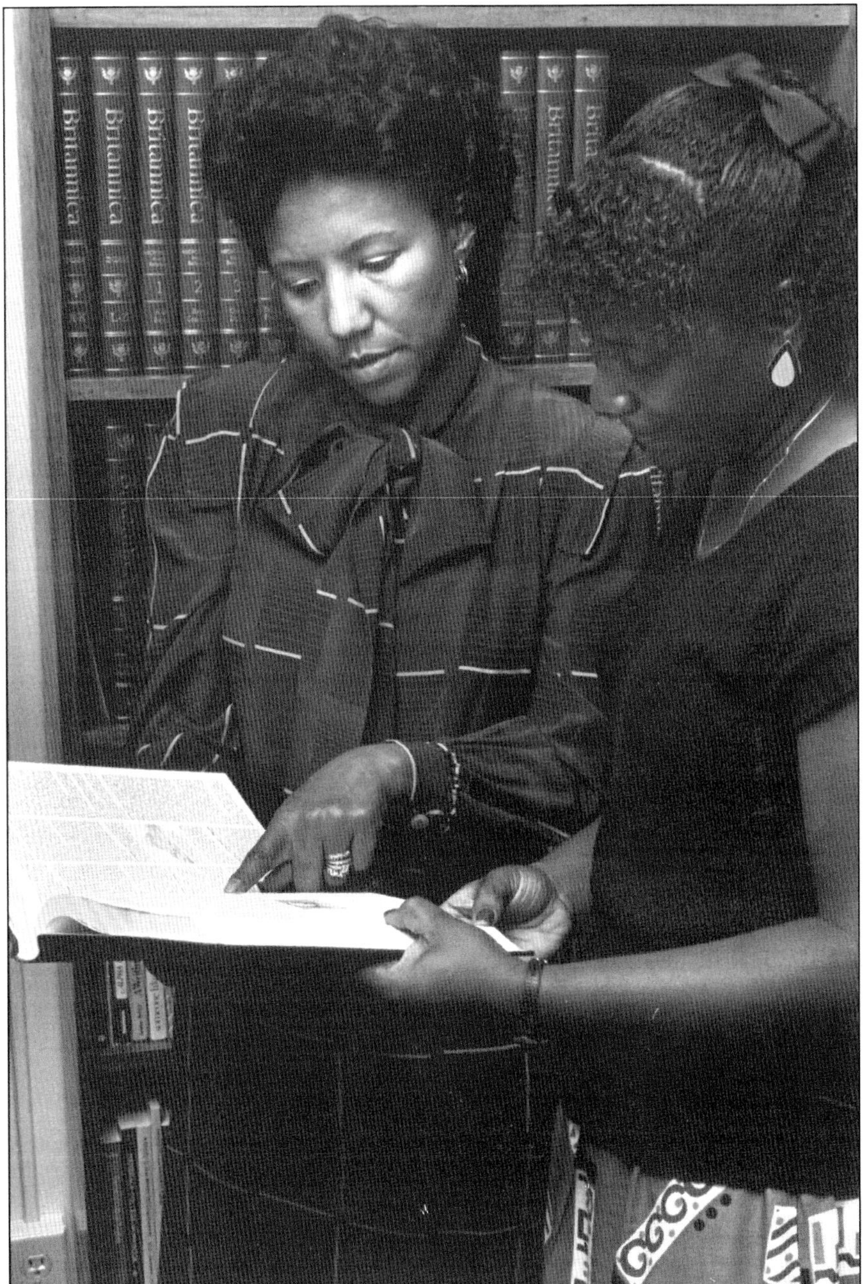

Joan Mathis Instructing a Student. Joan Mathis, pictured here on the left, has spent her life in service to Paris. Mathis holds a master's degree and teaches at Paris Junior College. After earning her master's degree in English in 1985, Joan Mathis entered the teaching field; teaching first at local high schools and then at Paris Junior College. Mathis was honored for her service to the community by being selected as the parade marshal for the 2011 Celebrate America Parade. She is a longtime member of St. Paul Baptist Church in Paris. St. Paul was founded by Elisha Barnes in 1867. At one time, Booker T. Washington spoke to the congregation. As of 2011, the Reverend Kenneth Rogers serves as pastor.

Five

IMAGES OF FAITH

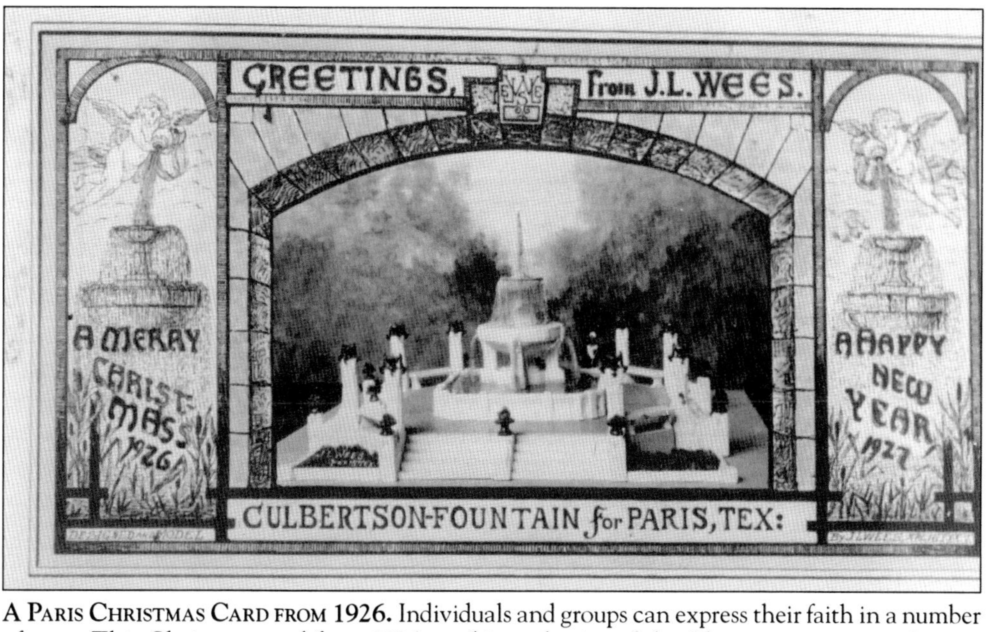

A PARIS CHRISTMAS CARD FROM 1926. Individuals and groups can express their faith in a number of ways. This Christmas card from 1926 combines the joy of the Christmas season with civic pride. This card surely depicts Paris's pride in how quickly it rose from the ashes of the 1916 fire. The architect of the Culbertson Fountain, J.L. Wees, used this card on the 10th anniversary of the great fire.

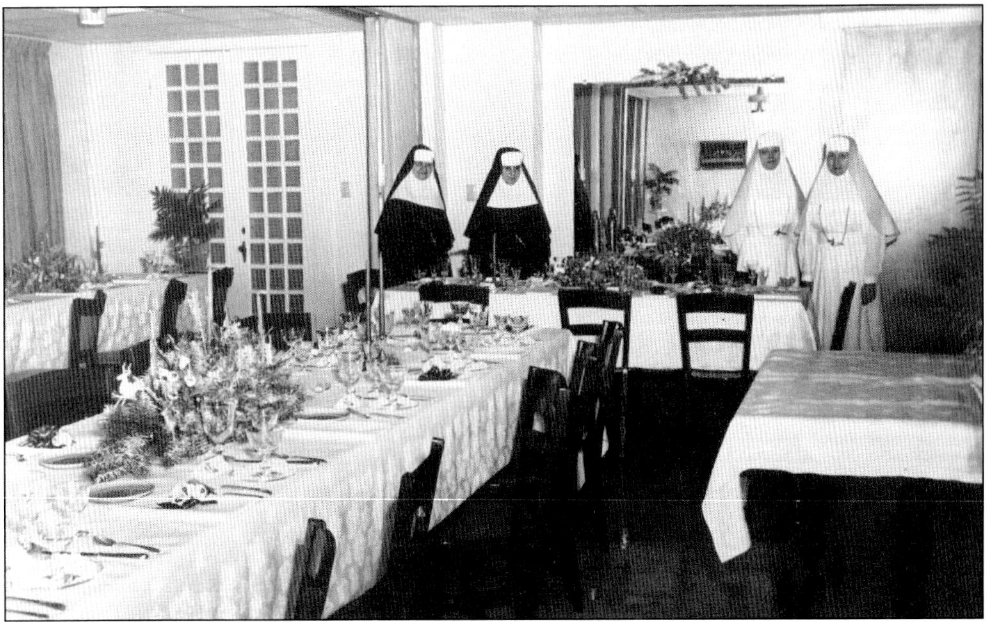

A CHRISTMAS CELEBRATION. Participating in a grand feast to celebrate Christmas is a long-practiced Christian tradition. Here, the Sisters of Charity of the Incarnate Word prepare to celebrate the birth of Jesus with a delicious meal, probably in the 1920s. This photograph was taken in Paris, possibly at a local hospital. The four nuns pictured here seem to be members of two different orders.

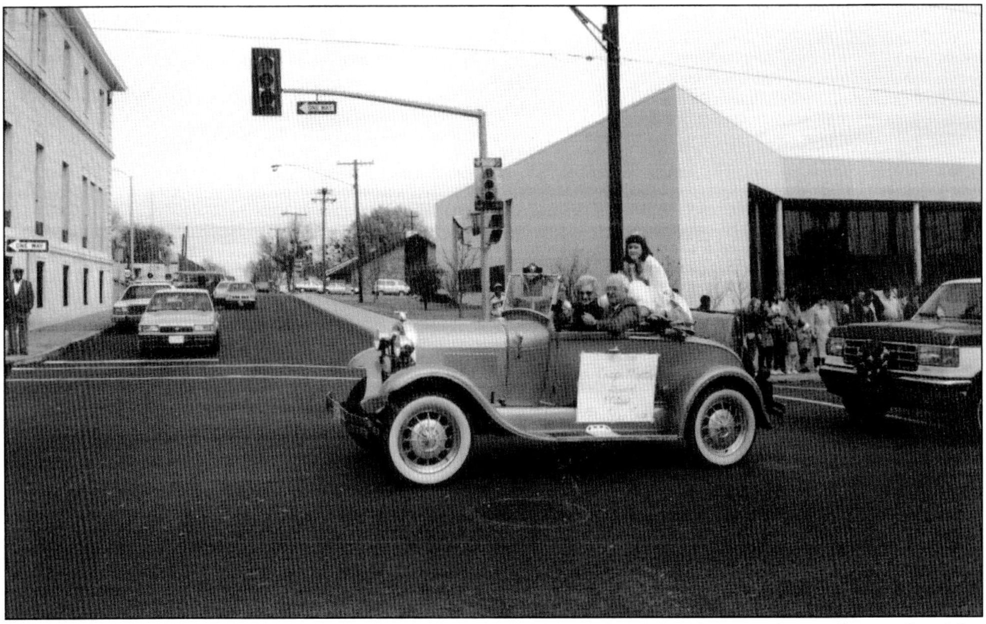

A NEW CREPE MYRTLE QUEEN IS CROWNED. Paris has a long tradition of parades and public expressions of civic solidarity and values. The Paris Crepe Myrtle Queen of 1987–1988 rides proudly in the grand marshal's car at the annual Christmas parade in 1987. Paris has been crowning Crepe Myrtle Queens since 1978. The festivities are sponsored by the Paris Council of Garden Clubs. (Photograph courtesy of the *Paris News*.)

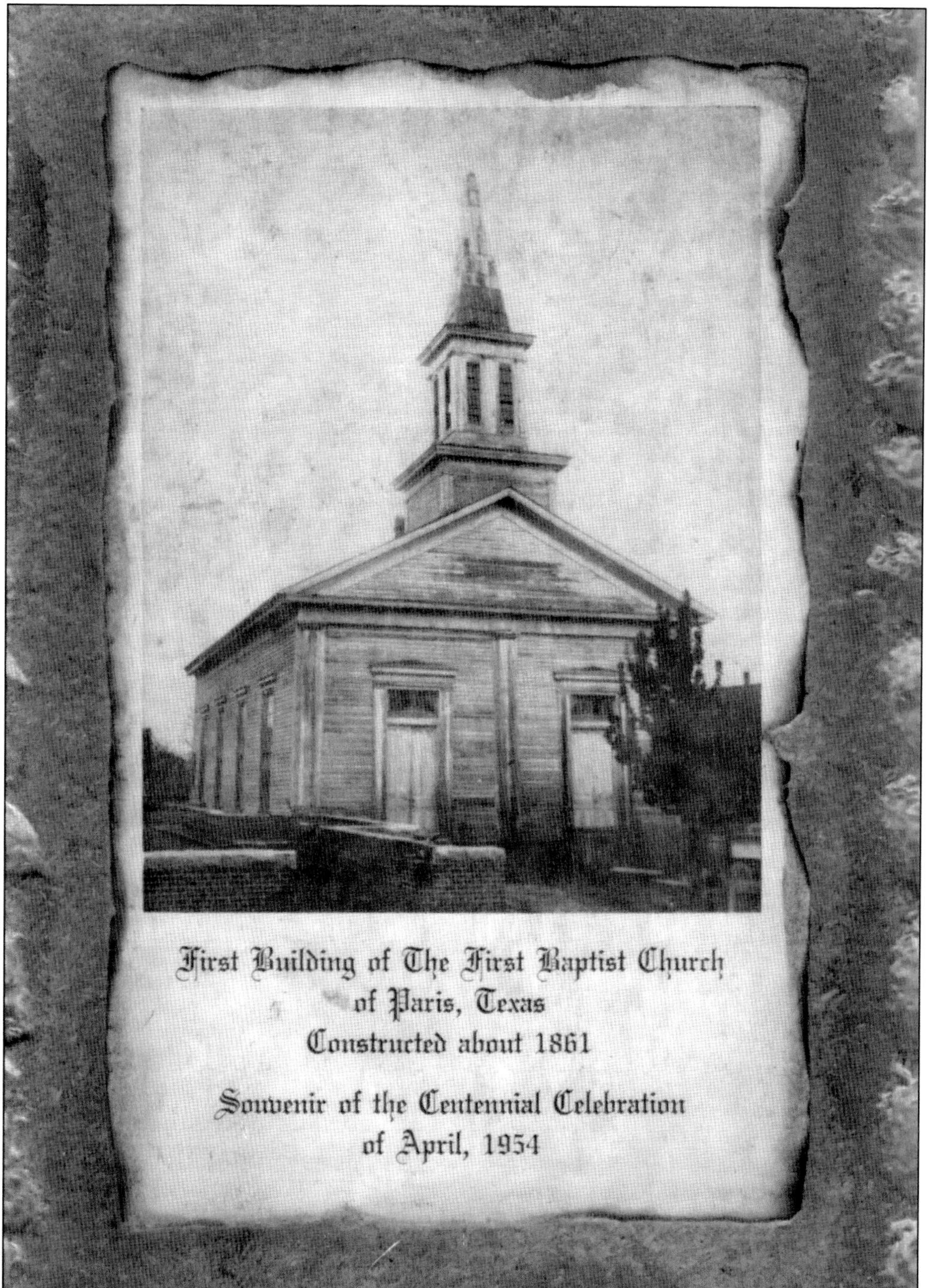

The Original First Baptist Church Building. Lamar County Baptists organized themselves formally in 1854. The first pastor of the flock was Rev. Willis Pickett. The congregation did not, however, have a formal meeting place until 1861, when the first church building, pictured here, was constructed. The original structure was replaced in 1895, and this second church building was destroyed in 1916. (Courtesy of the First Baptist Church.)

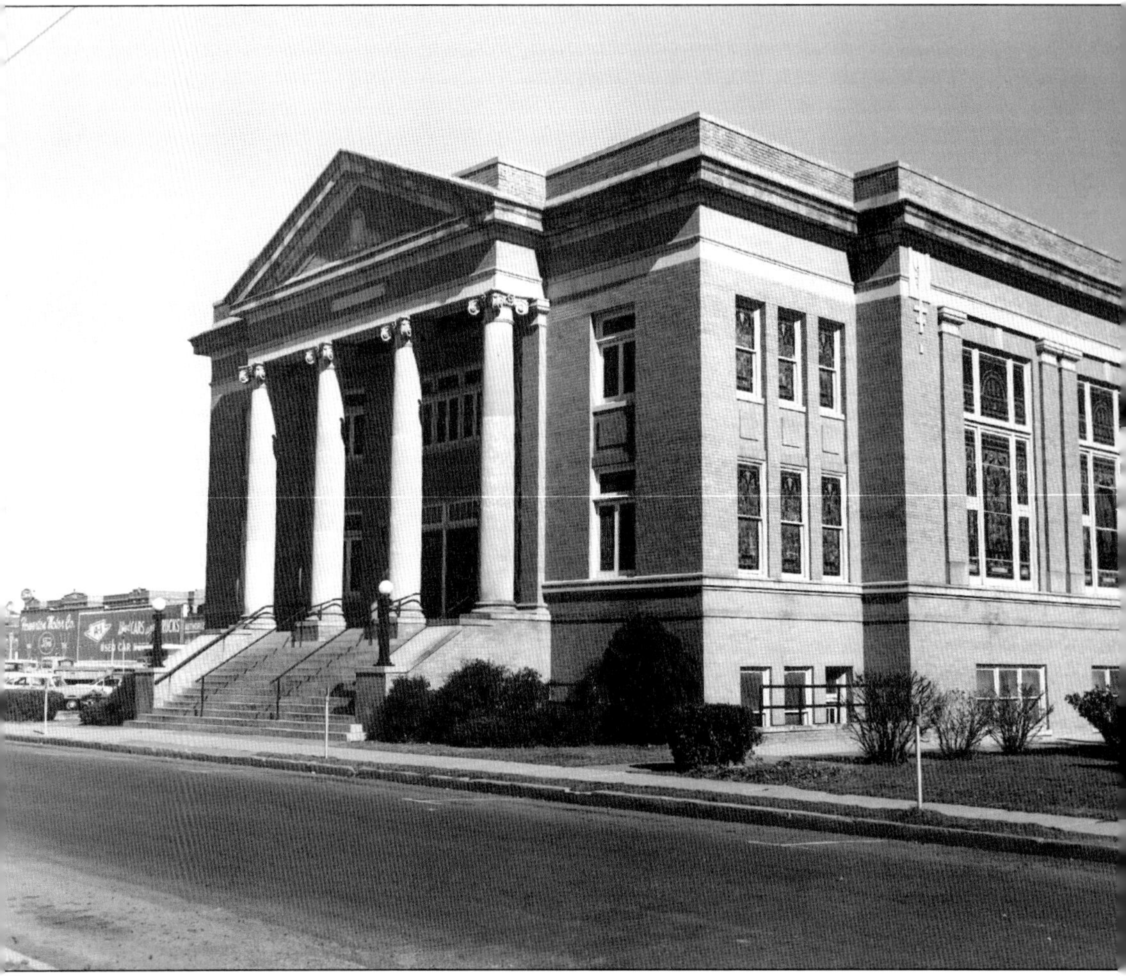

PARIS'S FIRST BAPTIST CHURCH. The current sanctuary, built in the Greek Revival style, was completed in 1918. The First Baptist Church of Paris is probably best known for its association with the Buckner Orphan's Home in Dallas. The children's home was the 1877 brainchild of Paris's own Reverend Buckner. As of 2011, First Baptist has had over 1,500 members.

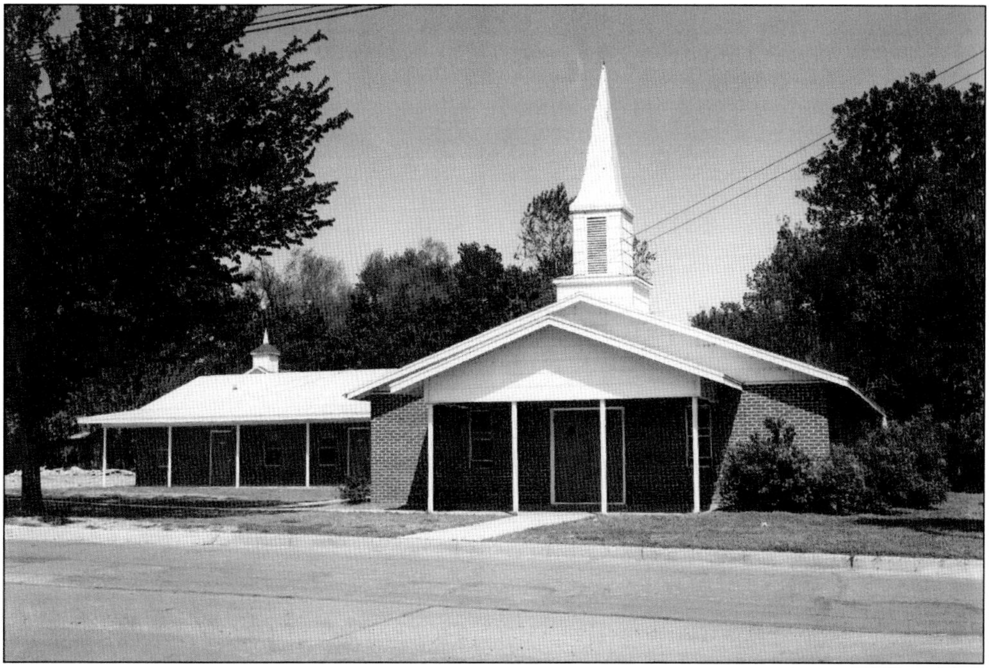

The Seventh Street Baptist Church. This photograph was taken sometime before 1951. In 1951, a severe ice storm swept across North Texas. One result of that storm was the destruction of the small spire seen on the left part of the building. The church is located on Seventh Street SW.

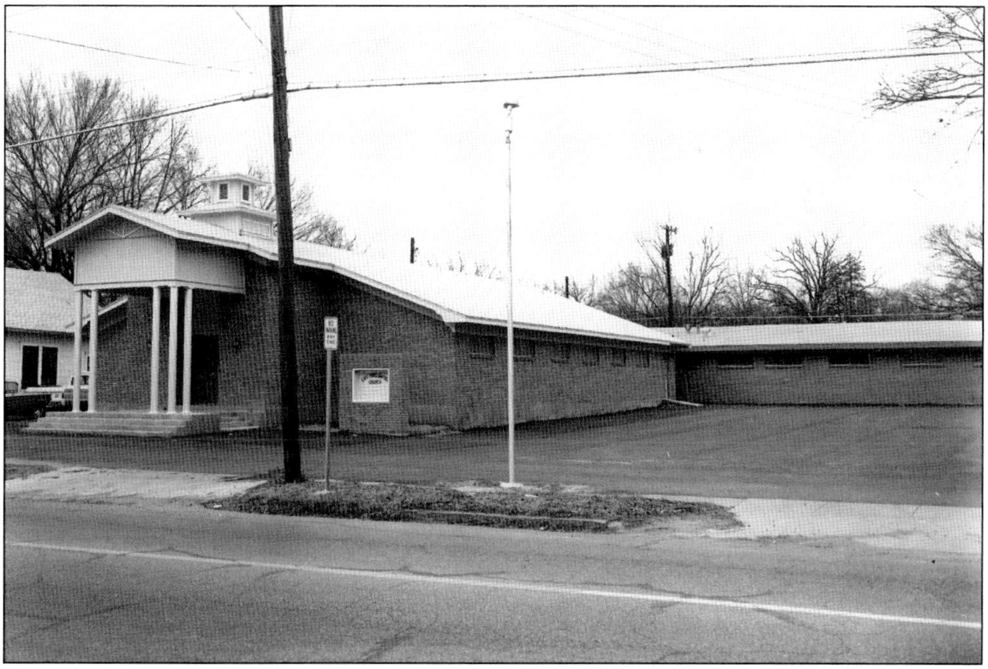

East Paris Baptist Church in the 1960s. The Bible Baptist Church of Paris was established during the hectic early days of the World War II in 1942. Worship services were held on Clarksville Street. In 1946, the name was changed to East Paris Baptist, and the sanctuary was moved several times. The sanctuary is currently located on North Collegiate Drive.

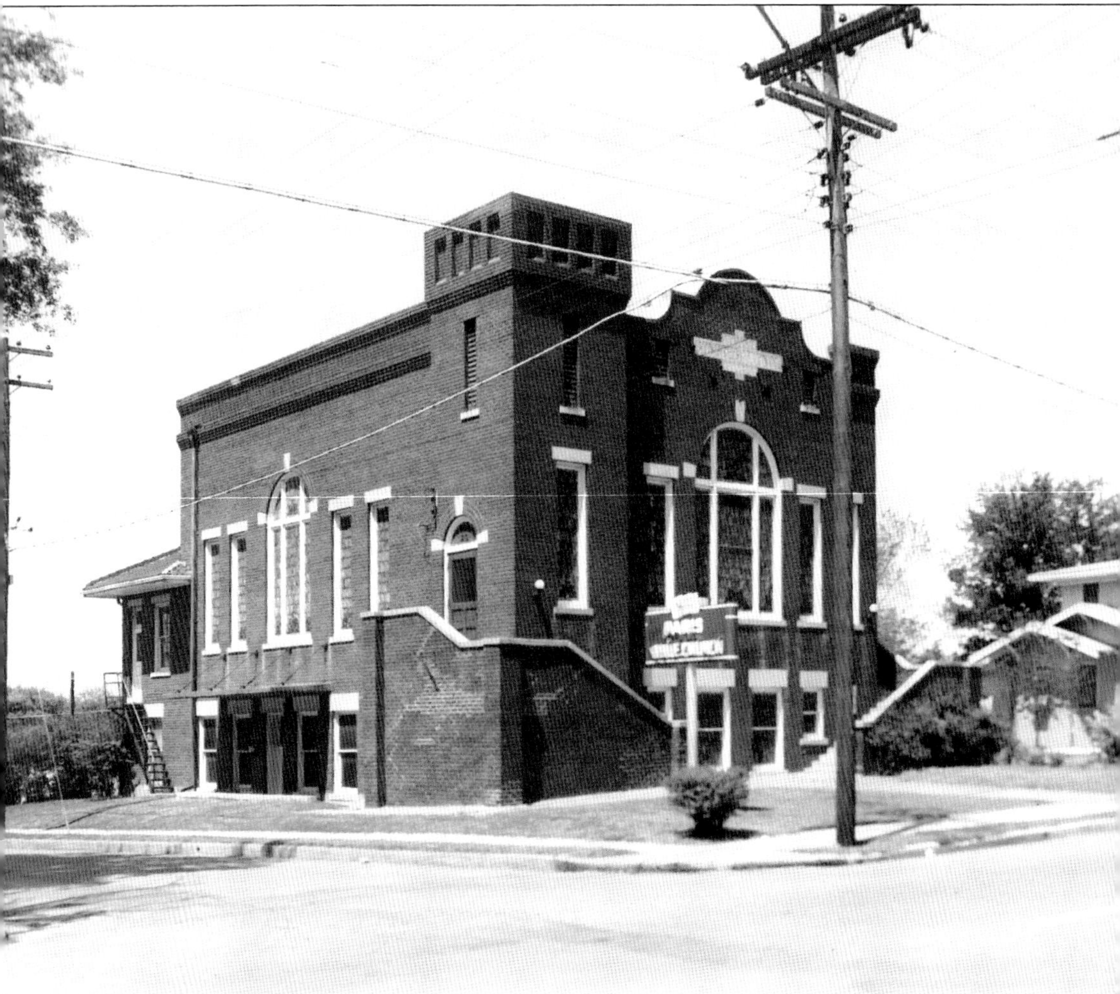

The Paris Bible Church in 1962. The original Paris Bible Church was known as the Paris Congregational Church. This church was founded in the late 19th century, and its building was destroyed in the fire of 1916. The building shown here was constructed soon after that disaster, located just down the street from the Gibraltar Hotel. The name of the church was changed in the 1950s. Although this building is now abandoned, members of Paris Bible are still active in the Paris area and worship on Nineteenth Street NW.

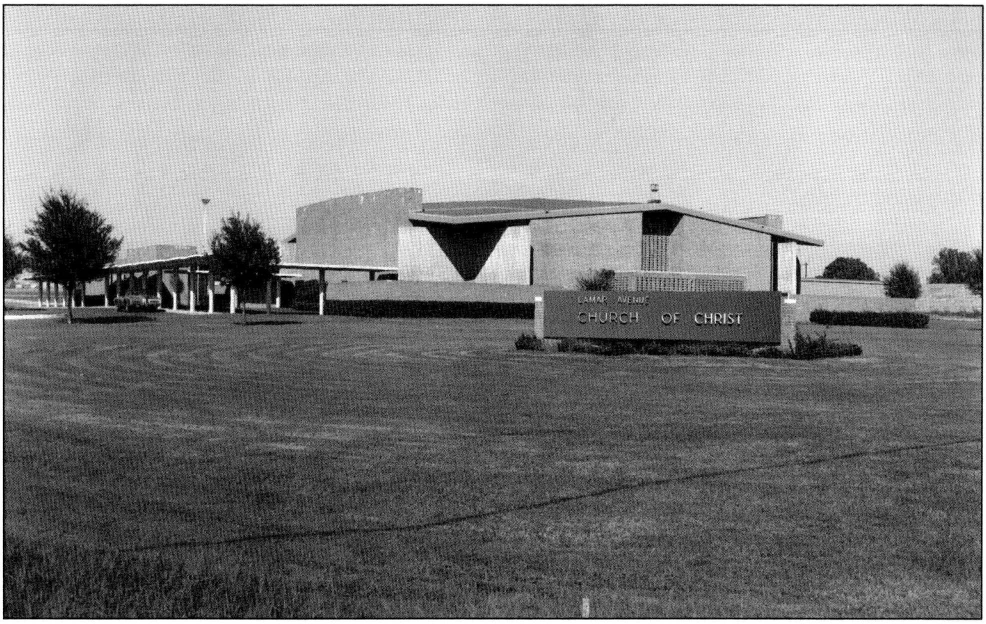

THE LAMAR AVENUE CHURCH OF CHRIST. This church was formally established in 1869 and has been a central player in the religious lives of many Paris citizens for over 140 years. In addition, this congregation sponsors missionary efforts in Estonia, Romania, Brazil, Peru, and Mexico. The date of the above photograph is unknown. The image below shows the Lamar Avenue Church of Christ. In this 19th-century image, the street is unpaved, but the sidewalk is paved. Also, in the background on the left, the steeple of another church can be seen.

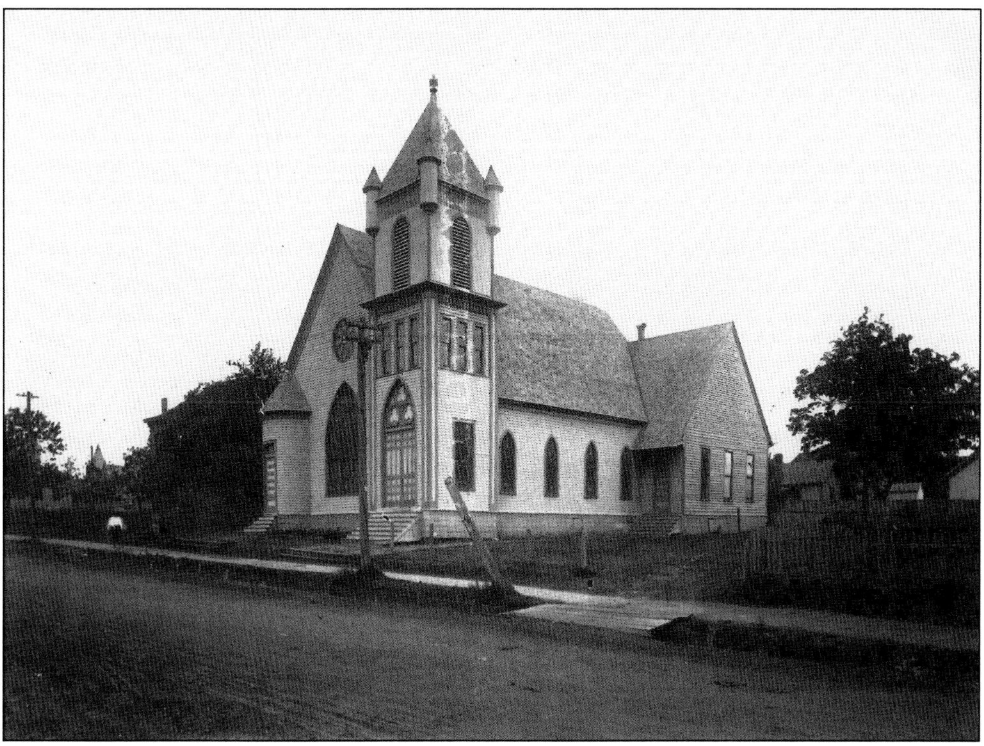

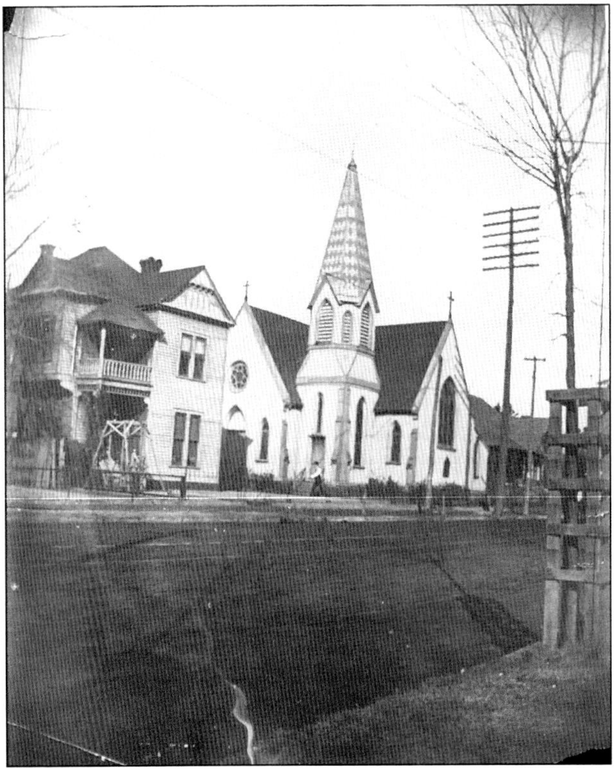

Two Views of Holy Cross Episcopal Church before the Fire of 1916. Episcopalians have been active in the Lamar County area since the late 1830s. Episcopal bishop Leonidas Polk (later a Confederate general killed in action in 1864) engaged in missionary activity in the area in 1839. The beginnings of the Holy Cross parish can be dated to February 7, 1870, when Rev. Francis R. Starr became the first rector of the congregation. The original church building was located on the site of the present courthouse. The church was moved to a location on South Main and West Sherman Streets in 1897. That structure shown at left was destroyed in 1916. The below image, taken sometime between 1897 and 1916, is of three vestrymen in front of Holy Cross.

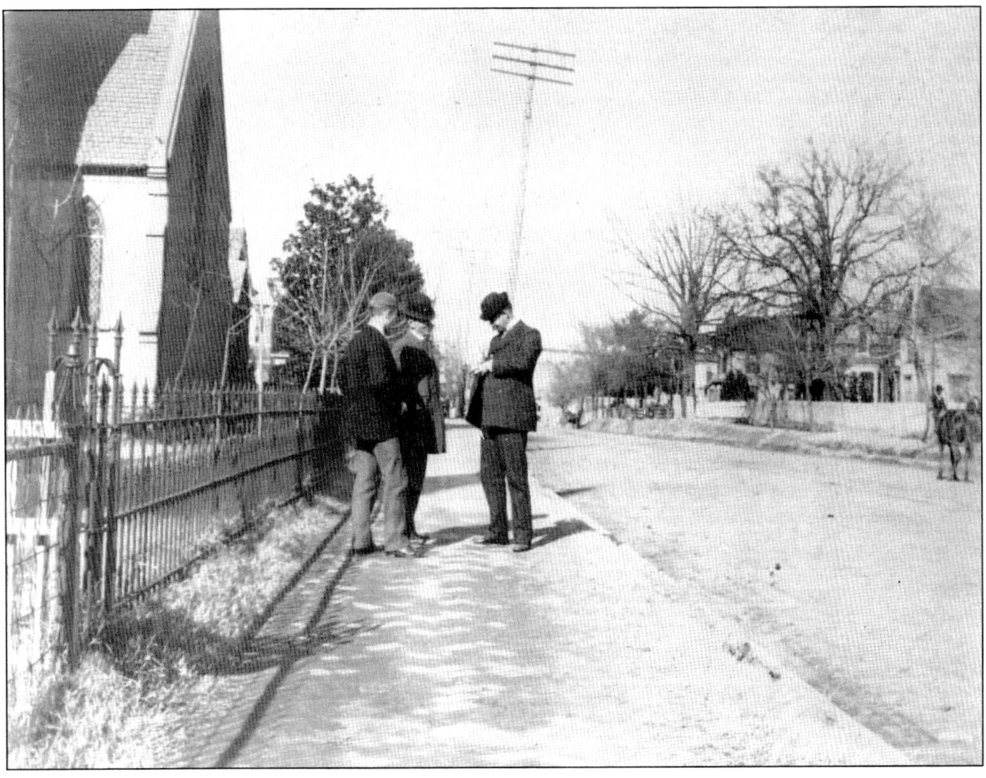

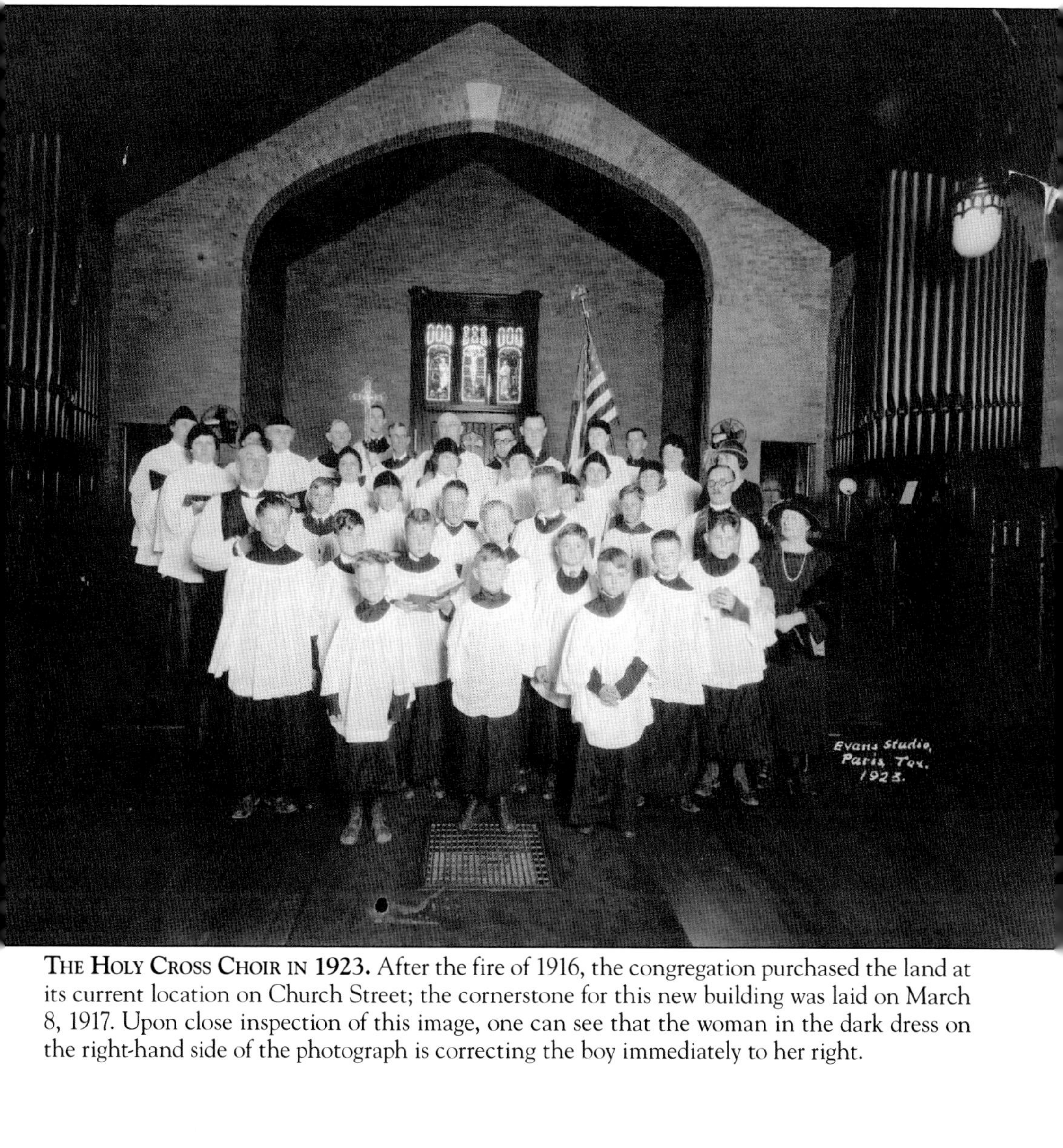

The Holy Cross Choir in 1923. After the fire of 1916, the congregation purchased the land at its current location on Church Street; the cornerstone for this new building was laid on March 8, 1917. Upon close inspection of this image, one can see that the woman in the dark dress on the right-hand side of the photograph is correcting the boy immediately to her right.

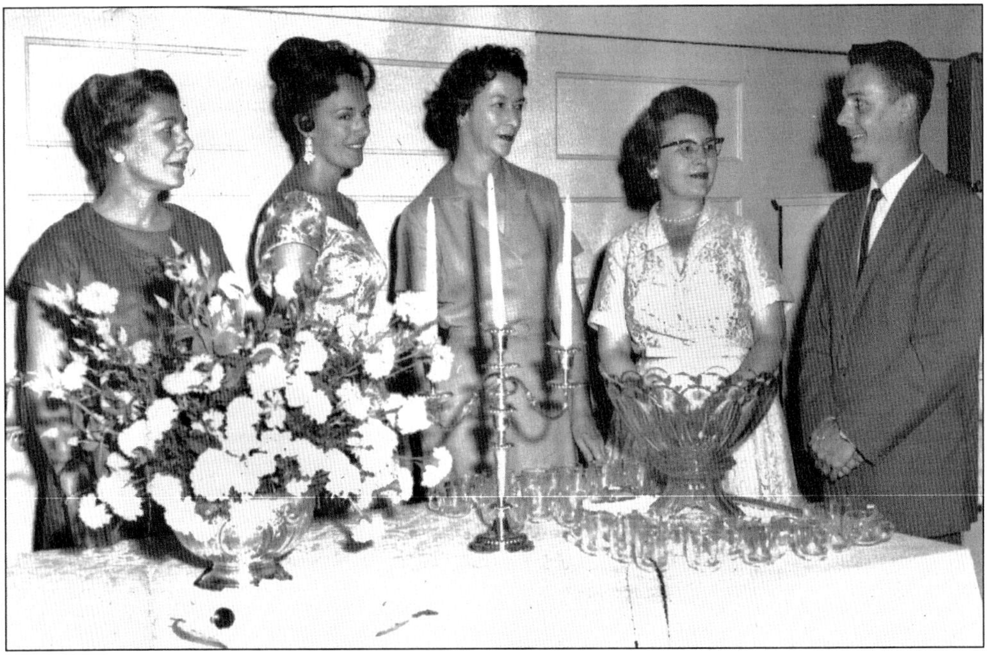

WOMEN OF HOLY CROSS PREPARING FOR AN EVENT IN THE 1960S. The Holy Cross Parish Hall was completed in the 1920s. Pictured are, from left to right, Catherine Anderson, Myrthé Dirks, Isabel Willoughby, Margie Bell, and unidentified male. As of 2011, Holy Cross boasts about 250 members.

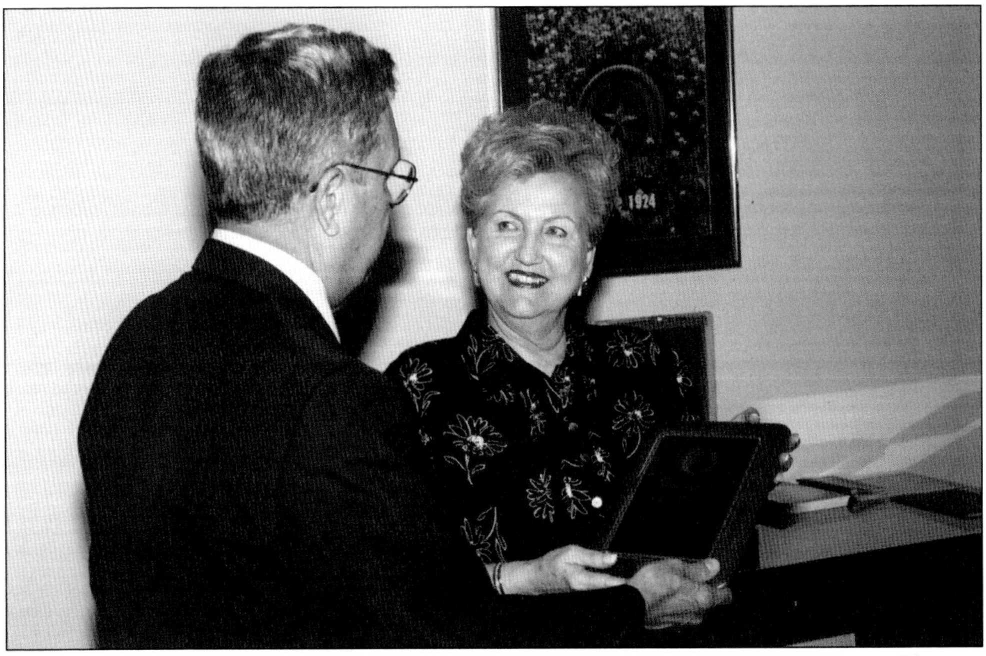

BETTY CLEMENT AT HER RETIREMENT CEREMONY FROM PARIS JUNIOR COLLEGE. Betty Clement taught English at Paris Junior College between 1967 and 1999. During her time at the college, Clement also served as communications division chair for a number of years. Clement went on after her retirement to become the first female deacon of Holy Cross Episcopal Church in Paris.

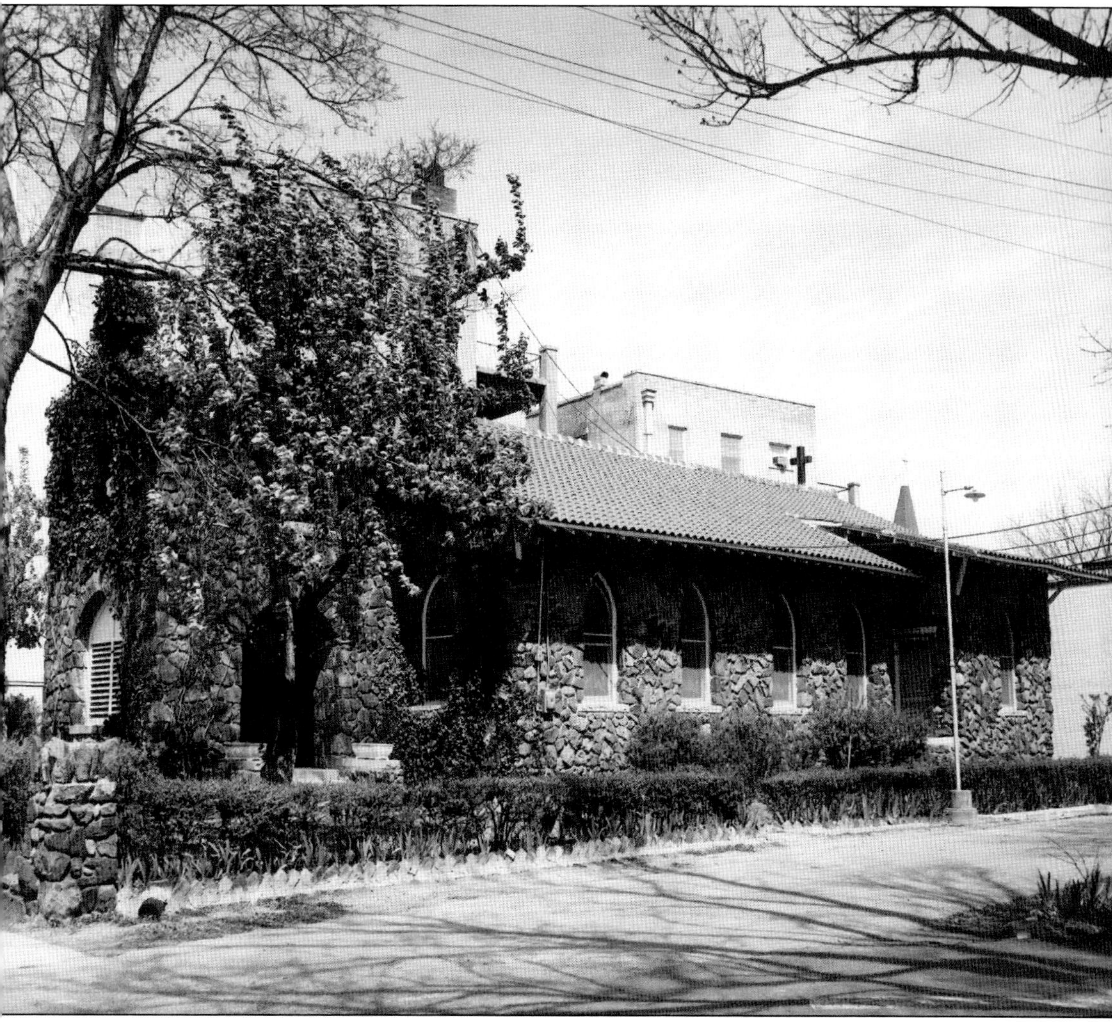

St. Joseph's Chapel in Paris. St. Joseph's Hospital Chapel was located on the grounds of St. Joseph's Hospital. This lovely old building was a much-loved place of worship prior to its demolition. The specific mission of this chapel was to minister to the spiritual needs of patients and their loved ones.

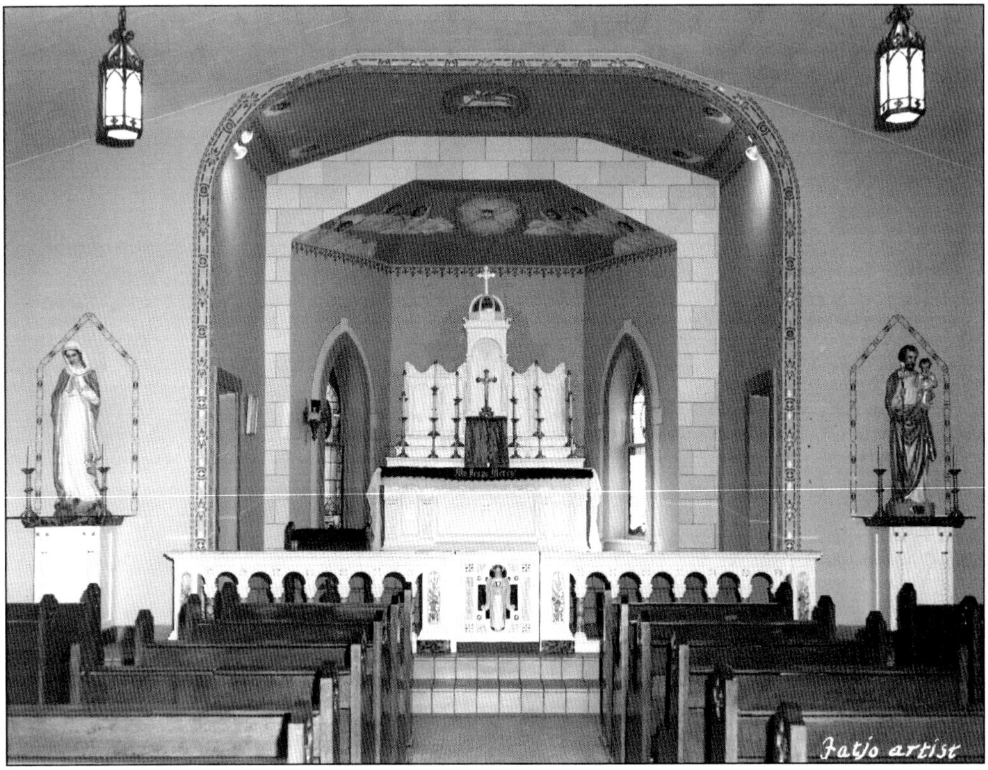

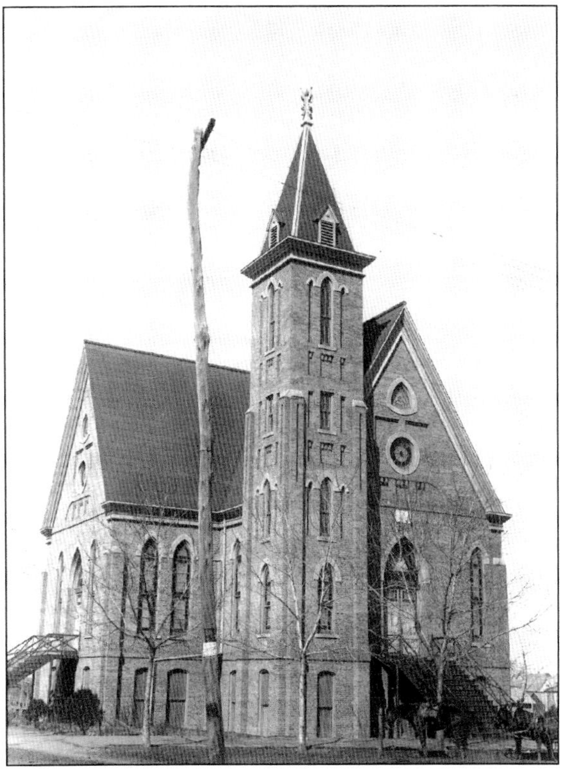

The Interior of Our Lady of Victory Church. The first recorded Catholic Mass in Paris was held at a private home in 1863. In 1880, Our Lady of Victory Catholic Church was consecrated. After worshipping in several locations over the years, the congregation moved into a new building on Austin Street in 1964. In 1986, a new Our Lady of Victory Church was built on Clarksville Street. That facility continues in use today. Our Lady of Victory was associated for many years with the Sisters of Charity of the Incarnate Word; this order of sisters played a significant role in Paris's health care.

Centenary Methodist Episcopal Church South around the Turn of the Century. This building was located in downtown Paris and survived the fire. Unfortunately, stability problems with the structure required that it be torn down in the 1920s.

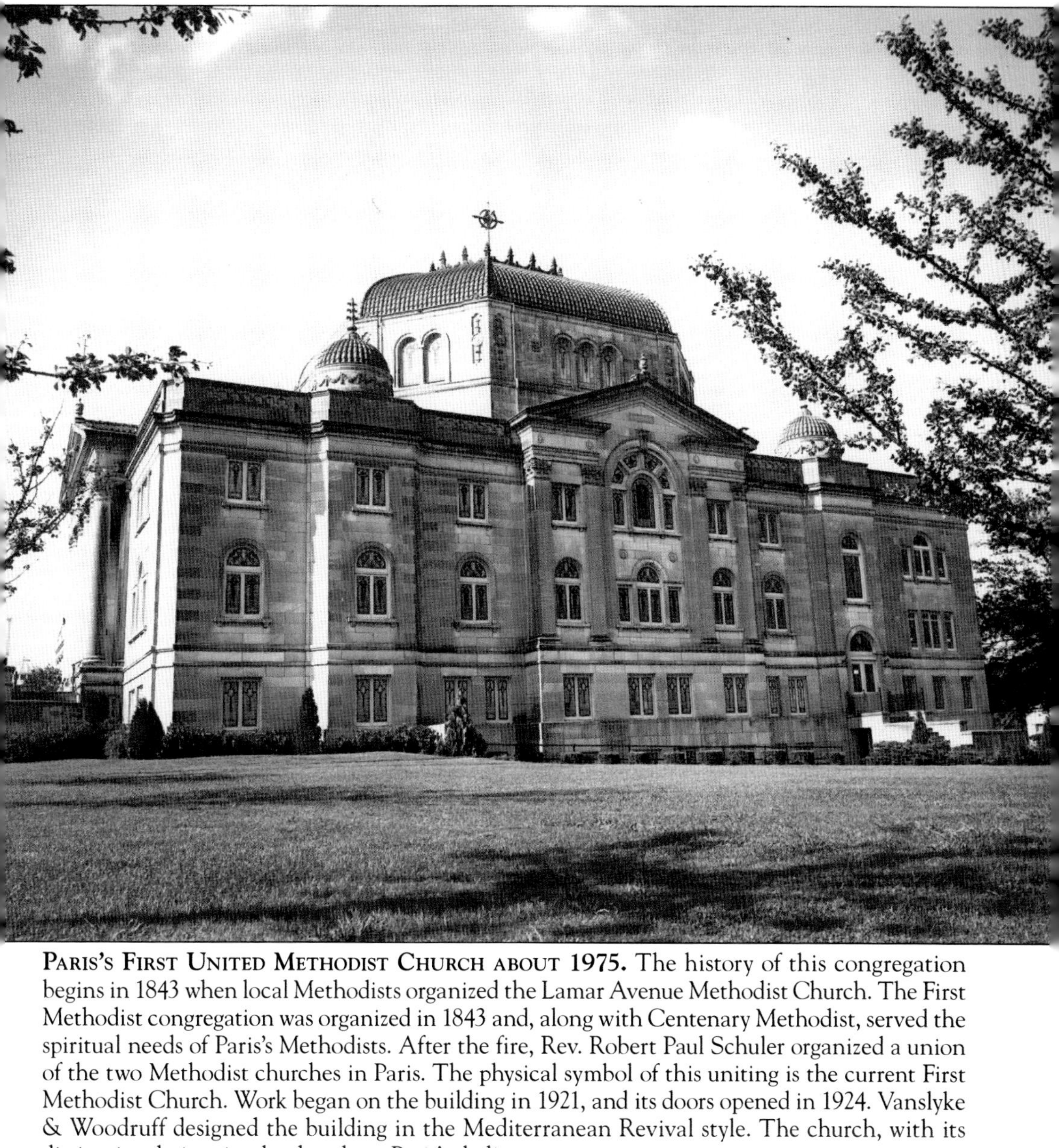

PARIS'S FIRST UNITED METHODIST CHURCH ABOUT 1975. The history of this congregation begins in 1843 when local Methodists organized the Lamar Avenue Methodist Church. The First Methodist congregation was organized in 1843 and, along with Centenary Methodist, served the spiritual needs of Paris's Methodists. After the fire, Rev. Robert Paul Schuler organized a union of the two Methodist churches in Paris. The physical symbol of this uniting is the current First Methodist Church. Work began on the building in 1921, and its doors opened in 1924. Vanslyke & Woodruff designed the building in the Mediterranean Revival style. The church, with its distinctive design, is a landmark on Paris's skyline.

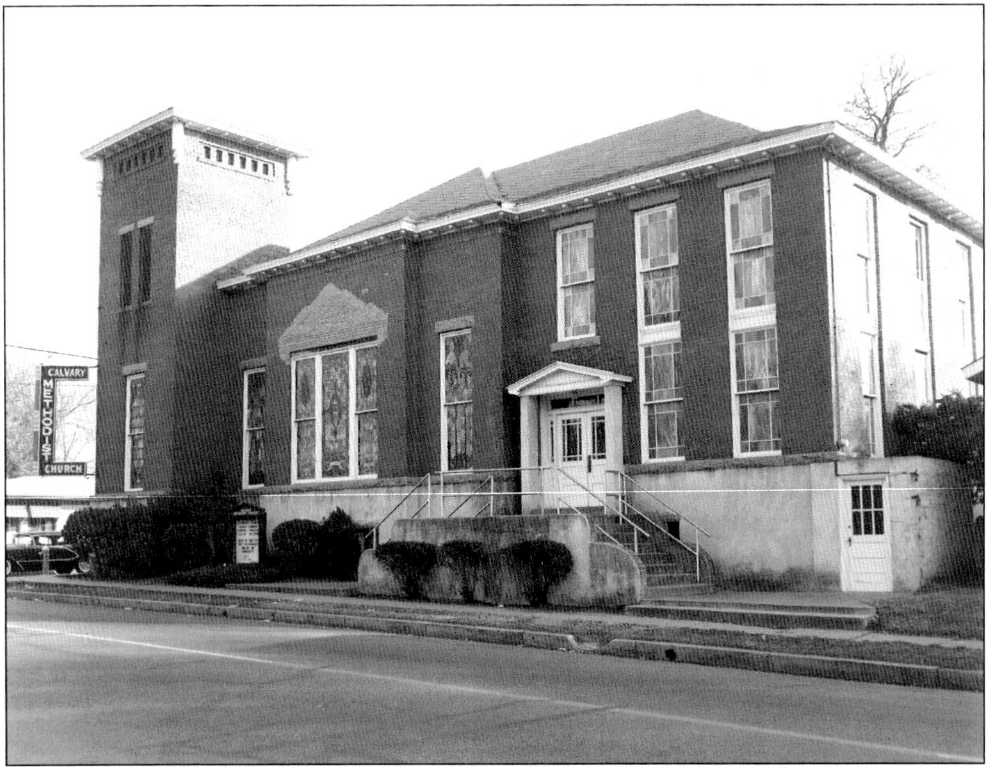

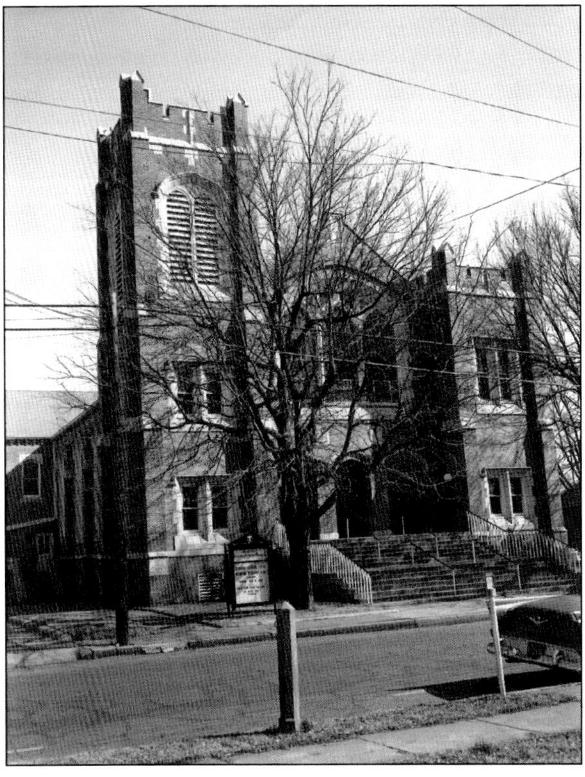

The Calvary Methodist Church on Lamar Avenue. The Calvary Methodist congregation was established in 1905. The building pictured here was demolished in 1980. This photograph was taken probably in the 1950s or the very early 1960s. The Calvary United Methodist congregation still worships at a new facility on Lamar Avenue.

Central Presbyterian Church on February 8, 1959. Interestingly, the phrase on the bulletin board in front of the church reads, "When Your Past Catches Up With You." This congregation was organized in 1844, originally known as the First Cumberland Presbyterian Church. The first church building for this congregation was completed in 1847.

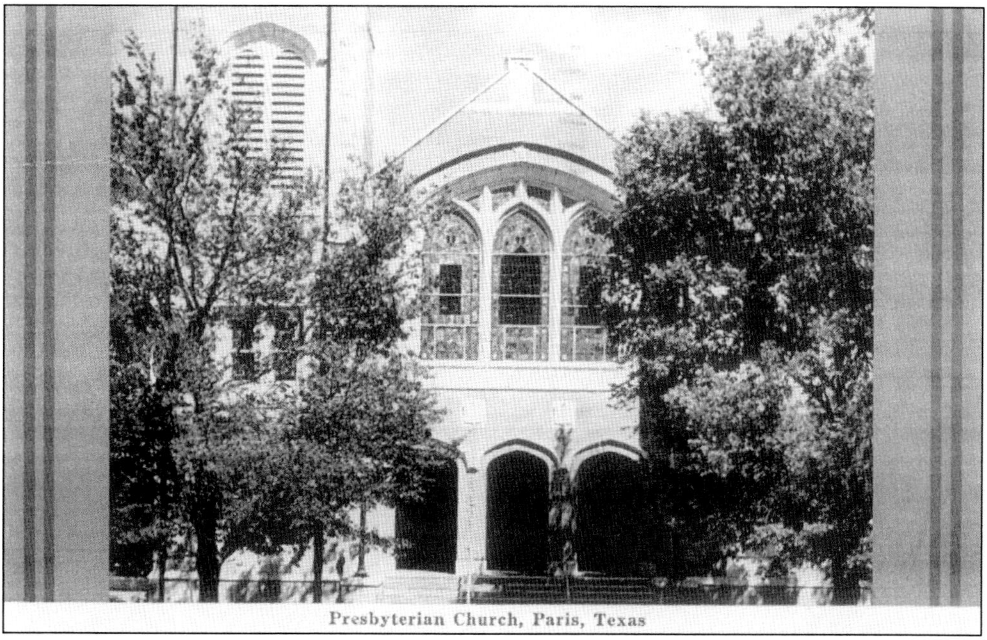

ANOTHER VIEW OF CENTRAL PRESBYTERIAN. The current church building for Central Presbyterian was completed in August 1917, replacing the older 1891 structure that had been destroyed in 1916. This building is a Texas Historic Landmark. (Courtesy of the Lamar County Historical Society Museum.)

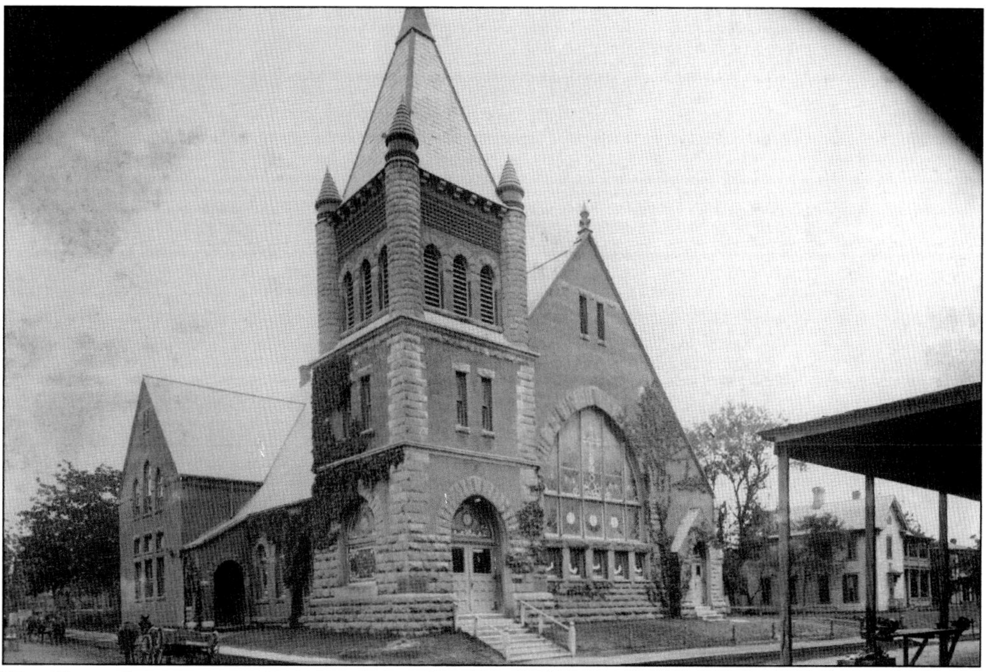

THE FIRST CUMBERLAND PRESBYTERIAN CHURCH. The First Cumberland Presbyterian Church was located on the northeast corner of Houston and Rusk Streets. The building was constructed during the 28-year pastorate of Charles Manton and dedicated in September 1892. This structure was destroyed in the fire of 1916. This photograph may have been taken in 1905.

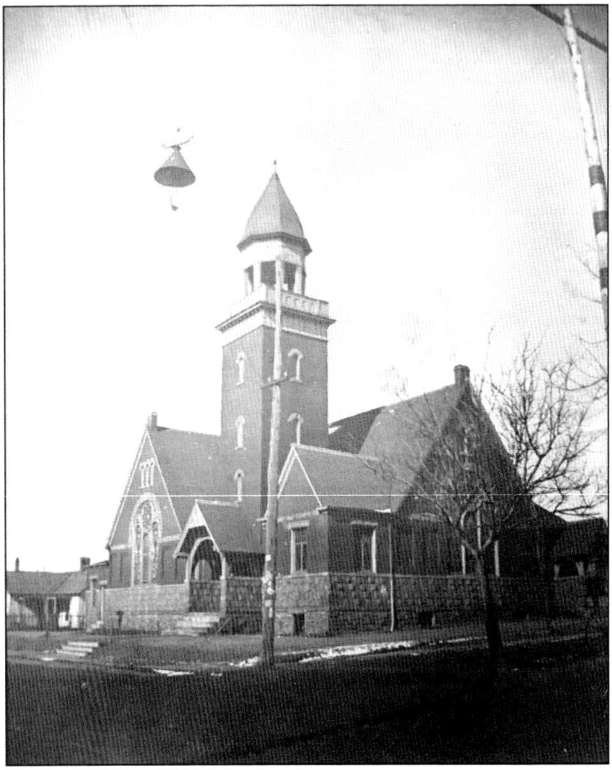

First Presbyterian Church around the Turn of the Century. First Presbyterian was built in the Romanesque style. W.R. Eubanks designed the building. The streets seem to be unpaved in this photograph. Note that the snow on the ground is in the last phase of melting away.

First Presbyterian Church. This photograph of First Presbyterian was taken sometime after the preceding image. One can see here that the streets are now paved. In addition, there has been a new home constructed to the left of the church.

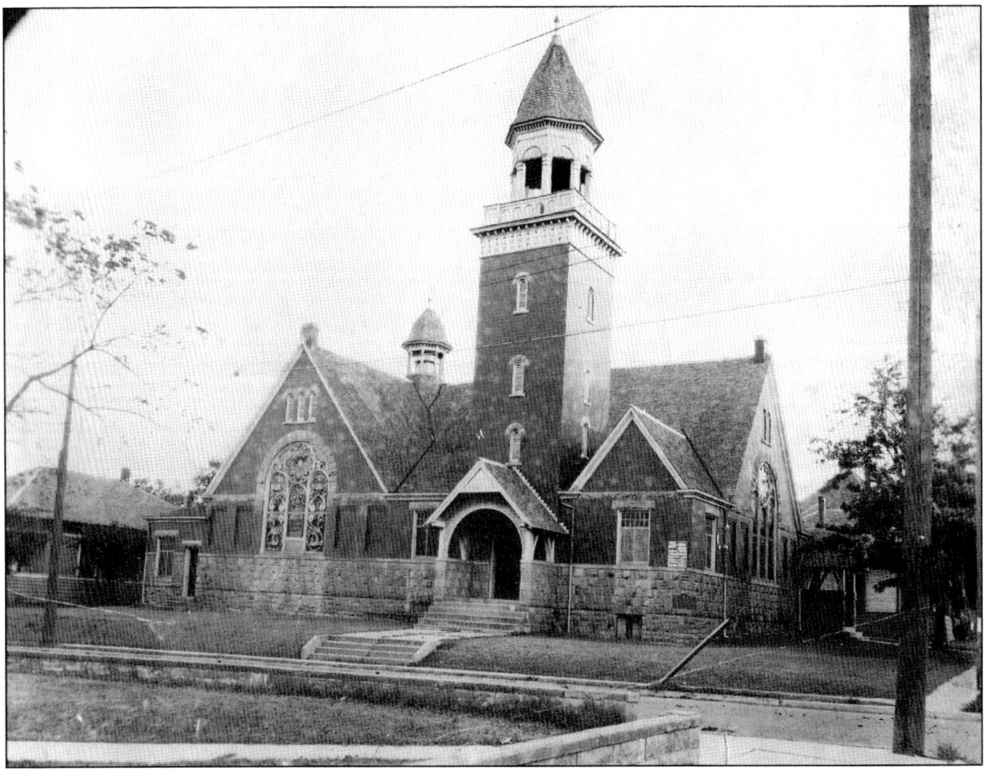

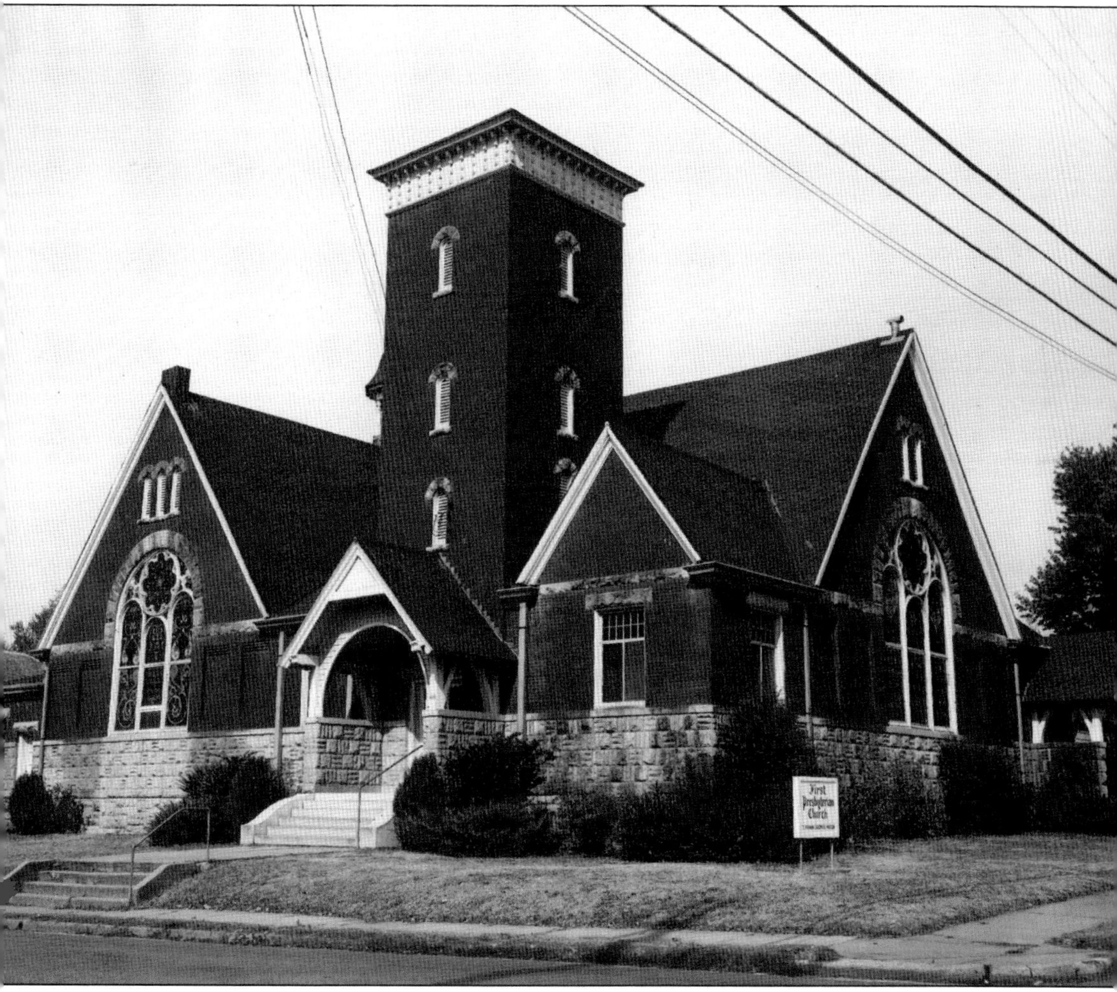

First Presbyterian in the 1950s. One can note that the spire on the bell tower is no longer extant. The pastor at the time this photograph was taken was Rev. T. Frank George. The current church was built in 1892 and was one of the few churches to survive the great fire. It replaced the original 1874 structure on Price Street.

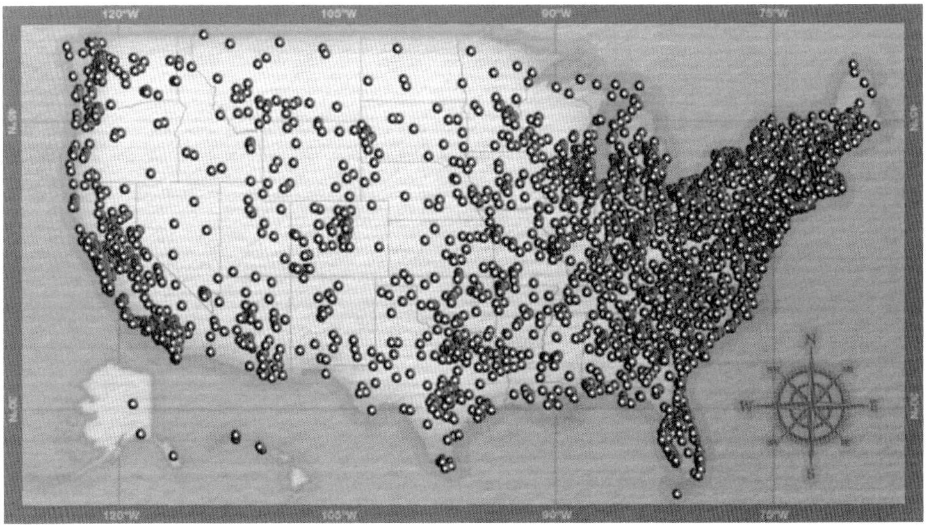